Steve Beard dropped out of Cambridge University in 1987 and began writing for *i-D* magazine just as the acid house scene hit London. Since then he has contributed to *The Face, Arena, RAY guN, Skin Two, Wired, Sight & Sound* and *Artscribe* and appeared at Pharmakon and Virtual Futures '96: Datableed. He is the author of the conceptual novel *Perfumed Head* and the cypherpunk novel *Digital Leatherette*.

Logic bomb

Transmissions from the edge of style culture

Steve Beard

Library of Congress Catalog Card Number 98-86427

A complete catalogue record for this book can be obtained from the British Library on request

The right of Steve Beard to be acknowledged as author of this work has been asserted by him in accordance with the Copyright, Designs and Patents Act 1988

Copyright © 1998 Steve Beard

First published in 1998 by Serpent's Tail
4 Blackstock Mews, London N4, and
180 Varick Street, 10th Floor, New York, NY 10014

Website: http://www.serpentstail.com

Set in Palatino by Intype London Ltd
Printed in Great Britain by Mackays of Chatham

10 9 8 7 6 5 4 3 2 1

for Victoria

'My advice to anybody in any field is to be faithful to your obsessions. Identify them and be faithful to them; let them guide you like a sleepwalker.'

J G Ballard, *i-D* no 53 November 1987

Contents

Acknowledgements ix
Preface by Matthew Collin xi
Introduction xiii

Celebrity burn
    Damien Hirst 1
    Dennis Hopper 6
    Elvis 16
    'Mark Leyner' 18

Gender fucking
    Sex crimes 20
    Mad love 22
    Virtual porn 26
    Gender hacks 30
    Cyberfeminism 31

Cinephylum
    Hollywood Babylon 39
    Bachelor machine #1 41
    Bachelor machine #2 44
    Vampiria 47
    Suicide cinema 49
    Image bombs 52

Human interfaces
    J.G. Ballard 54
    William Gibson and Bruce Sterling 61
    Jim Thompson 72
    William Burroughs 73

Techgnosis
    American psychonaut 75
    Electronic flaneur #1 77

Electronic flaneur #2	79
Hobo emperor	82
Media prophet	84
Free theory DJ	92

Fetish boys

Talent spotter	98
Otaku	102
Film fan	105
Conspiracy buff	108
Doll collector	110

Letters

Cosmo Landesman and Julie Burchill	112
Paul Dave	113
Male subject #1	122
Male subject #2	122
André Breton	123

Abysmal simulacra

Japan	125
Euro Disney	133
Sovietland	139
Burbclave	140

Media wars

Slacker	143
Mod	145
New romantic #1	148
Punk	154
New romantic #2	155

Slow memes

Shadow enlightenment	161
Archaic modernity #1	163
Archaic modernity #2	196

Index of Concepts	205
Index of Names	211

Acknowledgements

Victoria Halford for inspiring the book as well as providing its cover image.
Pete Ayrton, Paul Westlake, Laurence O'Toole, Emma Waghorn and everyone else at Serpent's Tail for publishing the book.
Stephen Hayward for advising me how to compile the book and acting *in loco agentis*.
Micha Weidmann, David James and the other guys in Great Sutton Street for designing the book cover.
Stewart Home for letting me know how to cope with the publishing industry.
Kodwo Eshun for being so positive; Paul Dave for being so negative.
Jim McClellan for setting such an example.
Dylan Jones, John Godfrey, Matthew Collin (big shout), Avril Mair; Kathryn Flett, Peter Howarth, Sheryl Garratt; Julie Burchill and Cosmo Landesman for commissioning the journalism.
John Kerrigan and Francis Barker for supervising the thesis.
Terry Jones and Nick Logan for infrastructural support.
The staff at the Cambridge University Library and the British Library for their labour.
Pam Downe (big hug), Julia Monk, Roy Hutchens, John Hardy, Nana Yaa Mensa, Janet Lee, George Barber, Mark Waugh, Nick Corstin, Suzi Q, Nick Tantis, Nick Land, Sadie Plant, Mark Fisher, Angus Carlyle, Robin Rimbaud, Paul Claydon, Adam Scrivener, Tony White, James Pyman, David Eimer, Deirdre Crowley, Chris Wroblewski, Omaid Hiwaizi, Alix Sharkey, Jo Peters, Michelle Stavrinou (RIP) and others for their various acts of hospitality.
Ken Beard, Dawn Beard, Karen Brooks, Tim Brooks, Clive Dreyer and Annette Dreyer for keeping me safe.

Preface by Matthew Collin

Who remembers Style Culture? Even the phrase, when repeated today, sounds peculiarly nostalgic – if not simply peculiar. The Style Culture era – which spanned the mid-to-late '80s and the early years of the '90s – although so recent, seems so far away now. The posturings and peccadilloes of the style media during those years form a shadow history of the Last Days of High Thatcherism: one part aspirational materialism (ie: flash), one part entrepreneurial verve (ie: blag), plus a whole lot of self-referential hype.

Logic Bomb, the edited journalism of Steve Beard, transports us back to that time and lets us live it again with a little distance. But *Logic Bomb* is more than an archaeological dig; it doesn't simply pick aimlessly at the fossilized bones of a long-extinct meme. Steve Beard refers to it as a kind of map; a tracing of the psychological contours of an era whose values now seem as peculiar to us as those of a distant cargo cult – yet much more fascinating, as they were our own.

Who can recall when (or why) the 'psychedelic skinheads' and the 'Gen-Xers' captured the imagination of fashionable society? Who cares now that the *Modern Review* and Tank Girl were once the talk of all Soho? A friend of mine often remarks how, on leaving Britain (he scratches out an itinerant living overseas), the fervid obsessions of the Brit-pop media-bubble cease to make any sense. Their relevance has no passport; their importance fades on exit from UK jurisdiction at Dover or Heathrow. 'In Budapest, no one knows who Julie Burchill is,' my friend declares. 'In Lisbon, they don't give a shit about Chris Evans.' And so it is with the Style Culture era: its references have slipped their moorings and are cast adrift in history.

Which is not to say that *Logic Bomb* is all about the past. There is a heap of smart stuff in here which remains almost frighteningly relevant, and stunning pieces that somehow slipped past the liberal-humanist gatekeepers of the style press, like the razor-sharp deconstruction of 1993's pernicious Asylum & Immigration Appeals Bill, or Avital Ronell's musings on the class-race profile of the War On Drugs.

Steve Beard's mission, so he says, was to loiter with intent amidst the flash and trash of the style media, to suck nourishment from it while simultaneously providing its critique. A double agent, in other words. He describes himself as a smuggler: bringing ideas from the margins into the mainstream, cloaked in the language of style but bearing ulterior motives: logic bombs. There is another word for his sort – blaggers; those who try it on to see just how much they can get away with before authority (in this case, editors and publishers) rein them back. As Steve's editor at *i-D* magazine in the early '90s, I was generally more than willing to collude in his blags, as he invariably delivered the extraordinary. He was among the few writers who temporarily banished the encroaching despair that all our efforts amounted to no more than cheap R&D for the advertising and marketing mills. Although he hides it beneath his world-weary demeanour and his big black coat, Steve's work is very much driven by an idealism that is the antithesis of the job description 'hack'. In other words, he gives a shit.

Style Culture itself was washed away in the tidal wave of euphoria that was Acid House. It leaves its traces in the heedless hedonism of the club press and the brutish masculinity of the lad mags. And they, too, need their own Steve Beards, their critiques from the margins – people who will snipe and gripe and prick at their complacent bubble. But right now, *Logic Bomb* will do just fine.

Introduction

What have I been doing for the last ten years? The short answer is that I've worked as a hack for the London style press. The long answer is that I've sanctioned – often against my worse instincts – one definition of what it means to function as an 'organic intellectual' (Antonio Gramsci) within a media simulacrum that has bought up the property rights to the old bourgeois public sphere.

I've spat out pic caps for double-page fashion spreads and I've filled pages with the musings of trendy French philosophers. But one thing I've never done is get paid the union rate for the job. It's perhaps a reason why at the age of thirty-seven I still struggle to make the rent each month. (There is a street beneath Grub Street.)

The pieces collected in *Logic Bomb* were written fast under the sweatshop conditions of industrial production that prevail in the glamorous world of the style press. I offer them up as they were originally crafted with only a few minor alterations (suggested by my editor for the improvement of sense). This is part of the reason why some of them (like the profiles of Jim Thompson and William Burroughs) are rather sketchy, why others (like the account of Iain Sinclair) terminate abruptly and why still others (like the *otaku* story) are a bit clunky. I am not attempting to excuse myself here. I am merely warning the reader that a lot of what follows is not witty salon exhalation. It's assembly-line prose.

I have structured the book into thematic sections (like Gender Fucking, Techgnosis, Media Wars) to give it the feel of a personal album or scrapbook (the inspiration behind this was partly suggested to me by ethnographic surrealist Marcel Mauss). Each section is introduced by a condensed memory blip which attempts to open out career psychogeography into the wider terrain of media history – so establishing the 'user's guide' kind of vibe that might prove useful to media studies kids or popcult antiquarians.

In many ways, I have approached my past in the spirit of a curious archaeologist wishing to curate the ruins of the style press. I think that some of what magazines like *i-D*, *The Face* and *Arena* have done in the eighties and nineties is provide marginal spaces within their pages for the kind of pop theoretical speculation that fails to occur within either midcult media or articled academia. This is not to deny that these mags supervise a revolt into style that is then commodified by the ad world. But it is to suggest that their vital connection has always tended to be with the legacy of the sixties counterculture.

There are two sections in particular that I feel deserve further explanation:

1 Letters In this section I have included the proposal I wrote to media don Julie Burchill when she was first setting up the *Modern Review* (I figure it's now forensic career evidence); a letter I wrote in response to my friend the intellectual underclass booster and Marxist critic Paul Dave on his thesis on 'eco-power' (the material here marks the horizon of my imaginative world at the time and gives some indication of the alcoholic rhapsodies I was unable to indulge in on the style press); two letters I made up while working on *Arena* (they demonstrate the queer subjectivity which was in the process of being evicted from the UK's first men's mag); and a highly personal review of André Breton's *Communicating Vessels* (which very much functioned as an imaginary letter to the Pope of Surrealism). All document the spirit of the times in their different ways.

2 Slow Memes In this section I have included the introductory chapter to the thesis on postmodernism which I was in the process of writing at the University of Cambridge in the late eighties (whereas my journalism was often criticized for being 'too academic', my academic work was criticized for being 'too journalistic' – a situation which gestures towards one definition of an organic intellectual discourse). I have also included the original footnotes to the chapter (a partial record of the parasituationist derives I used to take around the open stacks of the University Library in Cambridge, they archive the sampladelic operating system on which my subjectivity has been built). Some of the insights in this section are directly reworked in the journalism and I beg the reader's forgiveness if any repetition offends.

I had a lot of fun putting *Logic Bomb* together and hope that it shows in the finished result. What does it amount to? I'll let history be the judge. One thing I will say. As the style culture of Theme Park UK is displaced by the chemical culture of our Altered Nation-State, as Thatcher's punk-era visage morphs into Blair's smiley face, all the slash-and-burn brand names of eighties 'regressive modernization' (Stuart Hall) are aesthetically recommodified as nineties heritage sign crimes. (Coming to a multiplex near you soon: the Poll Tax riots retold as a feelgood musical comedy.) All of which is another way of suggesting that this book is already a brilliant nostalgia item. You must rip it off now.

Celebrity burn

You're sitting in a room near the British Museum about to interview David Duchovny long before he became a global TV star. This is the position you occupy in the culture industry – the position on the edge, the limen, the signifying margin. You catch gonna-bes and has-beens but very rarely the full-blown presence of celebrity (all celebrities are the same; it's only how they get it and how they lose it that's interesting). You remember what Lloyd told you when you were holed up together in Namibia. How he used to rent a room at Le Parc in LA and then bag a few celebs to take back home. Make a few quid. The wages of the aura harvest (seasonal, like any form of casual labour). You load a used SA90 into the breech of the Sony and say to David Duchovny: You're going over Noam Chomsky. He cracks wise.

Damien Hirst

Big Issue, no. 248, 1–7 September 1997

There are two Damien Hirsts. One is the London restaurateur, man-about-town and businessman who manages to keep his face in the papers by banging out outrageous works of art for astronomical prices and hanging with his buddies at the Groucho Club. This is the Damien Hirst who appears in his tasteful new Bloomsbury office – white walls, bare boards, a landscaped fireplace – to be interviewed. He has a two-hour window before meeting his dealer Jay Joplin at two. By five to two he's out of the building.

Then there's the Damien Hirst who makes his appearance the next day. The geezer, the practical joker, the big man who brandishes fifty-pound notes in the boozer as if they were fivers before proceeding to lose gracefully at pool. The one who rolls into his studio in a breaker's yard in Brixton ninety minutes late for his scheduled appointment to whiz up a spin painting for the *Big Issue*. The one it's very hard to dislike.

'I may not know much about art, but I know what I like.' Hirst beams at the completed canvas after it has been removed from the giant spin machine that occupies one end of his chaotic studio and transported to the other. The swirling pinks and yellows and whites that spatter the circular canvas are the results of a game of 'objective chance' played by Hirst – dipping plastic beakers into the pots of MacPherson's household paint assembled on makeshift tables and then casually chucking them on to the canvas as it rotates like a psychedelic platter – at his spinning wheel. He sticks the acetate with the *Big Issue* logo over a yellow splurge of paint so it's illegible and then stubs a trademark B&H into the canvas as a final gesture.

How many do you smoke a day, Damien? 'Not enough!' The rejoinder is instant and a clear demonstration that Hirst – despite the clowning with the photographer as he unzips his paint-spattered white paper suit to reveal his pubic hair ('Don't you want a picture of it? Everyone else does.') – is nobody's fool. He grins. 'Besides it's how many you smoke a night that counts.'

Spending time with Damien Hirst is a slightly bewildering experience. The *Guardian* carries a front-page story a few days later that hammers home the point about the numbers – Hirst spends eight minutes at the spin machine for the *Big Issue* and delivers a canvas worth £40,000. What can you say? The painting rests like a Day-Glo coffee table beneath a sombre fourteen-foot diameter spin painting which stands at the back of Hirst's studio like an altarpiece. He's been working on it all morning to get it to New York on time. The *Big Issue* painting by comparison is just a sketch.

'The trick is knowing when to stop.' Hirst is commenting on the progress of one of his assistants, who has been stuck at the spin machine for half an hour now, chucking paint at the canvas in a despairing attempt to produce something lively. Another of Hirst's team stands at the top of a ladder in the regulation white paper suit, witnessing the event with a Casio digital camera. 'Memory full,' he announces. Hirst's assistant keeps on going regardless. 'I only like the painting when the wheel's turning,' muses Hirst. 'After that I get bored.'

One of the reasons why Hirst has come out of hiding and agreed to do an interview is that he wants to promote *I Want to Spend the Rest of My Life Everywhere, with Everyone, One to One, Always, Forever, Now* (Booth-Clibborn Editions), the door-stopping retrospective of his work designed by Jonathan Barnbrook in the form of a pop-up book. It's a clever idea. Not only is the book the perfect introduction to Hirst's work but it's a work of art in its own right.

It includes press cuttings, photos, court transcripts (from the episode when a frustrated artist attempted to sabotage one of Hirst's works), letters and complicated pieces of 'paper engineering'.

Flipping through the book is like fast-forwarding through the back pages of Hirst's career. His big creative period was 1990–92 when he produced most of the work for which he is famous – *The Physical Impossibility of Death in the Mind of Someone Living* (the shark suspended in a glass tank of formaldehyde), *The Acquired Inability to Escape* (a chair, a desk, a pack of Silk Cuts and an ashtray full of butts inside a glass tank), *A Thousand Years* (a rotting calf's head, a sample cloud of flies and a UV insect-o-cutor inside a glass tank) – while in 1995 he won the Turner Prize for *Mother and Child Divided* (this time a bisected cow and her calf suspended in a glass tank of formaldehyde). Since then he has been concentrating on the spin paintings and the spot paintings – grids of dots that look like industrial colour charts.

These icons define the nineties as much as anything produced by Tony Blair, Oasis or the National Lottery. They are emblems of the global authority of 'Cool Britannia', tributes to the commodification of London. They are also the works on which Hirst's reputation will probably rest. So are they any good? The critics can't agree. Commenting on the post-punk roots of Hirst's aesthetic, the art pundit Matthew Collings states: 'When you think about the older artists going around in their suits and being in *biennales* and giving the same interviews all the time about their concerns and being a bit gratingly half-intellectual, you feel refreshed by this frankly abject juvenile style.' The imperious Brian Sewell, by contrast, considers Hirst a charlatan.

Not that Hirst is bothered by anything the critics have to say.

He's gone way beyond that. For the last 150 years, art has tended to exist in the avant-garde space reserved for it by what the scholar Hal Foster calls a 'self-critical bourgeoisie'. It's possible to argue that Hirst's glass tank work has operated within this space, that it returns to the Victorian scientific interest in anatomy and taxonomy in order to expose its limitations as an imaging system and transgress the taboo that surrounds death.

But Hirst is quite happy to see himself as a showman rocking the crowds. 'I think art is fundamentally theatre,' he says. 'A lot of people believe in truth-to-materials and things like that but I think if you can fake it then fake it because if you can't tell then it doesn't really matter. A lot of people see my work as high realism, like in order to justify your integrity you have to have a dead animal in there. But I'd be willing to use a prop 'cause I think you've only gotta make people think something and you can use whatever is at your disposal to do that. I mean, there's a lot of things that go on behind the scenes anyway. I'm constantly topping up the fly piece with new flies and changing the head. It's a high-maintenance sculpture.'

If Hirst has done one thing it's demonstrate that an artist no longer has to play the avant-garde game. To a certain extent, he's gone right back to the bourgeois origins of art as a luxury commodity available only to those with money to burn – which nowadays means private collectors, museums and corporations. Hirst is under no illusions about who his buyers are. 'I think there's a handful of eye people and billions of ear people, that's to say people who buy with their ears. Some people go look at it and think it's great so they buy it and all these other people hear that they've bought it so they buy it too. I don't think it matters. People are buying it because they are buying it. It's like Andy Warhol said, he only goes to his private views to see who goes.'

Hirst is notorious in the art world for 'Freeze', the warehouse show he curated while still a student at Goldsmith's College in 1988. He cut a deal with the property developers Olympia & York for the lease of the space, put out a professional-looking catalogue and managed to get hold of some gallery mailing lists. The result was that art bigwigs such as Norman Rosenthal from the Royal Academy and Nicholas Serota from the Tate Gallery turned up. By the time of Hirst's next exhibition, 'Gambler', Charles Saatchi had got the message. He duly turned up and bought a prototype version of the fly sculpture. Hirst's reputation was made.

So is he interested in business? 'I'm definitely interested in the business side of it. I'm interested in all aspects of life and money's just a tiny part. The thing is with the spot paintings no one wanted them in the beginning and now they're like forty thousand pounds each and they'll probably be a hundred thousand pounds and then they'll probably go back down to no one wanting them again. But I've done my job. They always look great on the wall – that's all you can do as an artist. But it's important to know how value affects things.'

It sounds as if Hirst is bored with the art world. 'I've done it,' he admits. 'I still love art though. But the art world was set up to deal with artists and it's a bit out of date I think – white spaces, boring shops. You're running out of things you can do now. I mean if you can do the art world at thirty-two it means there's something wrong with the art world, not that you're a genius. But I think that's pretty logical.'

Hirst's boredom with the art world has led him into the restaurant world. He has an arrangement with the Soho restaurant Quo Vadis to showcase his private collection of art and is meanwhile setting up a restaurant in Notting Hill called Pharmacy ('I'll be designing the salt pots, ashtrays, menus, everything'), at which he will exhibit his own work. 'I'm more excited about that than I am about doing things in the art world. If you blur the boundary between where the art is and where the restaurant is and where the food is and what's art and what isn't then it just becomes a great place to be.'

That's the great thing about being an artist. You can do what you like. Hirst has made a pop video for Blur, a film for Channel 4 with Pulp; he's licensed his spots to Rifat Ozbek; there's the book and the theme restaurants. Can the soundtrack album be far away? Are artists like Hirst, Tracey Emin and the Chapman Brothers more famous than most pop stars? Is art the new rock'n'roll? 'I think art's about life and the art world's about money, and money and celebrity and things like that are just tiny aspects of life. So if you keep your perspective on that then it's fine. I think art should be able to deal with celebrity and things like that. I don't think you should ever let celebrity become more important than art but I think it's a part of it. I think a desire to be famous is a desire to live for ever, which is very fundamental to art.'

Hirst certainly enjoys high-profile company when he's not chilling in his Devon farmhouse with his wife and baby son and Vietnamese pot-bellied pigs. The *Evening Standard* recently identified the members of his set as Keith Allen, Dave Stewart, Neil Tennant, Lou Reed, Jarvis Cocker, David Bowie and Eddie Izzard. Is he conscious of being famous? 'I hang around with people who are a lot more famous than me so I don't really notice it. I'm a small fish in a big tank. I don't get attention really. I've just cut my hair and people don't recognize me. If I'm in a bar and say I'm Damien Hirst people make me get my credit card out. Even then they don't believe me.'

Some say that Hirst is running out of ideas. That he reached his creative peak with the glass tank work and is now eking out his celebrity with kids' stuff – spin paintings and spot paintings. Hirst scoffs at such notions and insists that he's only interested now in impressing himself. The fact that he is increasingly able to scorn both critics and buyers alike (there's a waiting list for his work) means he is free to pursue his obsessions – which seem to have to do with that critical threshold at which decomposition becomes fruitful, or a poison becomes a medicine (the best part of his early work consisted of medicine cabinets with titles adapted from old Sex Pistols songs). Or as he himself says, 'I've only just started!'

Dennis Hopper

Arena, no. 39, May/June 1993

Dennis Hopper's gleaming black Mercedes turns off Ocean Avenue into Arizona and slithers into the bowels of the Shangri-La Hotel. The hard, clear light of Los Angeles almost pops in its abhorrence of the departing vacuum. Ten minutes later and Hollywood's oldest living delinquent is in the penthouse suite.

Does the interview, throws some shapes, drinks some coffee and is gone.

He looks like he's been dressed by a tornado. Navy blazer, pink and blue striped shirt, paint-spattered Levis, beat-up alligator shoes. Whatever came out of the closet first.

'Let's not fuck around,' he says lightly as he changes into a Comme des Garçons sweater for the shoot. The grey flashes at his temples are bleeding into his quiff and there are liver spots on his hands. But he moves fast for an old-timer.

Yesterday, he was casting for *Chasers*, a road-movie-cum-comedy-thriller that he is to direct starring Tom Berenger; today, he is promoting *Red Rock West*, a deft pastiche of film noir and Western in which he plays the Hit Man from Hell to Nic Cage's dumb drifter; tomorrow, he has to check on the progress of a travelling exhibition of his paintings and photographs in Germany. Somewhere down the line there is press to do for the movie version of *Super Mario Brothers*, in which he appears as the Nintendo super-villain King Koopa.

He's got very little time.

'They have festivals once in a while where I see my work,' he says at one point. 'They had one in Sweden where I got to pick my ten best movies. I picked the six I've directed and four that I've starred in. But it's hard for me to see myself as having a body of work. I feel my career has been very sketchy.'

This, from a man who has worked with everyone from James Dean to John Wayne, Marlon Brando to Sean Penn, Wim Wenders to David Lynch, Elizabeth Taylor to Jodie Foster. He started out playing nervy young punks; now he specializes in crazy old bastards; in between, he's done psychos, dipsos and weirdos. He's lasted in the business for nearly forty years without sliding into either cult oblivion or camp self-consciousness. He has made a small but significant contribution to the cinema.

But he wanted to do so much more. During the moments when he is counting the cost of the past, Hopper's shoulders droop and his gaze shrinks. His voice sinks to a low croak, as if sustained by fading batteries. He's almost talking to himself. 'I feel that I haven't really done a substantial amount of work. I should have done a lot more.' Then, out of nowhere, comes this crazy, yammering laugh and he's back up.

Way up. Hopper at full blast is Hopper in his element. It's like his whole body is riding a sudden power surge. His spine stiffens, his hands fly out in rapid bursts of eloquence, his discourse melts into a fluid jabber. On one occasion, when rehearsing the pantheistic beliefs of the Navajo tribe, he fixes me with his deep, subtle and coldly furious eye, and I am mesmerized.

'They say that we are the rock, we are the water, we are the sky, and that in all this there is a Great Spirit. That's easy for me to accept. I think my molecules are the same as the rock, the same as the water, the same as the sky. Whether there is life after death or not, certainly our molecules become part of what we came from, so in that sense we are still alive.'

I am almost ready to drive into the desert and eat peyote with the Navajo when out comes that weird laugh and Hopper comes back down. It's the story of his life. Highs following lows following highs in quick, nervy succession. Hopper has had more comebacks than Jesus H. Christ. And he's got nearly as many disciples, from Matt Dillon to Mickey Rourke to Sean Penn to Crispin Glover.

There is an authorized version of the Dennis Hopper comeback legend and it comes in two parts. Part One: Started out as a contract player at Warners in the fifties but refused to play the studio game, fell out with old-school director Henry Hathaway and was banished to the outer rim of the industry. Stuck to his guns and came back in 1969 as director of the low-budget biker-Western, *Easy Rider*, a movie that gave the finger to Old Hollywood, crystallized the hippie counterculture and made money into the bargain.

Hopper was thirty-three at the time. 'I thought nothing was gonna fucking stop me,' he says from the mournful shade of a twenty-four-year distance. 'A big mistake.'

Part Two: Blew his new-found Hollywood credibility with the self-indulgent piece of epic myth-mongering that was *The Last Movie*. Took drugs in Taos, New Mexico, had visions of James Dean and went crazy. Cleaned up his act and placed a call to David Lynch saying, 'I *am* Frank.' Found a new, post-punk audience with his portrayal of the archetypal American psycho, Frank Booth, in Lynch's *Blue Velvet*. Has never looked back.

Like all good legends, this one preserves the outlines of its subject's history. But it skirts complexity. It emphasizes Hopper's extremes at the expense of his subtleties, transforms his career into an allegory of repeated martyrdom when it is actually a more complicated figure of grand refusal and last-minute repentance.

Hopper was born in 1936, the elder of two brothers, and was raised on his grandmother's farm in Kansas. His mother managed a swimming pool in Dodge City, while his father worked for the government. More importantly for the future imaginative life of Hopper, his father was a Methodist lay minister. Methodism was a narrow Puritan sect distinguished by its emphasis on the personal nature of salvation, its rejection of traditional forms of worship and its suspicion of art and sex. This was the cultural heritage that Hopper rebelled against. His parents wanted him to be a lawyer or a doctor. He knew he was an artist. And art for him was intimately connected with the sacraments of intoxication. He would sniff gasoline from his grandfather's truck and lie back and trace shapes in the clouds. One time, he took too much, picked up a baseball bat and smashed in the truck's windscreen.

But, hey, to create you had to destroy. At least this was the implication of Gene Fowler's *Minutes of the Last Meeting*. Hopper's bible during childhood, this book celebrated the dissipation and self-destruction of such legendary Hollywood piss-artists as John Barrymore. 'All the people that I admired – all the great actors, musicians, writers and painters – were alcoholics and drug addicts. Whether it was Charlie Parker, W.C. Fields, John Barrymore or Edmund O'Keane.'

Hopper followed their example. At the peak of his addiction, he was on half a gallon of rum a day, plus a few beers, with an ounce or so of coke thrown in to keep him standing. In 1984, he holed up in an LA hotel room for three days and took speedballs every ten minutes as if taking a crash course in suicide. Soon after he went into detox.

Now that he has been clean and sober for nine years he

can afford to look back on his past excesses with something approaching wry amusement. 'I remember, when people said I might be drinking a little too much, I would say, "Well, you know Van Gogh said he had to drink for a whole summer to find that yellow." But it was probably because he was so drunk he couldn't find the tube the yellow was in.'

In 1949 the family moved to San Diego for the improved climate. It was at this time that Hopper took up acting in the local theatre. It caused problems with his parents and led to a lot of bust-ups. But he was determined to be a great Shakespearean actor. He eventually attracted the attention of actress Dorothy McGuire at the La Jolla Playhouse, who armed him with a list of contacts and advised him to try Hollywood.

Hopper remembers the first day he hit town as if it were yesterday. It was a balmy afternoon in November 1954; he rode the bus in from San Diego and was picked up at the depot by an old high-school friend. 'He drove me through Beverly Hills and I looked at all these huge homes and I just had a feeling of total defeat. I had fifty dollars in my pocket; I had a letter from a casting director. I couldn't understand on any level how I could live in one of these places or cope with this city. I was eighteen years old. It just looked impossible.'

He did a few bits and pieces of TV work and survived by stealing milk from neighbouring doorsteps. Eventually, he had to move back home and deliver telephone books while waiting for a show called *Medic* to air in January. He had a part in it as an epileptic and was sure it would be his big break.

It was. The morning after it was on, Hopper was offered seven studio contracts. You can understand what they saw in him. Even now, at the age of fifty-seven, he has a wonderful movie-star face. His bold forehead and straight nose look as if they have been chiselled from marble. It is his sardonic mouth and twitchy brows that convey all the seething doubt and intensity.

He and his agent sifted through the offers carefully and eventually decided Harry Cohn at Columbia Pictures was offering the best deal. Cohn was one of the legendary tycoons of Old Hollywood, one of those immigrant Jewish vulgarians who spun dreams from celluloid as if they were making cotton gloves or shirts. Hopper met him just a year before he died.

'He said that I was the most naturalistic actor that he'd ever seen. He was sitting smoking a cigar and said, "Well, tell me about your background." I was sweating profusely, looking through the cigar smoke at this rainbow of Academy Awards. And I said, "I'm in San Diego playing Shakespeare." And he said, "Oh my god, not Shakespeare. We'll have to put you in school for six months, take all that Shakespeare out of you." And then I suddenly went boom! I stopped sweating and I said, "Go fuck yourself."'

The way Hopper tells the story, it takes on the lurid glow of a Faustian encounter. The minister's boy confronted by a cigar-smoking Mephistopheles in a cheap suit. Hopper was an artist, he was going to be the greatest Shakespearean actor ever seen. Who was Harry Cohn? He was the embodiment of Hollywood in all its trashy splendour, a philistine showman, an inflated version of his father.

Hopper was tapping deep into the collective American unconscious with this fantasy. From Melville and Hawthorne to Twain and Faulkner, there has been a common effort to redeem the values of Puritanism by shifting them from the religious to the artistic domain. Such cultural transgressors, according to the literary critic Leslie Fiedler, 'consequently find it easy to view themselves in Faustian terms, to think of their dangerous vocations as a bargain with the devil'.

Hopper's big problem was that he never made up his mind about Hollywood. Was it sanctified by the aura of art? Or was it Babylon? He would hedge his bets throughout his career. In Fiedler's words, he ended up playing 'the typically American game with damnation'. He may have refused to bargain away his artistic integrity to Harry Cohn. But that didn't stop him signing a contract with Jack Warner.

Hopper still had to meet his real Mephistopheles, the glamorous creature who would entice him away from work, family and sanity with the promise of artistic rewards and haunt him for the rest of his life. 'I was an actor, man. I thought I was the best young actor around. I didn't think there was anybody better. Until I went up to Warner Brothers and saw James Dean.'

Hopper's second film as a contract player was Nicholas Ray's *Rebel Without a Cause*, the talismanic youth picture that made stars out of James Dean and Natalie Wood. He had a small part as a leather-jacketed juvenile delinquent. But what was important about the film was his induction into a subterranean world of casual sex, drugs, talk about art and dreams of taking over Hollywood. Dean became his idol and Hopper appeared beside him in his last film *Giant*.

When Dean smeared his Porsche Spyder over the highway in September 1955, before he had a chance to make good on his promises, Hopper was devastated. He continued plugging away in Hollywood for two more years but things finally came to a head on the set of Henry Hathaway's *From Hell to Texas*. It was his last scene. Hathaway wanted him to walk on and read the line. Hopper wanted to improvise around it. Eighty-six takes later, he walked on and read the line.

Then he quit Hollywood in disgust. The Dennis Hopper legend has him in exile for the next twelve years, whereas things were actually a bit more complicated. While it is true that he moved to New York, studied Method acting with Lee Strasberg for a couple of years, concentrated on his photography and painting and hung out with the early Warhol crowd, Hollywood was never far away. He married into Hollywood royalty in 1961 when he got hitched to the actress Brooke Hayward. She persuaded him to move to Bel Air and tried to put back together the broken pieces of his career.

Hopper was impossible. He was drinking heavily, prowling the neighbourhood late at night with his guns, railing against fate. He regularly assaulted industry people who failed to believe how he and Dean would have done great things together. Hathaway finally invited him to do *The Sons of Katie Elder* with John Wayne and Dean Martin in 1965 and Hopper, far from telling him to go fuck himself, turned around and grabbed the part.

Hathaway used him again in *True Grit* and he also appeared alongside Paul Newman in *Cool Hand Luke*. At the same time, he worked with independent producer Roger Corman on a couple of films that drew more directly on his personal circumstances. There was the biker flick, *The Glory Stompers*, and the Jack Nicholson-scripted acid odyssey, *The Trip*, in which he played a hippie high priest who dispenses LSD to Peter Fonda's burnt-out corporate hack.

Hopper was playing a double game, shuttling between the Old Hollywood he publicly despised and the inchoate beginnings of a new cinema he could barely define. *Easy Rider* was conceived by Fonda in 1967 as another in the line of low-budget exploitation films they had been doing. Hopper was always slated to direct, but Corman was originally going to produce. When he backed down, Hopper and Fonda arranged the financing themselves.

The fact that the film would become a cultural phenomenon and make Hopper a millionaire was not something anyone could have predicted. (Least of all Brooke Hayward, who was disappointed her husband was doing another 'biker-druggie' film and filed for divorce.) Now, it seems tricksy and portentous. At the time, it caught the mood, defining the counterculture for mainstream audiences.

The success of *Easy Rider* was an accident of timing. But it made the whole declining edifice of the studio system think Hopper was the Last Tycoon, a new Harry Cohn, the only man who could save them. Universal Pictures offered him a million bucks to do whatever the hell he wanted. In a characteristic gesture, he accepted the offer and promised he would bury Old Hollywood.

Hopper had come up with the idea for *The Last Movie* when filming *The Sons of Katie Elder* in Mexico. He saw that the film company was leaving behind a simulated Western town on the outskirts of the village of Durango and wondered what the natives would make of it. *The Last Movie* speculates that they would have had a primitive understanding of cinema as a sacrificial death cult.

Hopper tried to film the movie in Mexico, but was unsuccessful. In the end, he dragged his cast – which included Sam Fuller, Peter Fonda, Dean Stockwell and a host of other cronies, drug buddies and hangers-on – to Peru and shot in a remote village in the Andes. Stories filtered back to Hollywood of dissipation and excess on a grand scale, but Hopper brought his movie in on time and under budget.

He lost it in the editing room. He was meant to take six

months to edit forty hours of footage. He ended up spending sixteen months obsessively working and reworking his material in a secluded lodge he had bought in Taos, New Mexico. When he finally delivered his film, the Universal suits were horrified and declared it to be an 'attack on Hollywood'.

Which it undoubtedly was. But it was also meant to be the first artistic statement of a New Hollywood, a place that would resolve the Faustian contradictions that had tormented Hopper for so long. In a typical kind of megalomaniacal reasoning, he thought he was destroying Hollywood in order to save it.

The Last Movie is a sprawling, overambitious, incoherent piece of film-making. It is simultaneously a conceptual Western, a Passion play, a James Dean tribute, a pastiche of *The Treasure of the Sierra Madre* and a Godardian anti-movie. Pauline Kael, while sympathetic, called it a 'gigantic classic paranoid fantasy'. Universal gave it a token run and shelved it.

Even now, Hopper seethes with a sense of betrayal. 'I was the first American ever to win the Venice Film Festival. I came back like a kid who had won the World Series all by myself and Universal Pictures says, "We don't care, we're not gonna distribute the movie, we don't understand it." It was the end of my career, that was the end of it and then came Steven Spielberg, then came George Lucas, then came – dah-dah-dah – Francis Ford Coppola, and I was just sitting in Taos, New Mexico eating peyote and dreaming about James Dean, you know?'

The New Hollywood was built without Hopper. *The Last Movie* was meant to be that impossible object: the last Hollywood movie and the first American art film, a simultaneous act of refusal and gesture of penitence. It was a crazy dream. No wonder Hopper buried himself in Taos.

He got work during the next twelve years, but it was scattered and thin. Wim Wenders used him best in *The American Friend* as a distressed American icon adrift in the seductive coils of Europe. He appeared in *Tracks*, Henry Jaglom's hysterical anti-Vietnam war movie, as a violent and paranoid vet. Francis Coppola used him twice. In *Apocalypse Now,* he played the scrabbling, jittery Fool to Brando's ponderous Lear, while in *Rumblefish*, he was the stumblebum father of Matt Dillon and Mickey Rourke.

It wasn't until he dried out that he rediscovered the full extent of his powers. *Blue Velvet* showed what he was capable of. When he mimes to the kitsch Roy Orbison ballad, 'In Dreams', he distorts it into something menacing and uncanny. His face is a mask of rage and pain, but he remains absolutely still. His eyes penetrate the void and seem to reflect back on themselves.

It is in moments of abstracted trance such as this – not in the obvious scenes of assault and battery – that Hopper's astonishing intensity as an actor reveals itself. It's there even in *Rebel Without a Cause*, as he drives through the night, lightly tapping his face and looking at nothing.

Most recent directors have left this quality in Hopper well alone. (Stephen Gyllenhal has come closest to tapping it recently with *Paris Trout*, in which Hopper plays a murderously racist loan shark in pre-civil-rights Georgia.)

They have tended to play instead with his value as a condensed figure of sixties burn-out. Even Tim Hunter's excoriating vision of teen nihilism, *River's Edge*, uses Hopper in this way. The character he plays may be a paranoid, gun-toting, drug-dealing hermit but hey, when he kills, he kills for love.

Hopper had been to the brink and come back. He had played the 'typically American game with damnation' and not seemed like a jerk or a hypocrite. It was something that fascinated everybody. 'I've gone against all the principles of a Christian life,' he admits. 'I've enjoyed it. But I've still got the hangover.'

He returned to directing after his crack-up. (Although he directed the lowlife melodrama *Out of the Blue* in 1980, it wasn't a project he had entire control over.) *Colors*, starring Robert Duvall and Sean Penn, was a meticulously crafted cop movie that threw the gang culture of East LA under a liberal spotlight. More disappointing was *The Hot Spot*, a careless trawl through the file of noir clichés that Hopper optimistically described as 'Last Tango in Texas'.

By far the best film to come out of this period was *Backtrack*. A companion piece to *The Last Movie* disguised as a loping romantic thriller, it tracks Hopper's life back to Taos and juggles familiar Faustian motifs along the way. It also throws around a lot of art references. One of the most interesting occurs when

Jodie Foster contemplates a book of Georgia O'Keeffe's landscapes in the desert.

It suggests that maybe Hopper really has been a painter all along. He was painting before he was acting; he caught the tail end of the abstract expressionist boom in New York. The paintings he is doing at the moment combine computer-enhanced imagery from *Colors* with appropriations of LA gang graffiti as it has been repeatedly whitewashed by the authorities until it appears 'like a Rothko painting'.

O'Keeffe and Rothko are useful points of comparison for Hopper. Both painters belong to an American Romantic tradition of transcendental landscape which derives from a cultural interest in primitivist myth, primal forms of experience, trance states and pantheism. It makes you view Hopper's films in a new light. Makes you remember the straining for sublimity as Hopper and Fonda cruise the American south-west in *Easy Rider*; the vast panorama of the Rockies spread beneath Hopper's fevered brow in *Backtrack* as he transports Jodie Foster to safety in a helicopter.

The interview is drawing to a close and Hopper is becoming ruminative. He gazes out of the window at the imported eucalyptus trees and the heat rising off the asphalt next to the Pacific Ocean. 'You know, this whole town is a hallucination,' he says. 'It's almost like you have to invent something here because there's nothing here. It really is a dry, arid place. I think of Los Angeles as a place that was built temporarily. Anybody who says "Oh I really love Los Angeles" should go to a shrink, because there's nothing here. I mean, this town can come and go and it'll still be a desert.'

Elvis

i-D, no. 151, April 1996

Four years ago, Greil Marcus published *Dead Elvis* and the world of cultural studies was never the same again. Picking up from the rash of Elvis sightings that spread through the American tabloid media in the early nineties – Elvis popping up in a supermarket parking lot in Wisconsin, Elvis wandering around a trailer park in Syracuse, New York – Marcus went on to speculate that since his death in 1977 the King of Rock'n'Roll had been reborn as the focus of a bizarre pop cargo cult: 'Elvis Christ, Elvis Nixon, Elvis Hitler, Elvis Mishima, Elvis as godhead, Elvis inhabiting the bodies of serial killers, of saints, fiends.' In *E: Reflections on the Birth of the Elvis Faith* (Blast Books), John Strausbaugh takes this one step further by reconceptualizing Elvis fan worship as the beginnings of a whole new religion. In this he has been helped by science fiction writers like Neal Stephenson and Jack Womack, who have both reconfigured Elvis as a latter-day saint in the merchandising subworlds of America. (Womack even devoted a whole novel to the phenomenon, *Elvissey*, in which there appears a breakaway Elvis sect called the Jesseans who take Elvis's stillborn twin brother as the true messiah.) Strausbaugh is no match for Marcus as a cultural anthropologist. He lacks his scepticism, irony and alertness to the possibilities of redemption glittering amidst the trash of American consumer culture. He is more interested instead in hyping an official myth of 'Elvis Christ', and his book at times reads like a user's guide to the Holy Church of the King. To this end he relies heavily on extended metaphor – if Graceland is the Vatican of the Elvis cult, then the fan clubs are the missionary churches, the Elvis impersonators are the priests, the recordings and films the sacraments and those kitschy high-collar Vegas jump-suits the approved liturgical dress code. Strausbaugh understands that the polysemy of the Elvis icon (simultaneously black/white, male/female and hetero/homo) makes him an ideal candidate for a fully syncretic pagan media cult, but he is continually drawn back to the Christian Church as the recommended template for his new religion. He is, in other words, less drawn to the pill-popping Darkside Elvis that featured in Albert Goldman's 1981 biog than he is to the god-fearing Pentecostalist of the fan clubs. For him, it is Elvis's immaculate 'comeback special' on American network TV in 1968 that prefigures all the tabloid fantasies of a Second Coming. Written out of the record is the idea not that Elvis Died For Our Sins but that Elvis Died *Of* Our Sins, that he was the sacrificial victim of an orgiastic cannibal cult that only ever wanted (as gonzoid rock critic Lester Bangs memorably prophesied when he imagined scooping up handfuls of barely digested drugs from the King's still warm corpse) to eat him all up and spit him right back out.

'Mark Leyner'

i-D, no. 112, January 1993

After the cult success of My Cousin, My Gastroenterologist, his second book of language games, media samples, condensed techno-narratives, smart image bombs and general hip stuff, Mark Leyner was moved to confess that perhaps he was the world's first cyberpunk writer who was not a science fiction writer. That's to say, he was interested in science not as a formal device for reinventing the world (the flipside of which is still evident in the dystopian imagery of a J.G. Ballard), but as a rhetorical device for trashing it. Witness the chapter titles: 'i was an infinitely hot and dense dot', 'psychotechnologies of the somber workaholics'. Leyner is a hard-core comic fantasist, the anti-poet of the technological sublime. The boring tropes of the nineteenth-century novel – 'narrative', 'character' – do not register on his cultural radar. He is post-postmodern. As he has said: 'I never had to go through all the shit that postmodernists like Ron Sukenick and Steve Katz and Ray Federman had to go through back in the '60s.' Leyner's writing – dense, charged, lyrical – is the nearest equivalent to a Jackson Pollock action painting or the illegible soundscapes of The Orb, except that his material is the toxic debris of the postwar mass media. His latest book, Et Tu, Babe (Harmony Books, US import) is not quite as avant-garde as his previous, but is just as funny and inventive. Its subject is the phenomenon of cult celebrity and this time round there is the image of a central character: 'Mark Leyner', world's greatest writer, media Übermensch and pumped-up sex machine. 'Leyner' runs his global empire from his headquarters in New Jersey surrounded by deformed flunkies and protected by cybernetic bodyguards. He is up there with 'the Stephen Kings, the Louis L'Amours, the Jeffrey Archers', writes album liner notes in his spare time, and calls everyone 'babe'. He is so famous that Annie Leibowitz has photographed him nude with a spy satellite in geostationary orbit. Of course, it all ends in tears. It would be too much to expect Leyner to tell the story of his alter ego's fate in linear or conventional fashion. Instead, he offers a series of parodic media discourses (interviews, endorsements, press conferences, game-show transcripts, lists, blurbs, tabloid news items) and formal jokes (the introduction appears in Chapter 5, we are informed that a missing part of the novel has been confiscated by the government). Meanwhile, recurrent motifs include insects, mutation, junk food, pop anthropology, brand names, weird sex, DNA fingerprinting and Bruce Lee. 'Leyner' drives a VMW (that's 'Visigoth Motor Works') Piranha 793 and concedes that he's a part of the ' "I'm OK, You're Lunch" generation'. Actually, in the wake of the publication of Douglas Coupland's *Generation X* and the endless theorizations of the media-made generation ten years down the line from the yuppies, you can see that Leyner, despite being thirty-six, is a quintessential twentysomething. Same fascination with hyperbolic pop culture ('Imagine *Fiddler on the Roof* starring Bruce Lee'), specialized consumption, media terrorism, weird drugs (anyone for 'Abraham Lincoln's morning breath'?), conspiracy theory and chronic panic ('How do I know if I'm great or if I'm the victim of megalomaniacal delusions?'). The great thing about Leyner, though, is that he's still a punk at heart. Or as 'Leyner' says: 'we can't leave the exploration of inner space to New Age Milquetoasts like Terence McKenna.' *Absolument*, babe.

Gender fucking

You're carousing in Madame JoJo's in Soho near the desperate end of eighteen years of one-party rule. It's a loungecore night. Memories of our nursery days conjured on stage by a motley crew of nostalgia merchants (the Weimar moment). You've got your feet up. A bottle of Beck's in one hand, a Café Crème fag in the other and a cracking bird in your face (she used to be a bit of a name back in the eighties; how about that?). You think you're a big man. Some bloke with your first name is doing his Lenny Beige routine up above you – the sovs, the flash, the sleazoid charm. His mask is dripping. You remember the model of male subjectivity entertained by one of the men's mags you used to work for, the one that capital could not route through, the one that seduced you. *Diamond geezer.* 'Kitsch: the last degenerate form of myth' (Stalislaw Lem).

Sex crimes

i-D, no. 164, May 1997

Erotic delirium, necrophilia, unconscious sadism, ideal masochism, fetishism, exhibitionism, nymphomania, frottism, bestiality, homicidal mania – these are just some of the diagnostic buzz-words gleaned from *Psychopathia Sexualis* (Velvet), Richard von Krafft-Ebing's infamous collection of late nineteenth-century case histories. They point to the fact that many of the psychopathologies we are familiar with today were invented more than a century ago; they also demonstrate that many of them are well on the way to social acceptance. It was J.G. Ballard who said that the history of the twentieth century could in some ways be figured as the 'normalization of the psychopathic'. All he meant by this was that yesterday's abnormal behaviour becomes tomorrow's alternative lifestyle. This is nowhere more obvious than in the history of the gay scene. It seems outrageous to late twentieth-century eyes that 'homosexuality' and 'lesbianism' should be listed among Krafft-Ebing's sample of perversions, but he was working at a time when sexual norms were very strictly policed. If it was Freud who destabilized received ideas of normality by showing how much they were interrupted by the new depths of the unconscious, then it was Krafft-Ebing who actually went out and mapped the surfaces of this new continent of perversity. His judgements may be overtly moralistic ('Mr M, thirty-three years of age, of good family, which on the maternal side for generations had shown manifestations of psychic degeneration, extending even to cases of moral insanity') and his recommendations (abstinence, aversion therapy, incarceration) punitive, but the details are all there ('After undressing he had himself bound hand and foot, and then flogged by the girl on the soles of his feet, his calves and buttocks until ejaculation ensued'). So striking is Krafft-Ebing's muscular prose that it's tempting to read his work as a species of late Victorian fiction. The historian of knowledge Michel Foucault makes the point that the symbolic recompense of the 'abnormal' is its capacity to flip over into the 'transgressive'. This was certainly the case for homosexuality during the late nineteenth century (think Oscar Wilde), but a century later transgression in the broadest sense now takes its charge from more extreme forms of behaviour (think Jeffrey Dahmer). One of the reasons why *Psychopathia Sexualis* will find a readership today is that some of its case histories still manage to work as queer fictions. Take the examples of psychosexual metamorphosis ('he always spoke of himself in the third person and called himself the Countess V'), transsexualism ('small as my nipples are, they demand room, and I feel as though the pelvis were female') and lustmurder ('the eighth victim, a little girl, he enticed into his mother's shop, fell upon her from behind, and clapping one hand over her mouth, cut her throat with the other'). Indeed, given the antique language on offer ('heavy sexual neurasthenia', 'interdiction of masturbation'), they almost come across as instances of retro-Victorian steampunk SF. Not to be taken lightly.

Mad love
Arena, no. 36, November 1992

When Harriet and Randy hit the jackpot at Las Vegas, they decided to blow the money on a call girl whose expert ministrations sent 'bolts of tingling pleasure' through Harriet and gave Randy a pretty good time too. When Barrie and Gordon bought a house in the country, Barrie went riding one day and 'exploded' on the back of the horse; it was one of those special moments she just had to share with Gordon. And let's not forget Frank and Gina. Adept at turning sports events into sex games through an elaborate system of side-bets ('If the shooter makes the basket, I have to give Frank a blowjob'), they once managed to parley a televised boxing match into a whole weekend of 'excruciating excitement'. Not bad!

Such torrid tales seem to belong to the realm of fantasy. But according to Steven Finz, a 'professor of law' in Southern California, they are all authentic. He and his wife, Iris, have together compiled an anthology of true-life confessions to bring a blush to the cheek of any Barbara Cartland fan. The respondents in *The Best Sex I Ever Had* (Warner) have careers and everything. Gina is the assistant editor on a fashion mag while Frank is a 'radio disk jockey'. Gordon owns a car dealership, which means that Barrie can stay at home all day and practise being 'voluptuous'. Meanwhile, Harriet and Randy are in business together designing and selling mannequins (apparently Randy models the 'full-figured' dummies on his wife).

Steven and Iris (hey, let's not be formal) tell us that although, of course, no one buying their book 'needs instruction in the mechanics of copulation', everyone can do with pepping up their sex lives a little. For instance: 'You might never have considered pretending to be an armed assailant or a hooker from an escort service.' Well, we might have considered it, guys, but it's hard to find the right equipment in the local hardware store, you know?

What is the significance of this supremely daft little volume? Although it sells itself as a 'scorching collection of erotic revelations', most of the material it includes is pretty tame. It may flirt with lesbianism (Harriet and the call girl), bestiality (Barrie and that horse) and troilism (Harriet again, I'm afraid), but sodomy is a definite no-go area. This is safe sex for that nice young couple who live next door. Steven and Iris need hardly remind us that 'casual sex can be deadly'. Uh, right. Make sure Dobbin is fully protected, Barrie, OK?

Now that the equation between sex and disease is uppermost in a lot of people's minds, talking about it has replaced doing it. There is promiscuity only in the variety of books suddenly available on how to do it better than the next guy. Walk into any supposedly upmarket bookstore and look around. It is astonishing the extent to which soft porn has now become respectable under the guise of being therapeutic. But what is the exact attraction of the 'I came four times in one night' genre?

One clue is provided by the publication of *Investigating Sex: Surrealist Research 1928–1932* (Verso). A collection of documents edited by José Pierre and translated by Malcolm Imrie, they record the business of twelve symposia, chaired by surrealist founder member and chief manifesto-writer, André Breton, on the subject of sex. The first two were originally published in *La Révolution surrealiste*, the surrealist house magazine, but the others have not seen the light of day until now. They took place at infrequent intervals between 1928 and 1932 and included over forty people – of whom only seven were women. It has to be admitted that *Investigating Sex* is mostly boys' talk.

The list of participants reads like a roll call of the surrealist movement. The poet and novelist Louis Aragon, Antonin Artaud, the lyric poet Paul Éluard, Max Ernst, the poet Benjamin Péret, the poet Jacques Prévert, the novelist and parodist Raymond Queneau, Man Ray, the painter Yves Tanguy – all at one time or another were willing to expose themselves to the inquisitorial demands and hectoring submissions of Breton.

Breton was concerned to investigate the nature of love as much as of sex. More than anything else, he hoped to bring the irrational impulses of the unconscious into view so that they could be pressed into the service of the revolution (this was at the time when most surrealists were still sympathetic towards the Communist Party). A synthesis of Marx and Freud was the informal aim and the twelve sessions took their place alongside the surrealist interest in automatic writing and the recording of dreams.

It has to be stated that the material thrown up is beyond the wildest imaginings of a 'professor of law' like Steven Finz. Not because it is necessarily perverse, but because it is alert, sensitive and, well, imaginative. So, alongside the rather predictable interest in sodomy is a more curious sexual obsession with women's eyelashes and armpits and, in Queneau's case, an enthusiasm for women who limp.

A lot of the questions raised still resonate today. Is orgasm separate from ejaculation? Is love separate from sex? What is the ideal age for a woman? What is the best sexual position? Is it desirable to make love to a woman with a period? (Well, is it?)

Breton was obsessed with a number of personal questions, from how often a couple making love could reach orgasm simultaneously to how you could tell a woman was faking it. But the discussion often meanders out of his control into uncharted areas – fetishism, bestiality, voyeurism and homosexuality. This last practice is something that particularly bothered Breton. At one point, as Queneau and Aragon leisurely chat about doing it with another man, Breton throws a fit: 'If this promotion of homosexuality carries on, I will leave this meeting forthwith.' (The conversation switched to condoms.)

Some of the funniest exchanges occur between Breton, the intolerant sexual idealist, and Queneau, whose amused scepticism at times skirts cynicism. Queneau often seems as if he is winding Breton up under the guise of an objective pursuit of the truth ('What does Breton think of physical failures during lovemaking?').

Artaud is good value too. Already deeply involved in developing his idea of a shamanistic 'Theatre of Cruelty', he turns up for the sixth session in March 1928, gets by far the longest speeches and is only around for ten minutes. You can imagine everyone being slightly overawed by this charismatic figure. He raves on about the 'filthy urges' to which he is subject and claims that if he is going to fall into a state of 'rapture' with anyone it will be with himself. Then he walks out. At this point, Breton resumes control and the guys start batting around how many times they can do it in a night and how long it takes them to come (Breton: 'Twenty seconds maximum').

Some of the questions asked seem a bit of a give-away. For example, Péret: 'Would anyone allow themselves to be seen by a woman with suspicious stains on his trousers?' (To which Aragon quite reasonably replies: 'I don't see how there could be any suspicious stains on my trousers'.) And there are some great one-liners. Prévert on masturbation: 'I used to think about it a lot, once, when I practised it.' Aragon on how he can only manage semi-erections: 'I don't regret it any more than being unable to lift pianos.' (Aragon is sly, witty and slightly obstreperous throughout.)

Despite all the laughs to be had at the expense of these guys, it should be remembered that they didn't have access to a lot of the basic information we take for granted. When you think that the multiple orgasm was not 'discovered' – or produced as a talking point – until 1966 as a result of the research of American sexologists Masters and Johnson, it is understandable that Breton should have had such an obsession with female simulation.

It would be easy to see these sessions as the precursor of the modern vogue for group therapy. It would be even easier to see them as the nascent form of a confessional pornography which has today become commodified in volumes like *The Best Sex I Ever Had*. The name to invoke at this point would be Michel Foucault. The French philosopher, writing over ten years ago, made the point that confession was the quintessential method of transforming sex into 'discourse', and that it had been used as an instrument of oppression for centuries. Invented by the Catholic Church, it had spread into the disciplines of medicine, psychiatry and criminal justice. Something like *The Best Sex I Ever Had* is merely its latest refinement.

Like I say, you could slot *Investigating Sex* into this argument. But it would be too easy. The surrealists were attempting to subvert all the old control mechanisms; they were attempting to use confession as a tool to interrogate the way sexuality was organized in the bourgeois family, the Catholic Church and the state. They did not want to interpret their sexual impulses, merely record them. Unlike Freud, they were not looking for a 'talking cure', but neither did they want to establish a syllabus of perversion. Breton was equally dismissive of 'playboy sensualists' as he was of ' "doctors" of so-called love madness'.

The surrealists were searching for something powerful and estranging, a force that would impel a new way of looking at the world. As Breton asks: 'What kind of hope do you place in love?'

Virtual porn
Arena, no. 59, June 1996

What do you *want*? Your name is Beavis (or maybe Butt-head) and you want to know about porn on the net. What do you do? Check out a net directory, of course. One of the most exhaustive is the GoOd HeAd LoOks aT SeX on tHe NeT directory on a local server in Washington (http://maui.net/~gill/sex.html). So you download the page and what do you get? Invitations to participate in a Cyberporn Debate or to Fuck Big Brother. But that's not what you want. That's not why BT is clocking up the decimalized pennies on your modem line. You want the real stuff. A bit of Puss 'N Boots, a bit of T&A. Which is all a bit sad. Because the information you really want to get your hot and sweaty little hands on – whether it's Adult Links, Adult Pics, Sex E-Zines or even A Few Misc. Sex Linx Thangs – are all 'temporarily closed'.

This virtual porn business. The one where you no longer have to suffer the embarrassment of shuffling with your pocket change in the newsagents as you wait to get served. The one where you boot up the screen, slip unseen into alt.sex.bondage and wipe'n'go. You can see it's going to be harder to get into than you thought.

If the GoOd HeAd directory of sex links had been working, though, what might you have expected to find? Well, dearie, it depends on what you want. If you want to jump under the virtual covers with a bunch of other swingers then you can always dangle your credit card in front of one of the Members Only BBSs and get down and dirty in a text-based version of an 0898 chat line. What tickles your fancy? There's the Hot Tub

Club ('Better hurry up and get your clothes off! The Hot Tub is cumming!'), the Fantasy Party Line or the Honey Dripper. All the kinds of places where you can engage in 'serious adult erotic conferencing' while you browse the ads for mail order videos and curious leather and rubber goods.

If that doesn't raise the hairs on the back of your neck, then maybe it's time for you to check into the 12-Step Recovery from Sexual Addiction programme on Fidonet. Either that or log on to some of the Usenet alt.sex newsgroups and stroke the keys for as long as your fingers are up to it. What are you likely to find? Well, there's alt.sex.masturbation for a start. If that's a bit too close to home, then there's always alt.sex.fetish or even alt.sex.fetish.feet. The list of newsgroups devoted to sex scrolls past on the screen like a forbidding sendstorm of erotic signals . . .

Actually, one thing you soon learn from spying in this way on other people's hang-ups is that they take them desperately seriously. As J.G. Ballard noted long ago, the same quality of almost obliterating abstraction (*that* body part in *this* position with *that* connotation) becomes attached to any perversion when it's pursued rigorously and longingly enough. But that's not you, is it? You're a bit more, well, *normal*.

In that case there's plenty of good practical information for you to access on the net. Information about safe sex practices, information about sex and the disabled, information about how to deal with things like rape. Information about sex education? But let's not get too pious. You know all that stuff, right? (*Right?*)

What you want is . . . you know, the kind of stuff you get in the regular top-shelf wank mags. Well, why didn't you say? Take the dust cover off the hood of your terminal and step right this way. Where do you want to go? There's a gallery of smudged readers' wives and pixellated glamour girls just waiting to service you at either Fiesta (http://www.fiesta.org/), the X-Site (http://www.mailbox.co.uk/xsite) or Paul Raymond Publications (http://www.pr-org.co.uk/main/). All with the promise, according to a recent survey in *.net* magazine, that the pix on offer are just 'a little bit raunchier' than what the publishers can usually get away with on the high street.

You've got it. The porn barons are moving into cyberspace

and their sites are collecting upwards of a million hits per month. At the moment, it doesn't cost you a penny to download some T or some A. The publishers see their sites as virtual ads for their terrestrial wares and are happy for punters to browse around for nothing. But that will change. They're thinking of adding online dating services, hot QuickTime videos, breathless sound files, the lot. And that means you'll have to start unloading credit card numbers before you can say 'just looking'.

Still, there's always the GIF glamour babe sites to hit on. That's to say, collections of soft-core pix uploaded into cyberspace by horny dudes in college dorms and sundry other devoted admirers of the female form. These were the guys who pioneered the whole idea of putting their bedside fantasies up on the net and there's no reason why they won't be able to hold their own against the porn barons. (That's the beauty of cyberspace – it's a democracy.) Check out the CyberGirls Link Page (http://www.cybercity.dk/users/ccc2394/) for directions. Or else go to Modern Rome (http://www.xroads.com/~priapus) and Bill's Favourite Pics (http://www.whitman.edu/~burkotwt/porn.html) direct. What do you find? The virtual equivalent of those folkloric stories about shifty characters flashing you saucy postcards from inside the folds of their dirty macs while you're loitering on the street corner.

But what are you saying? You've seen this all before? You're *bored*? Well, you've got a point. The net is supposed to be about what's new and happening, right? It's about the hot breath of modernity shaving your neck as you fast-forward into the future. So why not experiment a little? After all, nobody's watching. It's just you, your modem and the World Wide Web. Forget about all those ditsy porn starlets who've got their home pages up on the net. Do something different. Drift over to Annie Sprinkle's site (http://www.infi.net/~heck) and drop into her MetamorphoSex Workshop. Surf the fine line between pornography, performance art and polymorphous perversity. Discover how in cyberspace identities are fluid, sexualities are plural and the body is one more touch-sensitive screen. See how Hunks on the Web (http://citynight.com/hunks) compares to alt.binaries.pictures.lesbians. Do these images do it for you? If not, why not? Slide into the Society for Human Sexuality (http://weber.u.washington.edu/~sfpse/) and see whether you only want what you want because that's the way you've been programmed.

Getting a bit dizzy? Maybe those crazy French guys Deleuze and Guattari (you know, they're always getting namechecked in alt.philosophy) were right when they said that sexuality was just a matter of flows, breaks and borders. Where do you want to stop? Uh-oh, what's this? A home page set against a black background with a blue ribbon attached. It's a protest against the US Communications Decency Act, which bans the transmission of 'patently offensive' material over the net and threatens offenders with fines of up to $200,000 and gaol sentences of up to five years. This is getting serious.

Now you know why all those sex links in the GoOd HeAd directory were 'temporarily closed'. You don't exactly want to Fuck Big Brother, but maybe there's something to this Cyberporn Debate after all. So what are the issues, exactly? You do a bit of research and find out that the authorities on both sides of the Atlantic are pursuing their completely understandable concerns with clamping down on things like alt.bestiality and cyber-kiddie porn. But, wait a minute, aren't these matters covered by the existing obscenity laws?

So what's the problem? Isn't this just another of those moral panics? Well, not entirely. There's the whole business of children accidentally stumbling upon adult material as they're toddling their way towards Make a Monster (http://www.rahul.net/renoir/monster/monster.html) or Kids Web (http://www.npac.syr.edu:80/textbook/kidsweb/). But hold on, isn't there plug-in software available that allows worried parents to screen out a hit-list of offending items from their browsers? There sure is. Chief among these 'parental control filters' is Net Nanny (http://www.netnanny.com/netnanny/home.html). But there are also related products like Net Shepherd, Cybersitter, Cyber Patrol and SurfWatch available on the market. Take your pick.

There's much more to the Cyberporn Debate than this, of course. But it isn't any different from the usual issues that are bandied about by the likes of Andrea Dworkin and Camille Paglia offline. So which way is the wind blowing in cyberspace?

Take a look at what Microsoft (always a good barometer of the zeitgeist) are up to and what do you find? They're hedging their bets. On the one hand, they've hooked up with Apple Computer and online service providers like CompuServe and Prodigy to file a suit against the CDA on the grounds that it violates their constitutional right to free speech. But on the other hand, they've teamed up with the WWW-sponsored Platform for Internet Content Selection and the Recreational Software Advisory Council to develop a common net ratings system. Which is it to be? Well, what do you want?

Gender hacks
i-D, no. 165, June 1997

When Steve Kurtz of the Critical Art Ensemble was in London recently he commented on the big ideological contradiction he saw existing in cyberculture at the moment. On the one hand, Internet talk still insists that the body is obsolete and we will all soon have the chance to upload our minds directly into cyberspace. On the other hand, biotech hype claims that the body is the ideal platform for micro-tech and that we shall all soon be wearing our minds on our sleeves. All of which is as good an introduction as any to *Processed Lives* (Routledge), an anthology of writings on 'gender and technology in everyday life', edited by Jennifer Terry and Melodie Calvert, which came out of a year-long series of events held at the Wexner Center for the Arts at Ohio State University during 1994/95. The primary theoretical motivator behind this anthology is Donna Haraway's idea that gender itself is a technology, that we are shaped as 'male' and 'female' according to historically constituted norms that settle across a marked anatomical difference. This leads to all sorts of speculations. Joyan Saunders and Liss Platt, for example, raise the idea that Kim Novak was a biological male who was raised a female because s/he was born without the 'standard male equipment' and go on to quote a case of gender reassignment that supports their argument ('You want me to tell you how we made the change-over from her being a boy to being a girl. OK, well, at the outset I started dressing her not in dresses, but, you know, in little pink slacks and frilly lace blouses'). Meanwhile, Judith Halberstam remarks upon the strict 'gender policing' that occurs in women's rest rooms and goes on to examine the difficulties faced by drag kings like Elvis Herselvis and Tony Las Vegas ('Why is femininity easily impersonated or performed while masculinity seems resilient to imitation?'). What is required is the invention of 'transgenders'. But this is difficult to achieve. Christine Tamblyn comments on the fact that despite the possibilities offered by the Internet for gender hacking, sexist behavioural codes still persist in cyberspace as panic reaction formations ('our identities are delimited by the poverty of our imaginations as much as by the abject biological markers of the organic'). Other contributors to the volume have other stories to tell. Evelyn Hammonds shows how *Time* magazine's computer-generated image of transracial harmony erases the facts of material history in its eagerness to construct a feminized Other. Lisa Cartwright examines how the National Institute of Health's Visible Man web site, which features scanned images of executed murderer Joseph Paul Jerrigan, projects the ideal citizen of cyberspace as a body stripped of civil rights. Kathy High looks at how the Human Genome Diversity Project acts as a form of 'bio-piracy' by cataloguing the genes of indigenous peoples as resources for First World profit. It all adds up to a provocative and stimulating book that cries out to be liberated from the hands of academics.

Cyberfeminism

i-D, no. 136, January 1995

Jack into All New Gen, the ball-busting computer simulation by radical femme performance outfit VNS Matrix, and suddenly the future looks female. Deliberately reversing the stereotypes built into most vidgame scenarios, All New Gen is modelled on a sex-based interactive fantasy in which the DNA Sluts are the heroines, Big Daddy Mainframe is the bad guy and Circuit Boy is a hot piece of cyber-totty along for the ride.

'Circuit Boy has become something of a pin-up back home in Adelaide,' says Julianne Pierce, one of the four founding members of VNS Matrix. 'That might have something to do with the fact that he has a permanent erection.' Or it might have something to do with the fact that he is symbolically castrated at the end of the game.

VNS Matrix were just one of an assorted bunch of tech-heads, cybertheorists and performance artists who took to the stage at the Terminal Futures conference at London's Institute of Contemporary Arts last October. Their brand of Barbie dyke feminism may have looked incongruous next to the bullish talk about VR military apps and speed-driven shoot 'em ups but it was by no means mere tokenism. In fact, what is striking about the rapidly expanding field of cybercult studies is how many of its leading practitioners are women.

Also on stage at Terminal Futures was Sandy Stone, a transsexual theorist from UT Texas's multimedia lab who is at the forefront of interrogating received ideas of gender, tech and language. Meanwhile, Sadie Plant – a lecturer at Birmingham University's cult studs department and perhaps the leading UK-based cybertheorist – was one of the chief speakers at the ICA's last tech conference and there are plans to bring over Avital Ronell – Berkeley's renegade comp lit professor whose groundbreaking *The Telephone Book* linked tech, gnosis and Heideggerian philosophy in provocative fashion – for the next.

Once you begin to compile a list of the women involved in cybertheory it can start to seem endless. There's Brenda Laurel, alt vidgame designer, author of *Computers as Theatre* and part begetter of *Wild Palms*. There's Lisa Palac, sex queen of cyberspace and leading contributor to San Franciso's *Future Sex* magazine. There's Constance Penley, film scholar at Santa Barbara and author of the forthcoming *Popular Science and Sex in America*. And then there's Donna Haraway, big-shot Santa Cruz academic, author of *The Cyborg Manifesto* and *Primate Visions* and the name held in most awe by the cybertheorists of Terminal Futures.

Like I say, this list can start to seem endless. It can also start to seem pointless. Isn't it patronizing and insulting to bundle together a diverse group of writers and artists just because they happen to be women who are into technology? Well, yes and no. While it is important to acknowledge that these figures have nothing like a shared agenda, the whole issue of how cybertech has transformed sex, media and power relations is so central to our understanding of post-industrial society that it doesn't seem unreasonable to run with at least a provisional idea of 'cyberfeminism'.

Tiffany Lee Brown, tech editor of *Future Sex* and virtual denizen of the WELL (Whole Earth 'Lectronic Link) in San Francisco, might be a good place to start. One of the chief contributors to a special 'chicks in psyberspace' issue of the Austin-based cyberzine *Fringe Ware Review* last year, she admits that she had to struggle to overcome her cultural conditioned technophobia before appreciating the benefits of getting online.

'Technology has typically been pretty cold and asexual,' she says. 'Most of us look at it as something that is opposed to human life. I think what's happening now is that a much larger segment of the population is getting involved with technology and wants to use it in different sorts of ways.'

What sorts of ways? Tiffany Lee Brown plugs the sex angle. She talks about the possibilities that the Internet throws up for gender hacking (where a man can pose as a woman and simulate sex using a strap-on dildo), goes on to suggest that VR-based sex applications have so far explored only a very limited sensorium (mainly based on the male gaze) and rhapsodizes about the possibility of transsexual – and even 'trans-species' – body contact.

All this certainly adds up to a very different take on the virtual world. While SF author William Gibson may have moved on from his initial conception of cyberspace as a disembodied info-matrix (check the weird saurian avatars in *Virtual Light*), the disdain that the console cowboys of *Neuromancer* have for their bodies (nicknamed 'the meat') fits in with a recognizably male strain of North American transcendentalism.

The huge irony is that many of the pioneers of the Internet back in the seventies – the data processors, librarians and archivists – were in fact women. While the big boys were out there grabbing the genius grants for their blue sky research projects, the women were inside the Net getting their heads around the whole messy business of information retrieval. It may have been low-status labour, but at least it was equipping them for the future.

This is one of Sadie Plant's big riffs. Remixing Foucault, Deleuze and McLuhan, she speculates that the relationship between computer technology, capitalism and subjectivity has been intensively zoned around the bodies of women. To paraphrase briefly, whereas the era of patriarchal dominance was associated with an industrial economy of brute labour power and female subjugation, the emerging order of transnational data flows is much more fluid, fractured and female.

Plant quotes the fact that Ada Lovelace was one of the first computer programmers (back in the nineteenth century) and goes on to liken the ability to jam together computer code to the traditionally female skills of spinning and weaving. Falling in step behind Foucault, she sees these subjugated knowledge indexes of the patriarchal order – these flighty ways of using hands, eyes and machines – as a powerful force of insurrection. Though not necessarily of liberation.

'If you look at patriarchy as a long-running command economy then you can say that what served in the past as its goods and services and media were its women,' says Plant. 'And you can go on to say that through their own activity, they too – like the machines – are now becoming self-organizing, intelligent and refusing to go along with their own regulation.'

The linked principles of self-organization, critical feedback and connectionism Plant sees as crucial to the development of capitalism as a global virus that breaks down older self-regulating structures like the state, the family and the market. She likes to look at the insurrection of 'women' as one local instance of this larger process of accelerated cultural erosion.

The dissemination of 'drugs' is another. Pointing out that the war on drugs – or 'Prohibition' as she likes to call it – is an instance of global capitalism fighting its own markets, she goes on to hypothesize that this is an example of auto-immune disease writ large. On the one hand, the coding of drugs as illegal is a useful control mechanism for the 'medico-military complex'. On the other hand, it leads to a loss of taxable revenue.

'There really is a crisis of such magnitude here that it can't really be underestimated. Prohibition is a disaster and clearly cannot continue – indeed in some sense it has long ago collapsed anyway. But by the same token it seems that if you did have global deregulation there would be enormous consequences for geopolitical power and the global economy generally – let alone its more immediate consequences on individuals and particular cultures. Either move seems impossible. Which I think sums up the dilemma.'

Plant has often been accused by left-liberal critics of being a gung-ho libertarian, cheering on the global spread of capitalism while ignoring the social injustices it leaves in its wake. This is rather unfair. Perhaps in order to rile her critics, she likes to describe herself as a cybernetic Marxist, one more interested in the revolutionary potential of 'the forces of production' than of 'the people'.

'Capitalism doesn't produce liberation for women – it would be naïve to say so. But it certainly does change and erode the old patriarchy and any change in that sense, even if it's not necessarily a good thing for women, is certainly a bad thing for the structures that have kept them in their place in the past.'

Which still leaves the point that while capitalism may be on a post-industrial curve in the West, it depends for its resurgence upon the peripheral industrialization of the East. And that that typically involves the exploitation of women in old-fashioned sweatshops.

'This is why it's not possible to talk about utopianism,' says Plant. 'But nevertheless, that process of industrialization which took two hundred years to happen in the West is happening within a generation in the Pacific Rim. And you have to say that even though to be working in a sweatshop is hardly a desirable situation, it's still a better option than being stuck in the village as a wife and mother. It may give you absolutely minimal economic independence but even that is thought and felt to be better than none at all. The real key is to continually speed that process up and get beyond it as quickly as possible.'

So speed is the key. Constance Penley has also been doing some thinking about women and technology, but where Plant sees the bottom-up erosion of old structures of domination, she sees the hysterical resurgence of old structures of feeling. She should know. As a result of teaching a course on the history of pornographic film at Santa Barbara, she has found herself caught in the crossfire between traditional anti-porn feminists and the forces of the Christian right led by Pat Robertson.

Part of Penley's interest in the films of Candida Royale, Nina Hartley and other post-feminist sex queens is to demonstrate that, far from lying back and taking it, women in the porn industry are more often than not calling the shots. This is especially so in the rapidly burgeoning genre of DIY porn, in which bored wives and mothers take advantage of the VCR revolution to document and distribute their sexual fantasies. In fact, so successful have these amateur odes to the female orgasm been that the established porn industry is producing its own simulacra of them, complete with stretch marks and shoddy production values.

If this is one example of how technology enables women to let it all hang out in public, then the ruckus Penley's course has caused is a reminder of the forces of reaction waiting in the wings. It's an old story. In a series of essays in *Popular Science and Sex in America*, Penley shows how the provocative linkage of women, technology and utopia has always aroused strong superstitious feelings.

She writes about how Biosphere 2, the bubble-top eco-community established in the Arizona desert, attracted all sorts of bizarre sexual rumours because of its high degree of female scientific involvement. Perhaps that's sadly unsurprising. What is interesting about Penley's research, however, is how she goes back to the pop science cults of the nineteenth century – like Spiritualism, Seventh Day Adventism, Christian Science and early Mormonism – to demonstrate a similar convergence of utopian, scientific and crypto-feminist discourses. And a similar backlash. Who would have guessed it?

It's a slightly different story as far as the history of women's involvement in the space programme is concerned. NASA's choice of teacher and mother Christa McAuliffe as their token female astronaut on the Challenger space shuttle was intended to domesticate the space programme and make it part of everyday life. It backfired. Once the Challenger had disintegrated on prime-time, McAuliffe became the butt of countless sick jokes and was implicitly scapegoated for the failure of the project.

Not that NASA's liberal credentials have suffered. Part of the value of Penley's research is that she shows how much the cultural histories of NASA and *Star Trek* are intertwined. Both have embraced multiculturalism, both have given important – if secondary – roles to women, and both are equally confused about their objectives.

'NASA, like *Star Trek*, doesn't really know if it is a military, a scientific or a corporate project,' says Penley. She points out that the American military has always been suspicious of NASA because it is a civilian organization. It opposed the development of the space shuttle (insisting that it could launch its spy satellites from unmanned rocketry) and loaded it down with multiple technical specifications in the hope that it would never get off the ground.

Another of Penley's useful bits of data-retrieval is to go back to a NASA research project of the late fifties in which twenty-five women pilots were put through the same tests as astronauts John Glenn and Alan Shepard on the Mercury training programme. Not only did they pass with flying colours, they were found to be more resistant to radiation, less subject to heart attacks and better equipped to deal with extremes of heat and cold. They even beat the men on cost criteria (being generally smaller, they used less food and oxygen).

'I'm not saying that women should be in space rather than men,' says Penley. 'All I'm trying to say is don't keep looking for reasons to keep them out. I mean, NASA are still looking for physiological reasons why women shouldn't go into space and the biggest one right now is the lesser amount of calcium they have in their bones. Apparently calcium leakage is a huge problem in even short-term space voyages.'

NASA have done zero research on the possibilities of sex in space and have tended to focus on the pregnancy issue as a way of avoiding the whole problem. Penley suggests that if they were serious about this then they would send only gays or lesbians into space. 'But I can't see that happening.'

It may not be happening in outer space, but it may just be happening in cyberspace. Part of the interest cyberfeminists like

Donna Haraway, Sandy Stone and Brenda Laurel have in the virtual domain is that it tends to be a sympathetic breeding ground for all sorts of alternative sexualities, transgendered identities and hybrid post-human modalities. Haraway in particular has done a lot of work on the significance of the cyborg as a symbolic figure which attends to the essential morphic slipperiness of most postmodern identities.

All of which gives the lie to the received Promethean myth of the great white male struggling to deliver his tech from the forge of his conscience. No more Frankenstein's Monster, no more Creature from the Black Lagoon, no more Rockets to Mars, no more Big Daddy Mainframe. In the future, our demons will be intelligent agents. Flitting about behind the screen in cyberspace, they will be quick, alert, deadly accurate and fe/male.

Cinephylum

You're slumped in the box-like theatre at Mister Young's in Soho watching Harvey Keitel run through the romance of male abjection in *Bad Lieutenant*. It's a special screening just for you (the film distributors understand that you've been hired to give their product editorial exposure in a Sunday colour supplement). No one else is around. This is a pure cinematographic moment: the projector, the screen, the spectator's imperial ego. You feel securely wrapped up in Harvey's bad dream. This is the value of the screening rooms of Soho for many idlers drifting through the media's twilight zones: asylum. (You remember a colleague who used to alternate between them and the crack-houses of Stockwell.) Cinephilia for you has never been just the manifestation of a 'cocoon principle' (Christian Metz), but the screen for a deeper alcoholic disturbance.

Hollywood Babylon

i-D, no. 120, September 1993

When *Wild Palms* aired on ABC earlier this year, Bruce Wagner suddenly became flavour of the month. The Oliver Stone-produced six-part mini-series was conceived by Wagner as a post-*Peaks*, post-cyberpunk soap opera with political subtext to spare and was hailed as the future of network television before it hit the screen. We are going to have to wait for the show to appear over here, but in the meantime there is always *The Wild Palms Reader* (St Martin's Press) to look at. Designed by Roger Trilling and Stuart Swezey to appear as if it were a commodity in the future universe of *Wild Palms*, it is a mix of conceptual doodles, sampled imagery and textual squibs that rounds up all the usual suspects (Gibson, Sterling, Hans Moravec), drops a few surprises (Malcolm McLaren, E. Howard Hunt) and is intermittently diverting. The Wagner contribution is disappointingly thin, but anyone curious to see how the man performs at length should check out the recently paperbacked imprint of his debut novel, *Force Majeure* (St Martin's Press). A rambling black comedy that frays into surrealism at its most extreme edges, it aims to do nothing less than deliver the Big Picture on present-day Hollywood by detailing the petty vanities, routine absurdities, bizarre humiliations – and sudden deaths – that go to make up life on the margins of the dream factory. Bud Wiggins is a not-so-young screenwriter still looking for his big break years after he should have packed it in and moved to Peoria. The only thing he has going for him is bluff, charm and self-delusion. Wagner remorselessly dissects the eloquent rationalizations with which Bud consoles himself, showing how they feed into a whole psychology of megalomania: every failed romance becomes a movie in the making, every nervous breakdown a creative decision. Bud's problem is not so much that he can't distinguish reality from fantasy – the whole industry is, after all, fuelled by this fundamental creative slippage – it's more that he can't separate his ambition from his talent. During the course of the novel, he writes a post-Vietnam script, a novel inspired by the memory of an old drug buddy and a play based on Tristan and Iseult, but the closest he gets to a real movie is when the producers of *Bloodbath* hire him as a 'script doctor' and he ends up in front of the cameras as a mad killer surgeon. Wagner is consistently strong on situation – Bud moonlighting as a limo driver gives him the rear-view mirror perspective on back-seat power plays, Bud going to self-help meetings allows him to refine his pitching technique. He is even stronger on characterization – Dolly Wiggins is the Jewish Mom From Hell, while Perry Bravo as a writer-sprung-from-the-joint outdoes Mailer. Plus there are some great one-liners (example: 'Who would have imagined the A List American directors to be the alumni of craphouse seventies sitcoms?'). Wagner is at his weakest, however, when he tries to turn Hollywood into a Grand Metaphor – for the loss of meaning or the end of emotion – and the Holocaust material in the concluding section of the novel is too weighty for the tone of immaculate irony cultivated earlier. What the hell, though. *Force Majeure* shows up the satire in Robert Altman's *The Player* for the charade it is and begs to be made into a movie by – if not Penny Marshall then at least Oliver Stone.

Bachelor machine #1
Arena, no. 51, May/June 1995

Atom Egoyan originally had a very clear idea of what he wanted to do in his sixth feature, *Exotica*. He wanted to explore the highly circumscribed ritual of the table dance. It was very clear in his mind's eye. The lush, overheated decor of an upscale strip club. A young woman pulling out all the stops doing her sexy schoolgirl number. And the client sat opposite, his eyes transfixed not by her expert ministrations but by the tabletop video screen before him.

'The idea was that he would be able to access bits of information from this person's history,' says Egoyan. 'On the one hand he would have this body draped all over him and on the other he would have access to home movie details of this person's life. I had this idea of a community of dancers travelling from club to club with their own personal laser disc collection.'

Sexual fetishism, techno voyeurism, cultural alienation – all compressed into a sardonic visual anecdote. It sounds like a typical Egoyan conceit. Which is why he decided to junk it. 'I must confess I have a fear now in my own work about dwelling on the effects of new technologies like video because it's too easy to simply dismiss it as "what I do". It prevents further investigation.'

He's only got himself to blame. Ever since the release of his first feature, *Next of Kin*, in 1984, Egoyan has been one of the few film-makers willing to tackle the difficult psychological terrain that links sex, technology and death.

Certain images stand out from the three films – *Family Viewing*, *Speaking Parts* and *The Adjuster* – that together make up the early body of his work. The psychotic suburban Pop who methodically erases his old home-movie footage and replaces it with pornographic imagery. The obsessive attempt to reconstruct a suburban home from the partial photographic records that survive a catastrophic fire. A vidphone masturbation scene. An eerie video mausoleum.

Egoyan looks back on his tech-head period with some bemusement. 'I was only ever interested in using video as a psychological device,' he says. 'But there was a danger that the device was becoming more important than what it actually signified.'

Hence the cancellation of the laser video idea in *Exotica*. The table dancing ritual is still present. But rather than being styled videographically, it relies much more on traditional theatrical details of costume, set design and camera placement to make its point. The client, Francis (Bruce Greenwood), is mourning his dead daughter and uses the young dancer, Christina (Mia Kirshner), to construct a fantasy image that will help him cope with his grief.

'This film's different from the others in as much as in the other films it was the technologies that allowed people to fetishize their experience and make a metaphor out of it. They felt that by fetishizing an image they somehow had access to what that image represents and it doesn't work that way. Because an image has its own properties. It moves and changes and the very fact that it seems fixed emphasizes a certain level of delusion. In *Exotica* it's not through technology but just through Francis's direct fetishization of Christina that I'm trying to deal with these ideas.'

The relationship between Francis, Christina and the club employee, Eric (Elias Koteas), who has fixated on her is the centrepiece of the film. Typically, though, Egoyan tries to pack in as much extraneous material as possible. Francis is a tax inspector employed to audit the accounts of a dilapidated pet store. He discovers that the owner, Thomas (Don McKellar), is making ends meet by smuggling exotic breeds of animals into the country and blackmails him into becoming a further prop in his fantasy. Thomas, in turn, likes to pick up guys at the opera house and take them back to his flat for casual sex.

Egoyan maintains that it is the three highly fabricated spaces his characters inhabit – the strip club, the pet store and the opera house – that interest him. And that he is trying to draw out the links between different species of hothouse 'exotica'. But whereas in earlier films the correspondences between different symbolic domains seemed almost too forced, here they threaten to explode into a mass of infinitely repeating fragments. There's the impression that, in trying to get real, Egoyan has lost control. hat he can't keep up with the beat.

Not that he's complaining. Whereas his previous films always earned him serious critical attention, *Exotica* has been his first commercial hit. Maybe his rep as a formidable intellectual film-maker is changing? 'I hope so. I always found it very frustrating when people told me that the other films seemed very cold and emotionally distant. Because to me it was such a denial of why I made those films – which was to deal with ideas of emotional loss and grief and mourning and loneliness.'

Maybe going to Armenia a couple of years ago had something to do with it. Egoyan was born in Cairo to Armenian parents and moved to the Anglo-Canadian suburb of Victoria when he was three. Hooking up with other Armenian immigrants only when he went to the University of Toronto in the early eighties, he has always seen himself as a bit of an interloper. Consequently, it's always been really easy to read themes of cultural impersonation and displacement into his work.

In the end, he just got fed up with it. Going back to Armenia to make a small arts-sponsored film for German television, *Calendar*, gave him the chance to confront the contradictions in his cultural make-up. It also gave him the nerve to break out of an increasingly imprisoning aesthetic. He experimented with voice-over, with improvised dialogue, with spontaneity. With everything he had sworn not to use. The result was an offbeat little gem – fresh, witty, reserved. But still complex.

Exotica is less successful. It looks bold and bright. It retains the playfulness of *Calendar* and has a lighter touch than any of his previous films, but there is the sense that Egoyan hasn't quite got the hang of cutting loose. Why, he even includes a fragment of video footage in the film. A blurry shot of Francis's wife laughing as she gently shields their daughter from the intrusive eye of the camera lens, it sums up in its studied negligence the artistic judgement Egoyan now needs to acquire.

Bachelor machine #2
Arena, no. 52, July/August 1995

Robert Crumb knows he's fucked up. Hailed by Robert Hughes as the 'Breughel of the twentieth century' and reviled by others as a woeful misogynist, the fifty-two-year-old American comix artist has made the long slow haul from underground notoriety in the sixties to gallery celebrity in the eighties (he was featured in one of the Museum of Modern Art's big po-mo exhibitions five years ago in New York) without once losing his edge of gnarly self-loathing. His work regularly changes hands for thousands of dollars and now, with the release of *Crumb*, an intensive two-hour documentary on the man's life and work, it looks like his asking price will soar.

'I've done him that favour,' says the film's laconic director, Terry Zwigoff. 'Whatever his work was worth before, it's gonna be worth twice as much now.' The film offers a new slant on Crumb. It opens with the artist demolishing his public image. (Everything he is identified with in the popular mind – the Keep on Truckin' logo, the LSD-fuelled cover artwork for Big Brother and the Holding Company's and Janis Joplin's album, *Cheap Thrills*, and the porno cartoon movie adaptation of *Fritz the Cat* – he hates for one reason or another.) And it ends with Crumb packing up his collection of vintage 78s and quitting America for the south of France in disgust at its overblown commodity culture.

Zwigoff is an old crony of the artist's, but *Crumb* is not the soft-soap job you might expect. It duly includes footage of Hughes, fresh from his PC-bashing stint in *The Culture of Complaint*, lauding Crumb for precisely those qualities – the depiction of women as intimidating sex objects, the uneasy appropriations of the 'coon' vernacular – that others find most disturbing in his work. But it also features the other side of the story, with journalist Peggy Orenstein claiming that Crumb's pornographic representations of women seem a little too lubricious to pass for satire.

It's something Crumb would admit to. It's something he *does* admit to. He's there on camera in the film talking about how hot he gets when he draws a particularly scabrous sex queen (one of the funniest moments in the film comes when Hughes is told Crumb enjoys wanking to his own artwork; he is momentarily flustered before recovering himself to go ballsing on about the onanism of Picasso). He also makes a point of depicting himself in his cartoons as a pathetically inadequate specimen – weedy, sunken, obscene, with pervy Coke-bottle glasses and a permanent frightened leer.

Sample Crumb cartoon. The author is alone in his room when he receives a visit from Mr Natural (icon of everything strung out, freaky and Reich On from the Haight daze of the sixties, he looks like a cross between God and Albert Steptoe), who presents him with an emblematic male sex toy – a strutting Amazonian mud-wrestler with no head. After several pathetic attempts to abuse her (which mainly seem to consist of jumping on her back and frotting like mad), Crumb eventually becomes so frantic with guilt that Mr Natural is brought back to fix things. In the *coup-de-théâtre*, it turns out that the woman *does* have a head. It merely needs to be retracted from her neck (the unpleasant implication is that someone has stuffed it down there in the first place).

Does this make it as satire for you? Is it funny? Zwigoff covers all the pros and cons in his film but admits that the question bores him. 'I thought it was important to cover it. But in the end these debates can go on for ever.' Instead he literally allows the artist to speak for himself and the audience to make up their own mind. My own take, for what it's worth, is that Crumb inflects the libidinal rush of the American mass media with a Puritan vocabulary of disgust that comes closer to the productions of therapy than of art.

But then, according to Dr Freud, there's no difference. You see, it all goes back to childhood. At least – as this film makes clear – it does in Crumb's case. Zwigoff was one of the first publishers of Crumb's work in the sixties and shares his passion for early blues and ragtime. When he started to make his film back in 1984, it wasn't Robert that fascinated him so much as the artist's elder brother, Charles, a medicated recluse who never moved out of the family shack in Philadelphia. 'I showed some footage of Charles – who's this wonderfully witty and intelligent man, every bit as much of an artist as his brother – to movie executives in the eighties. And they were like, we can't fund this, it's too depressing.'

It becomes clear during the course of the film that Crumb Senior, an ex-Marine Corps officer who embraced the American cult of 'business' with a vengeance, was a petty domestic tyrant who nearly crushed the life out of his three artistically talented sons. Crumb made the big time. Max escaped as far as San Francisco, where he paints in a ratty garret and consoles himself with the rigours of a homemade bed of nails. Charles never made it past the front door. (There are two sisters in the family as well, both of whom declined to be interviewed for the film.)

'The fifties was a very weird time in America,' says Zwigoff. 'There was just so much repression going on. So many people I know had severely damaged childhoods.' This is something that helps the film to resonate beyond its ostensible subject matter. It's certainly the reason why David Lynch allowed his name to be used over the title. It's summed up by an image of Crumb inspecting a copy of one of his father's business self-help books, which includes an author photo of Crumb Senior smiling like crazy. 'It reminds me of this smiling disease which they reckon Japanese salarymen have,' says Crumb.

What's distinctive about Crumb isn't so much the smile as the fixed grin he wears throughout most of the movie. As Zwigoff confronts him with old flames, new admirers and the wrecked remnants of his family, all Crumb can come up with is a creepy – half-insinuating, half-pleading – grin. It's impossible to deny the man's sardonic intelligence and black humour, but it all seems to be mobilised in defence of ancient grievances rather than projected outwards into an interrogation of the larger culture. Maybe Charles wasn't the only one unable to make it past the front door. Maybe, with his nagging compulsion to get down his fixations on paper, Crumb has his own, rather comfortable, bed of nails to carry.

Vampiria

The Face, vol. 2, no. 39, December 1991

What's the definition of a damned good myth? That it's elastic, a loose fit; it can be shaped into any meaning around. The Frankenstein monster is not a good myth; dumb, shambling, tragic, he always stands for the exploited working classes, brawn rather than brain, industrialism, plodding maleness.

Now look at Dracula. Vampires can be anything you want them to be. They can be male or female, they can stand for blood-sucking capitalists or moonlighting vagrants, they can be camp or tragic, sadists or masochists. As long as they're evil, it doesn't matter.

Which is why Gary Oldman is such a good choice for the leading role in Coppola's upcoming *Dracula*. He's elastic himself. You never know what you're going to get from him; you just know it's going to be good. And with Winona Ryder, Anthony Hopkins and Keanu Reeves also lined up for the movie, it could prove to be more than another of the director's autobiographical follies (how about Count Coppola, the tragic artist cursed by his strange desire to squeeze budgets until they bleed).

According to Christopher Frayling in *Vampires: Lord Byron to Count Dracula* (Faber), it all goes back to the hooligan reputation of the English abroad. The aristocratic English of the early nineteenth century, that is. Byron cut the prototypical figure. Mean, moody, magnificently promiscuous, he dragged his reputation through the boulevards of Europe and was never short of a satanic scowl. It was even rumoured that he had murdered one of his mistresses and drunk her blood.

The romantic image of Byron, itself partly adopted by the poet from old gothic shudder-novels, eventually found its way into Bram Stoker's 1897 masterpiece, *Dracula*. A satanic lord exiled in Central Europe, seductive and menacing, with a knack for blooding any spare young virgins, Dracula was Byron with swirling, oriental frills. As Frayling makes clear, though, he was also a lot more. The folkloric vampire of Romania – all posthumous magic and stakes through the heart – was also factored into the myth; as was the fatal woman of romantic legend, the awful sirens of Keats, Poe, Baudelaire and Hoffman.

Christian de Chalonge's *Docteur Petiot* offers the latest screen incarnation of the vampire myth. A baroque poetic horror movie based on the true story of a Parisian doctor who set up a private gas chamber in his basement during the Occupation, it stars Michel Serrault in the title role, complete with kohl-lined eyes and a seductive line in chat that proves fatal for his unsuspecting Jewish victims. A cloaked monster flapping around the streets on his bicycle at night, cackling and scheming, Petiot is the vampire as serial voyeur, as host-turned-parasite, healer-turned-killer, as small-time egotist.

He is also the vampire as cinephiliac. The equivalent of Dracula's coffin in *Docteur Petiot* is the warm plush interior of the picture palace. Petiot is forever in and out of cinemas, hiding out, basking in their nocturnal glow. The film opens with him watching an old vampire film, which, in a disorientating moment, he seems to enter and absorb. It ends with him arrested in a movie theatre.

All very appropriate, given the mutual attraction that has tended to exist between vampires and movies. It has to be something in their make-up. Look at the similarities. Both are fleeting and nocturnal, black and white shadows; both are hypnotic, silky and glamorous, a little bit too much of a good thing. Both are obscurely sexual. When the final strip of film rattles its way through the projector, the dreaming spectator gets a jolt, as if a stake had been driven through his heart.

Vampires have always been big in the movies. There have been three peak periods so far. The jagged camera angles, chiaroscuro lighting and beetling photography of German Expressionist cinema was picked out in F.W. Murnau's *Nosferatu* as early as 1922 (and left its mark in the European 'vamps' of early Hollywood, the Dietrichs and the Garbos). Then, in thirties Hollywood, there was the cycle of gothic B-movies starring Bela Lugosi – all cobwebs, castles and fearful peasants.

Most memorably, there were all those Hammer horror movies from the fifties starring Christopher Lee in red contacts and evening cape. With their Technicolor dash and suave gothic manners, their interest in tragic narratives of decline, they perhaps bore witness to the setting of the sun on the British

Empire (just as Stoker's original novel had observed it at its zenith).

Nowadays, the vampire myth is up for grabs. In last year's cult shocker, *Vampire's Kiss*, starring Nic Cage, it was used to explore fears of downward social mobility and class aggression; while in Kathryn Bigelow's *Near Dark*, it was the mark of the dispossessed, of those who have been excluded from the American Dream and are eager for revenge. Both highly prescient movies.

So much for politics. What about sex? There are all the obvious connotations of polymorphous perversity in a V-movie like *Red-Blooded American Girl* (which also has an intriguing AIDS subtext). And as far as drugs are concerned, both Paul Morrissey in *Blood for Dracula* and George Romero in *Martin* have used vampirism as a metaphor for addiction. Which just leaves rock'n'roll. There has never been a wholehearted vampire rock'n'roll movie. Francis Ford Coppola take note.

Suicide cinema

The Face, vol. 2, no. 30, March 1991

Once filming had wrapped, the producers of *Desperate Hours* took out a two-page ad in the *Hollywood Reporter* to congratulate Michael Cimino for bringing in the movie five days ahead of schedule. The spin on this surprise delivery wasn't too hard to read. 'See. This guy is reliable. Forget all the wild stories. We can do business with him.'

A remake of a creaky old Bogart picture, *Desperate Hours* fails to scale the mythic heights of previous Cimino efforts like *The Deer Hunter* or *Heaven's Gate*. Starring Mickey Rourke as a charismatic psycho on the lam and Anthony Hopkins and Mimi Rogers as the unfortunate suburban couple he snuggles up to with a handgun, it's fussy and slow for most of its length. But at least it proves Cimino can make a film without riding his reputation as an egomaniac.

Those were the days. Back in the seventies. When Hollywood was fumbling the move from dusty dream factory to sleek corporate conglomerate. When mass attendances were dropping, takings were down and studio bosses were willing to stake everything on an epic roll of the dice. The hour of the Bigshot Auteur. Of men like Cimino, Francis Ford Coppola and William Friedkin. All willing to slog through the mud of budget battles, delays and escalating controversy in pursuit of Academy Awards and high-grossing returns.

Coppola pulled out all the stops on the *Godfather* movies and *Apocalypse Now*. Friedkin baited the critics by pandering to the mob in *The French Connection*, *The Exorcist* and *Cruising*. Meanwhile, Cimino triggered equal measures of frustrated awe and smug outrage with *The Deer Hunter* by treating American involvement in Vietnam as one long game of Russian roulette.

Suddenly these guys were no longer hired hands squinting through a lens on a backlot. They were romantic rebels, heroic visionaries. No price was too high for their art. Coppola trashed the Philippines to make *Apocalypse Now*. Not to be outdone, Cimino deployed an army of technicians in Thailand during the filming of his own Vietnam epic. He even hired out the Thai air force.

It couldn't last. One by one, the Bigshot Auteurs went belly up. Friedkin hit the skids in spectacular fashion with *Wages of Fear*. Coppola built a dinky studio and splurged on lots of fancy video equipment. Made a couple of intimate little blockbusters and went bust. Cimino beat them all. With *Heaven's Gate* he bankrupted a major Hollywood studio.

Self-consciously conceived as the Last Western, the summation of a genre, *Heaven's Gate* had to be perfect. Cimino built and rebuilt sets in a frenzy, shot a million feet of film, agonized endlessly over the final cut. He rode round the set in a Jeep barking orders to thousands of extras. The film bombed. Not only that, it toppled United Artists and effectively put the brakes on Cimino's career.

In between he has directed only two movies. *Year of the Dragon*, a lurid and hyperviolent thriller that pits racist cop Mickey Rourke against New York's Chinatown. And *The Sicilian*, an epic gangster movie set in the Old Country, which is all peasant blood and soil and steamy Lawrentian symbolism.

The comparative modesty of *Desperate Hours* signals that Cimino is anxious to submit himself for renewed membership of the Hollywood club. Just like Friedkin was with *The Guardian* last year. Or like Coppola is at the moment with *The Godfather Part III*. The Bigshot Auteurs are staging a comeback.

Too bad the industry doesn't need them any more. Their scope is too epic, their attachments too mythic. An old-fashioned romantic like Cimino is a lost figure in the new Hollywood Playhouse. The mystic tug of the American landscape, frontiersman values adrift, the beat of community ritual. These are Cimino's concerns. And increasingly they have the aura of a peeling billboard on the highway. Marlboro Country. Purest American corn.

A new breed of film-maker has the run of Hollywood now. Hip young popsicles like Tim Burton and Michael Lehmann. Kids at home in the synthetic landscapes of Hyperreal America. Where the prevailing aesthetic is all gore and sampled signs rather than blood, sweat and tears. Why move heaven and earth to carve a statement about the Making of America when there's a whole media cosmology to splash around in?

In retrospect, *Heaven's Gate* looks more like the Last Movie than the Last Western: Old Hollywood as the burial mound of the American Dream; Commerce sacrificed on the altar of Art; Professional suicide as a solitary ritual of purification; Cimino embodying his own myth of tragic heroism.

These equations don't hold up any more. But they're everywhere in Cimino's work. In his very first film, the heist movie *Thunderbolt and Lightfoot*, Jeff Bridges expires the moment he fulfils his dream of gliding down the highway in a white Cadillac. In *Year of the Dragon*, Mickey Rourke dutifully hands over his weapon to the defeated bad guy so he can die an honourable death. Christopher Lambert commands his sidekick to assassinate him in *The Sicilian* once he recognizes his mythic career as a desperado is finished.

And so it goes on. The most memorable phrase from *The Deer Hunter* is 'One Shot' – a slogan that encapsulates its twin ideologies of the hunt and the sacrificial death. Even in *Desperate Hours* there's a suicide scene that manages to combine lonely nobility, mountain scenery and heavy weaponry.

As for the *Heaven's Gate* crisis, Cimino came through it all with a movie that's a mess. A glorious mess. Despite the reams of spent celluloid, he probably figured he only had one shot.

Image bombs
i-D, no. 149, February 1996

Latest neat little tech primer from French theorist of speed, urbanism and military technology Paul Virilio is *The Art of the Motor* (University of Minnesota). Divided into seven chapters, this looks at the way in which what Bruce Sterling calls the 'military entertainment complex' is increasingly responsible for moving around the tech scenery and adjusting our means of perception in the post-Cold War world.

This can, paradoxically enough, make Virilio seem conservative. His interpretation of the global media complex, for example, as a nomadic war machine that abolishes the distances between events and triggers panic rushes of mimetic violence leads him to ignore the political and economic causes of social change. He's happier seeing the LA riots of 1965 and the more recent overturning of Soviet statues in Moscow, for example, in the context of media terrorism rather than as specific and highly local struggles against oppression. He takes quite a few pops at the colonization of the global 'image market' by the corporate American media. And he sees the fashion for politically correct language as an indication of the way technologies of mass communication move irresistibly towards a logic of 'general incrimination'.

Where he scores is in his more gnomic and even anecdotal flashes of insight. Thus he talks of opinion polls as information bombs designed to pacify a demassified population comprised of 'marginals, divorced singles, the unemployed, members of ethnic, sexual or health minorities and children of single parents left to their own devices'. He sees Benetton pointing the way forward to a time when terror will be the only aesthetic capable of keeping the advertising industry in business. He thinks that the 'paraconstitutional' power of the media will be increasingly responsible for making or breaking regimes according to their news value. And he thinks that the consumer society is coming to an end.

What will help sell the book, however, is that Virilio finally turns his attention to the new virtual and nano technologies for which his previous writings have done so much to prepare us. As usual, he's done his research. He comes up with the stories no one else does. Had you, for example, heard about plans to set up a 'Military Channel' in the US? Had you thought about VR as a development of a tourist industry that had already reached 'the end of the line' in its colonization of beachscapes and mountaintops. Perhaps you had. But had you thought about it in the context of 'extremist sports', like bungee jumping, that attempt nothing less than to simulate a near-death experience?

This is typical of Virilio. He takes a familiar trope and completely defamiliarizes it. There's plenty of this in *The Art of the Motor*. It's a valuable little book.

Human interfaces

Jim Kelman takes your call on Boxing Day. You've always been grabbed by his writing. Now working for the style press has given you the chance to get back to him (journalism: an access protocol). Jim Kelman says: Diacritical marks are the 'literary' stigmata of class war. There is no space in your story for this insight (it's simultaneously too technical and too epistemologically condensed). But it makes you understand for the first time your childhood irritation with, say, Dickens's strict punctuation of the Artful Dodger's speech (writing: a coming-to-consciousness). Years later you catch Jim Kelman in a pub in Wood Green. He remembers you. You know it's time to get out when you start interviewing people the second time round and they fail to recognize you. Burn-out: the sign over the exit in the media simulacrum.

J.G. Ballard

i-D, no. 97, October 1991

A terminal posture

The aircraft rise from the runways of the airport, carrying the remnants of Vaughan's semen to the instrument panels and radiator grilles of a thousand crashing cars, the leg stances of a million passengers.

J.G. Ballard, *Crash*

Notes towards a mental breakdown

The subject has sealed himself inside a London suburb for the past thirty years and has shown few real signs of any willingness to leave. Throughout this period of self-incarceration he has been engaged by an obsessive compulsion to transcribe his multiple fixations and considers himself a successful author with fourteen novels and innumerable short stories to his credit (you should see some of the crazy stuff he's written, Travis, it's really sick; how he can begin to imagine some publisher touching anything with a title like *Why I Want to Fuck Ronald Reagan* is beyond me, but then you know schizophrenics). He is now sixty-one. Although he talks increasingly of departing – for Miami, Los Angeles or some other exotic city half-remembered from the TV screen – it seems unlikely he will ever be able to gather the required imaginative momentum. Perhaps he has been exhausted by the strain of constantly writing. Or perhaps he is waiting for some apocalyptic event, a transformation of the surrounding landscape of semidetached houses and manicured lawns into a contaminated ruin (that, or a rerun of *Miami Vice*; I tell you, he used to watch that goddamned show every week – with the sound down, if you can believe it).

Answers to a questionnaire 1

'It's such a great loss. I miss it. We're so frightened of violence here. We've got this terribly censored and tightly controlled Eastern European-style television. It's so silly.'

Answers to a questionnaire 2

'I'd be quite happy to live in LA. Of all the American cities I've visited it's certainly the most intriguing. It's a remarkable place. Everyone visiting it for the first time already knows it so well. Because you've seen fragments of it in literally thousands of TV episodes and movies, you have a curious sense that you're in a TV episode yourself when you're driving round the place. You constantly see buildings, hotels, road junctions and store fronts that you instantly recognize.'

Answers to a questionnaire 3

'The boundaries of the Third World shift. Los Angeles is really the capital of the Third World. The Mexican/US border should be redrawn to run along Wilshire Boulevard, because north of it is Hollywood, Westwood, Santa Monica and Beverly Hills, where the LA professional classes live, and then south of it is 90 per cent of Greater LA, which is multiethnic – driving around there you feel you're in Mexico.'

The shabby voyeur

Ballard gazes beyond the open French windows at the scruffy luxuriance of long grass and flat light visible from his sitting room. Does he take a secret pleasure in offending the well-tended sensibilities of his bourgeois neighbours? Or is his indifference to the orderly status hierarchies of Shepperton an unconscious expression of helplessness, a revenge against his bachelor existence? Maybe he's just a slob. He sips a whiskey and soda and contemplates the huge surrealist canvas that takes up half the length of the room.

Answers to a questionnaire 4

'Dali, Magritte, Yves Tanguy, Max Ernst.'

A sophisticated entertainment

They make the pilgrimage to see him every year. Serious young men in wire-framed spectacles eager to discuss the aura of the nuclear sublime, the unconscious sexual charisma of high technology, car crashes, the secret meaning of the Kennedy assassination. All the obsessions that inform his novels, all the neural firings that have sparked a hidden trail of excitement across the campuses and suburbs of the developed world. Sometimes they ask him incomprehensible questions ('Marcuse said that the consumer society is marked by the "repressive desublimation" of the libido. But your novels seem to deal instead with a "non-repressive desublimation". Do you agree?'), sometimes not ('Is life a nightmare?'). They always claim that *Crash* and *The Atrocity Exhibition* are his most interesting texts; they always insist that he is not a science fiction writer but a visionary. He is always unfailingly polite.

Answers to a questionnaire 5

'The decadence of the 1990s, instead of being an over-the-top relaxation of everything, a libertinism which suggests that anything goes, might be the opposite. You might get an over-the-top Puritanism. Look at what's springing up in America at the moment. Everything is forbidden, everything is proscribed

– from the glass of wine at lunch to behaviour which fails to be "politically correct". It's most peculiar.'

Answers to a questionnaire 6

'Not the whole of the Green movement, but the wilder edge of it. People who devote their whole lives to one tiny corner of the Green movement rapidly become single-issue fanatics. All they want to do is save the asparagus or something and they're prepared to kill human beings to bring that about. We'll soon have people wanting to save the smallpox virus.'

Stochastic analysis

His novels of the sixties and early seventies represent one of the few serious attempts to grapple with the engineered psycho-pathology of the postwar consumer boom. Even as it was being constructed, the landscape of motorways, concrete high-rises, mass media, nuclear airbases, resort centres and suburban developments was imagined by Ballard as something already ruined, entropic, deranged. By fast-forwarding anticipated cultural decay beyond the point of catastrophe, he hoped to map the secret fault lines of his immediate environment, to gauge how far the technological progress of the sixties was really an erosion of the collective unconscious. In that sense, he was the very opposite of a futurist.

Answers to a questionnaire 7

'I can't wait. It's all that's left, isn't it? When they develop, as I'm sure they will, a really user-friendly virtual reality system where you don't have to dress up like a deep-sea diver, it will transform, or rather replace, reality. After all, what we see around us now is a virtual reality system; the external reality each of us sees is a construct created by the central nervous system. All we're doing is getting an electronic aid to take over the heavy lifting. It's an extraordinary business. The consequences could be incalculable over a hundred-year span. The external world could effectively cease to exist in any real sense. It's so tantalizing. You'll have a two-tier planet, with those who run everything living inside a world of fantasy, of huge self-compensating and self-deluding internalized dreams, while those who have nothing but their central nervous systems to hang on to will be way down below trudging the pavements.'

Answers to a questionnaire 8

'Research in the neurosciences is proceeding at a really remarkable pace. I take for granted that the ultimate wiring diagram of the brain will eventually be unravelled in the way that the structure of DNA was unravelled and that the neural circuitry which generates transcendental experiences of all kinds – whether religious or imaginative – will be understood. One will be able to programme – and do it oneself – a religious or transcendental vision in the same way that neurologists can now stimulate pleasure centres in the brain. There's no logical reason why the mysteries of the human mind shouldn't be accessible.'

Kodachrome

J.G. Ballard's new novel is published in hardback on September 26 by Collins. A sequel to his earlier semi-autobiographical novel, *Empire of the Sun* (which was filmed by Steven Spielberg in 1987), it refracts the major events of his life – childhood in Shanghai, where he was interned during the Japanese occupation, his study of anatomy at Cambridge, a stint as an airforce pilot in Canada, retreat to Shepperton, the death of his wife, his experimentation with the alternative lifestyles of the sixties – through the lens of his previous fictions in a style that recalls the methods of time-lapse photography.

Answers to a questionnaire 9

'I've tried to link together obsessions of mine – car crashes, time, hallucinatory states of mind which have always drawn me to the surrealists – and find their sources in my own past in Shanghai. And also what I consider the important events of the postwar world, like the Kennedy assassination, which acted as a tremendous catalyst for me. It really represented the firing gun for the start of the sixties.'

The image maze

The Warren Commission. The rake-off on the book of the race. In their report, prompted by widespread complaints of foul play and other irregularities, the syndicate lay full blame on the starter, Oswald.

J.G. Ballard, *The Assassination of John Fitzgerald Kennedy Considered as a Downhill Motor Race*

Answers to a questionnaire 10

'Through the broken prism of the Kennedy assassination one saw the space race, pop, drugs, the whole psychedelia thing, the Vietnam war and major developments in the sciences and the consumer society – everything from the proliferation of data-processing and computer systems to advances in transplant surgery and molecular biology. All this generated the tremendously hot mix which was the sixties.'

Answers to a questionnaire 11

'Bush doesn't have the same mythic dimension as Reagan. To assassinate him would be nothing – because he is nothing. Whereas to shoot an anonymous person quietly having his lunch at McDonald's is a genuinely provocative act. In a curious way, you're making a point.'

The see-through brain

J.G. Ballard is fascinated by disaster, catastrophe, spectacular scenes of violent death, war, assassination and extreme states of mind. The first time I met him I expected to be greeted by some twitchy suburban crank – or, at the very least, an austere patrician aesthete – but the man is chatty, gregarious and pleasantly ironic. With his easy manner, his fruity vowels and his sheet of grey hair flopping indifferently over the collar of his open-neck shirt, he comes across as a mildly eccentric bourgeois bohemian, everyone's ideal image of themselves as a hip old geezer. He is a case study in how the return of the repressed, when treated with amused curiosity, can be good for you.

Answers to a questionnaire 12

'Norman Schwarzkopf was the Cecil B. DeMille, the P.T. Barnum, of Desert Storm, orchestrating events in the form of a bloody opera. But the mass-media coverage of the Gulf War and the war itself were out of sync in many ways. The whole thing ended inconclusively without a proper climax. The Siege of Baghdad should have been the climax, with Saddam bombed into oblivion in his bunker by a hand-picked team of Delta Force commandos.'

Answers to a questionnaire 13

'It was totally different from Vietnam, much more sinister in a way. Those nose-cone cameras relaying zoom pictures of missiles actually going through doorways and vehicles on your living-room TV screen, unconsciously inciting the viewer to become a cruise missile. It was bizarre.'

No U-turn

David Cronenberg is contracted to begin filming *Crash* after he has wrapped *The Naked Lunch*.

Internal émigré

Over fifty years after he left the mythical city of his childhood, Ballard has returned to contemplate its extraordinary metamorphosis. Street vendors hawk pirate videos of *Die Hard* and *Top Gun* in Hong Kong-Chinese-language versions while above them tower the glittering corporate temples of international finance. There are satellite dishes everywhere. Observing the ministrations of the BBC camera crew assigned to record his reactions for posterity, he is suddenly conscious of the factor of media multiplication involved in his perception of the city. He feels no nostalgia. Casting his gaze down the Bund, he anticipates his image spread out across the night of Shepperton on a thousand softly illuminated TV screens.

William Gibson and Bruce Sterling
i-D, no. 86, November 1990

Entry command

William Gibson wanders into the side-street office of his London publisher's, folds up his limbs, lets his tote-bag drop. It's a long way from Vancouver.

'I always have trouble finding this place,' he says. 'I don't know why, I should have gotten used to it by now.' Given that it's over six years since his first novel, *Neuromancer*, hit the submerged world of science fiction publishing like a graffiti-daubed smart missile, he has a fair point. But then Gibson has never been too impressed by his status as a techno-guru, a hip priest to the hardwired generation, the Godfather of Cyberpunk. He's more than happy to leave all that stuff, the jive oratory, to his buddy Bruce Sterling. Who turns up outside five minutes later. Rattles the front door like it was a makeshift airlock, bellows something in Texan through the glass and finally makes it inside by what seems like sheer force of personality. 'OK, where's the interview?'

Password

The term captures something crucial. The overlapping of worlds that were formerly separate: the realm of high tech and the modern pop underground. The work of the cyberpunks is paralleled throughout eighties pop culture: in rock video, in the hacker underground; in the jarring street tech of hip-hop and scratch music; in the synthesizer rock of London and Tokyo. This phenomenon, this dynamic has a global range; cyberpunk is its literary incarnation.

Bruce Sterling in his preface to *Mirrorshades: The Cyberpunk Anthology* (1986), the seminal SF collection, which includes stories by Rudy Rucker, Marc Laidlaw, Lewis Shiner and John Shirley as well as Sterling and Gibson.

Delete?

BS: I suspect it'll be chiselled on our tombstones.
WG: It has a life of its own. We've just had to get used to it. Trying to get rid of it is a Sisyphean task.
BS: I feel about it the same way I feel about the term science fiction, really. There are drawbacks to it and there are

useful aspects to it. Actually, after having met the Milanese cyberpunk movement, they're like these Italian sub-Red Brigade.
WG: Post-Marxist.
BS: Yeah, post-Marxist political punk anarchist philosophical types.
WG: With very nice jerseys.
BS: They were wearing, like, jerseys they'd made themselves that said 'cyberpunk' on the back.
WG: And a brain with lighning bolts leaping out.
BS: Yes, I felt quite cheered by the sight of it. The c-word's stock rose a bit there.

Alignment character option

They make an unlikely pair, Gibson and Sterling. The long, loose one dressed in cable-knit and turn-ups and the big, ballistic one strapped inside denim cotton and canvas. Both sporting little round specs. The hip professor and the cerebrating hustler, the slow cool guy and the fizzing dude. The jazz artist and the guitar hero. It's a neat double-act. Gibson lets his partner cut loose with most of the interview power chords, content to pick out the details, keep up the conversational beat, bounce around a few riffs. His laconic drawl twists its way through Sterling's rousing boom, deep in the mix, but always in tune. They're on the same wavelength, these guys. Hardly surprising, given that they've just finished work on their first joint novel, *The Difference Engine*. A project that took over three years.

List files

Subject: Gibson, William
Age: 42, looks younger
Residence: Vancouver, Canada (via South West Virginia)
Résumé: *The Difference Engine* (1990), co-written with Bruce Sterling (reviewed, *i-D* 85); the 'Sprawl' trilogy, comprising *Neuromancer* (1984), *Count Zero* (1986) and *Mona Lisa Overdrive* (1988); *Burning Chrome* (1986), short-story collection; Hollywood movie scripts and cover blurbs too

	numerous to mention
Trivia item:	Gibson was at Woodstock
Subject:	Sterling, Bruce
Age:	36, talks younger
Residence:	Austin, most definitely Texas
Résumé:	*The Difference Engine* (1990), co-written with William Gibson; *Crystal Express* (1989), short-story collection (reviewed *i-D*, no. 82); *Islands in the Net* (1988) (reviewed *i-D*, no. 76); *Mirrorshades* (1986), editor; *Schismatrix* (1985); *The Artificial Kid* (1980); *Involution Ocean* (1977); pamphlets and think-pieces too numerous to mention
Trivia item:	Sterling's favourite book is the Re/Search document on J G Ballard

Defining text parallel

Gibson calls it the Matrix, Sterling the Net. A satellite-linked sheet of data wrapping the globe, frayed at the edges by mutant subcultures, bunched into knots by sleazy city-states, spun into chaos by illicit cargo cults. An Electronic Babylon, a multinational glut of white noise. During the eighties the cyberpunks hot-wired a terminal vision of the future that was one long perpetual present. All serial numbers sawn off, all sell-by dates removed. A neon dystopia populated by information junkies and mirrorshade assassins, surgically enhanced posthumans and genetically distressed superbrights. For Sterling, the world had expanded into a cosmic black hole, for Gibson it had imploded into a computer-generated void, a virtual reality, a simulated landscape behind the green screen. Cyberspace.

Hard copy command

WG: The essential art of pop poetics is the art of neologism. Cyberspace was my contribution, a term which was hollow, senseless, waiting to receive meaning. I don't care what people pile on top of it. It's like with the Milanese cyberpunks, there's bound to be an inevitable accretion of meaning.

SB: What about when it's not a street subculture but a high-tech corporation which hijacks the term? Is Gibson still considering legal action against Autodesk, the Californian computer company who have been trying to patent Cyperspace as a trademark?

WG: I briefly retained counsel, but in the end I discovered just how expensive good copyright lawyers are.

Status line

At the start of the year, the pair were invited to a VR conference in Austria, where they delivered papers, messed about with development models of data gloves and video projectors, put on a show for the assembled high-wired boffins and generally hung out. Were they aware of their status as cognitive brokers in tomorrow's technology, futures traders? Gurus?

BS: We were gurus.

WG: Yeah, we were gurus. I'm afraid we were on the guru route that time, for sure.

BS: The guru rubber chicken circuit.

SB: Sounds like a change from the usual globe-trotting round of sci-fi conventions, anyway.

WG: Better hotels.

BS: Some of them, yeah. I don't really think it's entirely new.

WG: You've been doing it for years.

BS: Well, I do a certain amount of public speaking, yes. But I think these are the people who are our natural audience. The ironic tragedy is they're so busy they don't have time to read.

Switch cursor position

What do Gibson and Sterling make of the way their technosleazy image of the future has been cleaned up and turned around by the *Mondo 2000* lap-top brigade, the New Age space cadets, the synchro-energized visionaries? How do the original cyberpunk duo feel about the cyberhippies?

WG: Ambivalent.

BS: Yeah, I thought that's what you'd say. Although I read

Mondo 2000 with enormous joy, it's one of the very few magazines I subscribe to. It consistently astonishes me. I think their basic riff is that they would like to be taken as gurus leading people on to the broad sunlit uplands of some new techno-utopia. They'll never get there, but the places they are fumbling about in are inherently interesting. Their basic motive is to become posthuman superbrights.

WG: Yeah, I don't know any of them personally, I don't know what they actually do when they're alone. But they seem pretty driven. The style may flow a bit, but they're purposeful in a way I find remarkable.

Double indent

In the first issue of *Mondo 2000*, Gibson was interviewed by Timothy Leary, Silicon Valley savant, mind-bending blag-artist and all-round hippie dude, the Harvard psychologist who introduced LSD to the Woodstock Nation and was branded the 'most dangerous man in America'. Was it a meeting of minds? Or were wires permanently crossed?

WG: I spent a week getting pretty drunk with him in January in Barcelona and that sort of broke the ice. I hadn't quite realized before that the thing that's really great about him is that he's like William Burroughs. He's a very bohemian character, although he doesn't present himself that way. What did you say about him . . . ?

BS: A failed prophet is still a prophet.

WG: Yeah, right.

BS: There aren't that many around. Rare things, prophets. And prophets who survive are even rarer.

Mark text #1

Heroin was now out of favor in the West. The drug-using populace had dwindled with the aging of the population, and modern users were more sophisticated. They preferred untraceable neuro-chemicals to crude vegetable extracts.

Bruce Sterling, *Islands in the Net*

Tab reset

BS: I don't know about Ecstasy, it should have been called Equanimity. It doesn't live up to its press. It's a pity what happened to it; it could have been a quite useful marriage counsellors' drug.

SB: Either that or a quite useful chemical warfare reagent. Apparently the American military considered doping enemy food supplies with it.

WG: I remember one of the American chemical companies came up with something they called STP, which leaked into the drug market in about '68 or '69. The selling point was that it would keep you wrecked for three days straight. I checked that one out and I think the reason they dropped it was that you could really have gotten into killing. So that was probably a drawback.

BS: If you want a version of the drug of the future, it's not recreational, it's something like steroids. Because they convey no kick, they're not addictive. Instead they change the shape and properties of your body. It's a way for career people to deal with stress. They feel that insane demands are being made on them that are beyond the ability of a human being to cope with and the answer is not to drop out of the rat race but to become superhuman.

WG: Super-rat.

BS: To become a super-rat, yeah.

Mark text #2

Julius Deane was one hundred and thirty-five years old, his metabolism assiduously warped by a weekly fortune in serum and hormones. His primary hedge against aging was a yearly pilgrimage to Tokyo, where genetic surgeons re-set the code of his DNA, a procedure unavailable in Chiba. Then he'd fly to Hongkong and order the year's suits and shirts.

William Gibson, *Neuromancer*

Reveal codes

WG: If you want to see the posthuman thing manifesting right now, get *Los Angeles* magazine and read the medical advertisements at the back, read the ads for elective surgery. And I think by now there are probably more than a few longevity doctors, they're big in California. People start working on their longevity when they're thirty-five if they've got the money.

BS: Yeah, it's a great invisible literature, cosmetic ad copy. If you want to see what's happening in the culture, it's a good place to go look for clues. The subtext used to be, *We'll Keep Your Husband Faithful*. Now it's, *We'll Keep You 25*. They read like medical texts.

WG: The packaging is increasingly lab-oriented, too. They put things in ampoules.

Insert #1

Sex times technology equals the future.

J.G. Ballard, *Re/Search: J.G. Ballard*

Change default drive

WG: I saw a great example of some invisible literature recently. It was this long clip from a McDonnell Douglas promotional video for their Apache attack helicopters. It was so good. So much better than anything Hollywood has ever come up with. I mean, Jim Cameron would have eaten his heart out, because the things looked great, incredibly sinister and dynamic-looking. I'm fascinated by the semiotics of modern weapons. They're designed to look so mean, but they don't really have to.

BS: I saw some astonishing cheap plastic sub-machine guns at Vienna airport, really small-calibre things.

WG: Oh, those aren't cheap, they're expensive.

BS: Yeah, but they were all cast out of one single mould.

WG: No, no, actually, those aren't small-calibre. The magazine comes out of the brace of the butt. Probably a high speed .2.

BS: Yeah, I think that's what it was.

WG: That was the first thing I saw when I got off the plane. I thought, this is going to be fun.

BS: It's the sort of thing you carry when you have to gun someone down inside a plane and you don't want to pierce the fuselage during the flight. They fire, like, a clip of soft-nosed .2 slugs or something. Horrible fucking things.

Bin feed

Gibson has always maintained that he was never in the business of making social forecasts. That his books should be treated as cognitive aids to the decoding of contemporary culture, simulations of the present rather than visions of the future. But on one level at least they have been prophetic. The recent glut of Hollywood sci-fi spectaculars owes a lot to Gibson, movies like *RoboCop* (which he rates) and *Total Recall* (which he doesn't). Not that he's been ripped off, he's on the Hollywood payroll. He was handsomely rewarded for his *Alien 3* script, even though it's no longer being used. Meanwhile the options on his novels and short stories continue to wind their way through various studios (update: James Cameron is scheduled for *Burning Chrome*, Abel Ferrara for *New Rose Hotel*, *Neuromancer* has been put on ice, while conceptual artist Robert Longo is tinkering with *Johnny Mnemonic*).

WG: That's Hollywood! It's deal driven. I work down there like a carpenter or a plumber; I just do it for the money. It's a union gig. Really, really well paid and I can get my teeth fixed on the Writers' Guild. It's not like an art gig.

Strikeout function

Sterling has been rather more ambiguous on the question of science fiction's predictive capacity, quite enjoying the switch-back glory ride that is the career of the professional futurist. He was writing stories connected with Islamic culture, for example, way before all the recent headlines.

BS: In a way, Islam might be the one major force that could really dig in its heels and resist the entire set of values represented by the global Net, but every time Saddam Hussein goes on television, that's a defeat for him. Once you're on television, you have essentially accepted the Net, you have capitulated on some very basic level.

Mark text #3

She let her gaze follow steam-pipes and taut wires to the gleam of the Babbage Engine, a small one, a kinotrope model, no taller than Sybil herself. Unlike everything else in the Garrick, the Engine looked in very good repair, mounted on four mahogany blocks. The floor and ceiling above and beneath it had been carefully scoured and whitewashed. Steam calculators were delicate things, temperamental, so she'd heard; better not to own one than not cherish it.

William Gibson and Bruce Sterling, *The Difference Engine*

Random access memory

What would have happened if the Victorian inventor Charles Babbage had been given sufficient government funds to construct a working model of his Difference Engine, the steam-driven number cruncher that in actuality never got further than his drawing board? Gibson's and Sterling's joint novel simulates a response to this hypothetical question. A conceptual 'proof-piece' whose operational premise is that the Information Revolution tore through the social fabric of Victorian London mere decades after the impact of the Industrial Revolution, *The Difference Engine* is a highly controlled exercise in prefabricated archaeology, a landmark text, a complex piece of narrative machinery, dense with sideswipe irony, sampled documents and rejigged detail. It was Sterling who performed most of the research and development, sifting through boxes of old maps and archive material at the University of Austin, consulting his Marx and his Foucault; Gibson who fine-tuned the working parts. A neat double-act.

Insert #2

This month, researchers at the Science Museum will begin building Babbage's Difference Engine to find out if he really could have succeeded in his quest. Backed by British industrial sponsors led by ICL, the team in the department of computing have carefully analysed the original design drawings of the engine, and commissioned British component makers to build the 4,000 parts using Victorian tolerances and materials.

Sunday Correspondent, 16 September 1990

Preview function

BS: I see it as being weirdly parallel to our book. In many ways we were using the voices of the period to tell our own science fictional story.

WG: When I walked in and the Difference Engine was there, I just went for it. It was this really riveting object. They even had these disposable cotton gloves, which are actually in our book. It gave me an astonishing jolt.

Merge/sort

More a narrative performance than a novel, and in that sense not always a conventionally good read, *The Difference Engine* is constructed as a series of 'iterations', of information-processing runs. Why? Because its narrator is the Difference Engine itself (jokily tagged the Narratron by Gibson and Sterling). Each iteration is an attempt on the part of the hyper-evolved Engine of 1991 to approach autonomous self-consciousness by meditating on the circumstances of its own origin, by analysing the old restaurant bills and police mug shots that exist in its bowels and deducing the story behind them all. It's a brilliant conceit, the Victorian technique of omniscient narration reclaimed as a cybernetic simulation. Add to this the fact that the novel was actually composed on floppy discs Fedexed between Vancouver and Austin and what you have here is a radical postmodern cultural event.

Insert #3

Conspiracy theory (and its garish narrative manifestations) must be seen as a degraded attempt – through the figuration of advanced technology – to think the impossible totality of the contemporary world system.

Fredric Jameson, *Postmodernism, or the Cultural Logic of Late Capitalism*

Hard return

From the urban vortex of the Boston-Atlanta 'Sprawl' in *Neuromancer* to the monumental crunch of the Smoke in *The Difference Engine*. From cyberpunk to what some wags have already dubbed steampunk. What's going on?

WG: We were looking for some sort of radical move that would allow us to get a grip on contemporary reality

SB: So the surreal business of the novel, the printing-press situationists, Victorian fast food joint, Dickensian hackers, the whole empire espionage subplot, this is a way of smuggling the language of cyberpunk conspiracy fiction in through the back door of history? Of junking its overfamiliar vocabulary while retaining

Caution: text overload

SB: its usefulness as a cultural metaphor?

WG: Yeah, well put

BS: I think it has something of the structure of a conspiracy novel. It's essentially chaotic, there's a great deal in it about chaos theory, the notion of exploding complexity, beyond anyone's ability to sum up

Terminate run?

SB: Jean Baudrillard, the Prophet of Postmaderni$m, arhues thwt jue kiohgl zxopd
   *

Terminate run?
   *

WG: I think this is a tough one to recommodify. It's an indigestible artefact.

BS: The day they have Jean Baudrillard video games, where you can, like, fly through the black hole of commodification, the day they do that, there'll be a Difference Engine T-shirt.
   *
   !

Jim Thompson
i-D, no. 162, March 1997

Jim Thompson died early on 7 April 1977 in Huntington Beach having smoked his last packet of Pall Malls. One of the last things he told his wife was that he'd be famous within ten years. He wasn't wrong. The French began to make films of his hardboiled crime novels almost immediately. Alain Corneau got there first with *Serie Noire* in 1979; Bertrand Tavernier directed *Coup de Torchon* soon afterwards.

Then in 1984, Barry Gifford at Creative Arts/Black Lizard reissued *A Hell of a Woman*, *The Getaway* and *Pop. 1280* and, over the next three years, put out ten more Thompson novels. Hollywood soon got in on the act. Maggie Greenwald's *The Kill-Off*, James Foley's *After Dark, My Sweet* and Stephen Frears's *The Grifters* all saw the light of day in 1990, while in 1994 Sam Peckinpah's *The Getaway* was remade with Alec Baldwin and Kim Basinger. Now, twenty years after Thompson's death, comes the biography. Robert Polito's *Savage Art* (Serpent's Tail), like Ted Morgan's book on William Burroughs or James Mitchell's book on Michel Foucault, is one of those rare biographies that not only place the man in the context of the times but also lead to a renewed understanding of the work. Polito is quite conscious of what he is up against and that is the whole legacy of the Thompson myth as it was fashioned by him throughout his life. He used to insist that he had written hundreds of pulp novels, that they had often been banged out in hotel rooms in a matter of weeks in between drinking sessions, that he never received the credit he was due, that he was a victim of 'flukish Fate'. It is to Polito's credit that he carefully sifts the fact from the fiction in Thompson's past and gives us the definitive account of his creative life. He makes us understand that there are really two Jim Thompsons. The first Jim Thompson was the Depression-era hobo, Oklahoma City Marxist and radical humanist whose magnum opus – a proletarian novel called *Always to Be Blest* – was pitched out of the window of a bus when it failed to find a publisher. The second Jim Thompson was the jobbing hack, Californian booze hound and erratic family man who deep into middle age managed to reinvent himself as the Céline of American crime fiction. In an astonishing period of intense creativity between 1952 and 1954 he managed to squeeze out the books that made his reputation – among them *The Killer Inside Me*, *Savage Night*, *The Criminal*, *A Hell of a Woman*, *The Nothing Man*, *After Dark, My Sweet* and *The Kill-Off*. Polito makes the point that 'If he had died in the spring of 1954 his literary legacy would have remained essentially what it is today.' Writing against the grain of the fifties, Thompson dredged up memories of thirties marginal men – roughnecks, grifters, travelling salesmen, losers – and dumped them into a soiled American landscape of poverty, alienation and failure. His central characters are often psychotics who unwind during the course of a tortuous narrative and it was Thompson's special trick to observe them from the inside with a steady, unflinching gaze. Polito suggests that Thompson's subversive take on the American Dream was preparing the way for William Burroughs and the beats. But he was more than the sum of his influences. He was an American Original.

William Burroughs
i-D, no. 90, March 1991

Likely to be the best biography of the year by a long shot is *Literary Outlaw: The Life and Times of William S. Burroughs* (Bodley Head) by Ted Morgan.

Inducted into the American Academy of Arts and Letters in 1983 at the age of sixty-nine, Burroughs has lived long enough to witness his canonization as the hip priest of the postmodern avant-garde, but – as Morgan makes clear – he has always remained an enigmatic pariah, an authentic American crank. Banishing himself from the midwestern cultural heritage that threatened to become his lot, he drifted through a succession of cityscapes – forties New York, Mexico City, Tangier during its time as an International Zone, Paris, London, seventies New York – only to end up in Lawrence, Kansas, a home of sorts, an ironic return to his roots.

Throughout his wanderings, Burroughs refused to go native, he always stayed true to his obsessions, which explains why he has been uniquely cherished as a guru by three generations of the counterculture – the beats, the hippies, the punks. Each could read what they wanted into this obstinately contradictory figure. A bohemian in a three-piece suit, a homosexual frontiersman, a control freak and a junkie, an anarchist conservative, a criminal and an artist, Burroughs is a cult author whose fascination has outlasted such contemporaries as Jack Kerouac, Paul Bowles and Allen Ginsberg.

From the autobiographical *Junky* to *Naked Lunch* and its cut-up sequels to the more recent trilogy of novels completed by *The Western Lands*, his fictions have mapped the psychic landscape of post-nuclear America according to the swings of his own metabolism. Burroughs is a 'litmus person', in Morgan's phrase. The motifs that recur in his work – addiction, conspiracy, viral infection, mutation, control – are more than symptoms of personal distress, they are cultural metaphors.

Morgan emphasizes this shamanistic side to Burroughs throughout the course of his extensively researched 600-page book. Sometimes he stretches credulity, especially with regard to reported stories about black magic and the occult, but there's no disputing the honesty, wit and intelligence he brings to his appointed task.

Techgnosis

Michel Serres is talking at the ICA about the telematic angels of the Internet. You are attempting to interest the clever young man who runs the online pages of a national newspaper in the possibility of an interview. You fax him a proposal and follow it up with a phone call. When you manage to pin him down, he berates you for the poor technical quality of your fax. You say: No chance of a commission, then. What you don't say is that you've faxed him from a local convenience store. One thing you hardly ever admit to industry insiders is that you've been writing a tech column in a glossy for the past year now and still haven't got your home system wired. What interests you isn't technology, but human subjectivity. New media become invisible when inhabited; they need to be 'probed' (Marshall McLuhan) with the working/obsolete assumptions of older media.

American psychonaut

i-D, no. 144, September 1995

Philip K. Dick died in 1982 just at the beginning of a glorious career. He was alive long enough to see some of the rushes from *Blade Runner* – the Ridley Scott adaptation of his 1968 sci-fi novel *Do Androids Dream of Electric Sheep?* – and was ecstatic about the results. More film offers would surely have followed. He might even have become a local media celebrity. He would certainly have been a valued elder statesman in today's rapidly expanding cyber domain. But he died before the release of the film, leaving us with a legacy of books and short stories – chief among them *The Man in the High Castle, The Three Stigmata of Palmer Eldritch, Flow My Tears, the Policeman Said* and *A Scanner Darkly* – which have had a huge influence (on everyone from the avant-post-punk scene to the philosophy of Jean Baudrillard).

Like I say, Philip K. Dick died too early. He was short of

money for most of his writing career and locked into a sci-fi fandom scene that didn't really understand him. When things were particularly tough, he was reduced to living on dog food. *Worse*, he imagined he was committing some kind of crime by doing this (was it *legal* for a human to eat dog food?). This is just one of the facts to be gleaned from *The Shifting Realities of Philip K. Dick* (Pantheon), a collection of personal fragments, diary notes, autobiographical texts, TV proposals and lost chapters edited by Lawrence Sutin (who published a biography of Dick called *Divine Invasions* four years ago).

Dick's fictional universe is firmly anchored within a paranoid mindset. The world his characters inhabit is usually only a 'consensus reality' and a typical Dick novel will trip through five or six different worlds-within-worlds before finally crashing into some pseudo-gnostic godhead. Dick didn't need to invent cyberspace like Gibson did. For him the world was already a 'consensual hallucination' marked by synchronicities, leakages, coded messages and secret signs. What this collection makes clear is how much he lived what he wrote. He was constantly beset during his working life in California by visitations, psychic flashes and sudden illuminations. He was worried he was a schizophrenic (although one of the psychiatrists he consulted pronounced him perfectly sane). Presumably his experimentation with LSD must have complicated matters. In 1974, the defining moment of his life occurred. He imagined that he was possessed by an entity which he called VALIS (Vast Active Living Intelligence System), which set about reorganizing his life, calling in old royalty cheques and generally putting his life on a more coherent footing. There's not much on this episode in *The Shifting Realities of Philip K. Dick*. There's too much on his gnostic religious ramblings (Hakim Bey calls Dick the only authentic twentieth-century gnostic). But there's plenty here to keep even the most casual reader of Philip K. Dick fully entertained.

Electronic flaneur #1

Arena, no. 65, January/February 1997

It is spring 1996 at the University of Warwick's Virtual Futures conference just outside Coventry. The avant-tech musician Scanner has been invited on-stage by the conference's organizers to perform one of his unique sonic improvisations. A tele-screen flickers with images of a ghostly figure wandering through the concrete intersections of London with a three-foot long aerial quivering in his hands like a baroque dowsing rod. Static bleeds over the PA system against a background of gentle, quasi-abstract beats. Radio frequencies are being cast. Suddenly a human voice drops out of the ether. The audience lean forward in their seats to listen to the fragments of a cellphone conversation which in this new ambient context are weightless, disembodied, provocative. The performer himself is nowhere to be seen.

'Perhaps I was trying to hide. I'm easily embarrassed.' It is autumn 1996 in an elegantly appointed flat in London's Battersea and Robin Rimbaud, the man behind the Scanner mask, is busy fixing up some orange juice. He is smartly dressed in striped top, navy shorts and deck shoes and is filling me in on the explosion of interest in his recording career over the last eighteen months. Appearances at conferences and festivals from London to Berlin to New York, commissions for BBC Radio 3, a soundtrack for a bunch of MTV ads, CD-ROM projects with like-minded artists and musicians, invitations, faxes, e-mail requests. His schedule for 1997 is already starting to hot up. There's no way he could hide even if he wanted to. 'It would only make me look suspicious, wouldn't it?'

Robin Rimbaud in person is very different from the Scanner image that has accumulated over the last three years. The austere sleeves of his albums, the interest in scanning the airwaves, the phantom appearances on stage, the occasional press-shots revealing a pale, intense, underdeveloped figure. They add up for some to an impression of Scanner as a sinister audio voyeur. Whereas Robin Rimbaud is actually, of course, bright, chatty, extremely courteous and very English. The difficulty of translating an avant-garde aesthetic of memory, drift and psychogeography into a pop frame of reference inevitably leads to misunderstandings.

'I used to call myself a "flaneur electronique". Then I had a little jokey name badge made up with the job description, "cultural engineer". I also used to talk about taking "sound polaroids". But it wouldn't surprise me to learn that my albums are archived in the record shops under some all-purpose section labelled "perve".' It doesn't matter. What counts for Rimbaud ultimately is not the image but the work. His five albums (from *Scanner 1* to *Sulphur* through *Scanner 2*, *Mass Observation* and *Spore*) each demonstrate an almost painterly interest in the layering of sound which gives new meaning to the term 'uneasy listening'. Mixing slo-mo techno beats, repeat melody loops, found noise and intercepted voice traffic, they sift through the debris of the sonic landscape that envelops us in order to construct implied archaeologies of loss, pathos and missed connections. They're also mordantly funny.

Cyberspace has been famously defined in the past as the spot where a telephone call takes place. Rimbaud is one of the few artists to take the full measure of this, to work at the edge of the sonic rather than the more familiar visual envelope of data communication tech. 'I like using human voices because you don't know who these people are and in a way it doesn't matter,' he says. 'You work out your own connections. For example, on *Spore* there's a man talking to this woman at the beginning of one of the tracks. The real story is that she's broke and wants her ex-partner to help her out with some money. But whereas a reviewer in America said it's the housing department not being helpful to her, another person said it's her brother giving her a hard time. I know the real story because I edited it.'

The instrument from which Scanner takes his name is an item of consumer tech available from Dixon's or Radio Shack. 'It's no more sophisticated than a very broad-range radio receiver,' he explains. 'Whereas the FM radio dial is restricted to a frequency range of between 88 and 108 Hz, a scanner moves through all the different frequencies from 0 to 1500 Hz. From 0 to 10 Hz it picks up hearing aids, microwave ovens, fax machines, cellular phones and baby alarms. At the top of the scale, which is really exciting but unfortunately impossible to pick up, are earth-to-satellite transmissions.' He becomes animated. 'So it's astronauts talking to each other. You know, "I'm bored and want to go to the toilet but can't get out of this suit." Or whatever it is astronauts say to each other.'

Rimbaud bought his first scanner five years ago from some hunt-sab pals who had used it as a countersurveillance tool to stay one step ahead of the law. It didn't last long. 'I was playing at the Camden Palace in London one night and it blew up. I switched the thing on and it got really hot and smoke started coming out of it. Apparently, the internal battery had imploded.' He laughs. 'I felt like Jimi Hendrix. As if I should have stood there biting this thing with my teeth.'

He's come a long way since then. Up until the summer of last year he was still pursuing his day job in the music department of Fulham public library. ('It got a bit comical towards the end,' he remembers. 'I was having to phone in sick to appear on MTV.') Now at the age of thirty-two he suddenly finds himself in demand all over the world. Appearances in Belgium, Japan and Austria beckon on the horizon and he has just completed producing the *Memetic Flesh* album for Canadian cyber-gurus Arthur and Marilouise Kroker at the same time as writing a 'sub-drum'n'bass track' for the Dutch Conservatory of Music sampled entirely from the oeuvre of Stockhausen.

Rimbaud is moving fast. He enjoys collaborating with other artists and looks as if he's shaping up to be the Brian Eno of the nineties. So how does he feel about comparisons with the great man? 'He's one of the few people I admire,' he admits. 'He's somebody I was really impressed by as a genuine person. He's so modest and such a nice bloke. At whatever age he is I was impressed that he's still got a decent haircut, he dresses well and he's polite and good-mannered.'

Electronic flaneur #2

Arena, no. 60, July/August 1996

As the information economy fast-forwards into the twenty-first century like a runaway machine, it sometimes seems there's only one thing keeping it going. The drive for globalism. Whether it's China and the USA struggling to come to some common agreement about intellectual property rights, the World Trade Organization pushing for a reduction of international import tariffs or software manufacturers like Sony and Microsoft making sure their products are compatible, the transformation of the planet into one giant hypermarket is increasingly the name of the political game.

Of course, it's technology that makes the money go round. Auto manufacturers can now switch their assembly lines to the low-wage climes of the developing world at the touch of a button. Satellite news vendors are able to beam their wares across national borders. The computerized stock market runs twenty-four hours a day. But just because technology makes all this possible, doesn't mean it necessarily has to. It can always be hijacked, subverted and *detourned*. As SF prophet William Gibson is fond of saying, 'The street finds its own uses for things.'

This is a story of the streets of San Francisco finding their own uses for a piece of world-spanning software whose development was funded by Deutsche Telekom in Berlin. It begins a year after the fall of the Berlin Wall and the global ascendancy of free-market capitalism, when the design house Art+Com was commissioned to build a VR model of Berlin to help plan its post-Cold War renewal. The project leader, Joachim Sauter, started to collate old maps, canned film footage and architectural drawings in order to construct a point-and-click walkthrough of Berlin past and present. He soon discovered that the sky was literally the limit.

'I thought, why just visualize the city?' he says. 'Why not visualize the surrounding area as well? After that, things took on a momentum of their own. We found that there were some technical approaches that would allow us, theoretically at least, to visualize the whole Earth.'

The final result of such musings is Terra-Vision, a globe-trotting interface that allows the user to hack the planet all the way from real-time satellite data, through aerial photographs and computer models of various cities, down to local map coordinates. Art+Com have taken their system on tour and it's striking. Booted up on a classy SGI Onyx workstation (of the type used to code the SFX in *Jurassic Park*), it models a virtual image of the Earth that the user can access by manipulating a one-metre-diameter trackball. By rolling and steering the ball, it's possible to hop and skip across the planet, diving in and out of client databases, before pulling back and returning to the host server in Berlin.

If knowledge is power, then Deutsche Telekom looks well placed to make a pretty impressive land grab in cyberspace. There are plans to hook up all sorts of local servers to the T-Vision interface through a series of ATM broadband data connections. So far a German TV channel, the Smithsonian Institute in Washington, the Toronto Science Museum and Disney's Epcot Centre in Florida have all expressed an interest in climbing on board. Momentum is picking up.

The implications of all this are staggering. Once T-Vision has expanded its links as it intends – taking in data on global weather systems, archaeological sites, tectonic plate movements, polar ice cap shifts and human and animal migration patterns – then the world is its oyster. It could achieve its ambition of becoming a network to rival the World Wide Web in scope and influence on the Internet. It could also become the ultimate surveillance tool.

What a couple of trendy young American wireheads saw in the project, however, was something quite different. Mark Pesce, a self-described technopagan who helped to code the Virtual Reality Modelling Language so important in the field of computer simulation, and Paul Godwin, a CD-ROM composer and digital musician, hooked up in the cyberdelic rave scene of San Francisco in 1994 and made their connection with Art+Com soon after. Their ambition is to transform T-Vision into a browser capable of accessing the world's electronic folk music at the flick of a wrist.

'We call it World Song,' says Godwin. 'The idea is literally to activate the planet's songlines.' Godwin becomes quite animated when talking about his project. He spices his talk with buzz-words like 'rave science' and 'sacred art', namechecks American computer performance artists like Brenda Laurel, Rita Addison and Charlotte Davies and is heavily into English dance acts like Orbital and the Prodigy. More than anything, though, he's been influenced by the visions of American science fiction writer, Neal Stephenson. It makes for a heady brew.

Art+Com are eager to collaborate with the Americans because Pesce has the VRML code that would enable them to transform T-Vision into a proper simulation in its own right. The Americans want to hijack T-Vision for their own purposes, with musicians from around the world storing samples of their work on local servers so that a user can flip from the gongs of Tibet to the drums of London in one swerving motion. Godwin and Pesce are doing something more than just putting together another global jukebox with World Song. They are attempting to build the ultimate cut'n'mix sampling tool.

'That's what really disappointed me about something like Internet Underground Music Access. Madonna liked it, Warner Brothers got all their acts on it and now it's the Interactive Music Network. It's not sacred art. It's just an alternative distribution system. We want to transform World Song into a global database of samples which are simply there and not for sale.' All of which suggests that in the global switchback ride of the information economy, the currents of pleasure may outrun the movements of money. Well, it's a thought, isn't it?

Hobo emperor

i-D, no. 161, February 1997

Iain Sinclair is a history man ahead of his time. In early books like *Lud Heat* and *White Chappell, Scarlet Tracings* he created an imaginary London whose occult power/knowledge complex was shadowed by the leavings of Egyptian myth, the placement of Hawksmoor's churches and the ritual significance of the Ripper slayings. Since then, he's boosted the careers of figures as diverse as Peter Ackroyd, Stewart Home, Aidan Dun and Alan Moore and has set himself up as the Grand Old Man of London Psychogeographers.

He's also been responsible for parties of stumblebum delinquents wandering around London attempting to crack the code of the city's paving stones with nothing more to hand than an A–Z and a copy of one of his books. It's not something he's taken kindly to. When he was preceded onstage at a literary event in London in 1995 by a typical Sinclair casualty whose incoherent musings served only to baffle the audience, he was moved to comment that the loonies were out there doing his walks before he could get there himself. Given that in *Lights Out for the Territory* (Granta), his latest collection of mythopoeic ramblings based on his peregrinations around Lambeth, Westminster, the City of London and his native Hackney, he elevates the figure of the stalker (particularly in relation to his occult 'pursuit' of Lord Archer) to the level of some crypto-shamanistic visionary, this seems a bit rich. It seems that Sinclair can dish it out but can't take it himself. All of which begs the question. As he wanders around London riffing feverishly on graffiti, road signs, graveyard inscriptions, antiquarian tat and other sacred trivia does he know what he's doing or not? Sinclair would presumably like to think of himself as a latter-day William Blake dowsing the rocks and stones of London and forcing them to deliver their freight of occult cargo. But Blake created his own mythical system and few poets, nowadays, are up to that.

Sinclair is a postmodern *bricolage* artist; he samples the myths of the past and weaves them into dizzying fabrics of prophetic invention. If he bears comparison with any other contemporary writer it's with William Gibson. In *Count Zero*, Gibson explicitly modelled cyberspace as a gnostic dreamtime (populated by the ghosts of the Haitian voodoo pantheon) and, to a certain extent, all Sinclair is really doing is hacking the streets of London as if they were hyperlinks in some Web-like palimpsest laid down by the Spirit of History. What's interesting is that he's more of a Deleuzian than Gibson. Whereas, in *Idoru*, Gibson fixates on 'nodal points' as the bearers of geomantic information, Sinclair (like the ley-line hunter Alfred Watkins before him) understands that it's the lines connecting the points that actually do the work of mapping the dreamtime. So are Sinclair's flights of fancy worth following? Does he know what he's doing? He's a strong poet. The answer has to be 'yes'. It's just that some of the places he gets to (he traces his ancestry back to the Knights Templar at the end of *Lights Out for the Territory*) make you realize that he has little interest in Gibson's idea that pop culture is 'the testbed of futurity'.

Media prophet
Arena, no. 23, September/October 1990

They say the sixties are making a comeback and you can see what they mean. For those who've made their pile in the monopoly money industries of the last decade, pulled off that fifties patented conjuring trick of jumping a rung on the class ladder, it's time to unravel and get into some serious soul-searching, fritter away some of that bank roll on making yourself a Better Person. A meaningful philosophy of life, maybe a fancy new religion: something vaguely cultic to impress the dinner party guests. What's really needed is a bona fide guru, a Name to tickle the spiritual palate of the jaded. Only thing is the only real takers are the derided gurus of the sixties. There they all are, those longhair prophets, those wiggy shamans, nervously edging back into view – their manuals of do-it-yourself metaphysics dusted off, repackaged and propped up again on the racks of the Neo-Boho Culture Mart.

You can almost hear the breathless sales pitches: 'How about tripping out to the wellsprings of tribal knowledge with Carlos Castaneda? Or rediscovering New Age mysticism in the pages of Robert Anton Wilson's *Illuminatus* trilogy? Then again, there's always the electro-hoodoo groove of Marshall McLuhan.' Marshall Who? 'You remember: celebrated media guru, the Oracle of the Electronic Age. All those prophecies about the Global Village, the Electronic Sensorium, the mystic communion of souls at the living room altar of the Telstar god.'

Sounds weird enough. The only problem is that McLuhan at his best was a lot more rational than this and a hell of a lot more interesting than any hippie guru. He was no kaftanned clown, but a sober suited professor of literature with a glint in his eye, an eccentric academic who'd been dabbling in all sorts of extracurricular pursuits – technology, pop culture, the media – ever since the forties. How was he to know that the combination would prove to be so explosive by the time his third book, *Understanding Media*, was published in 1964?

Suddenly people assumed he had some secret understanding of the strange new world of computers, freeways, paperbacks, jet travel, credit cards, news leaks and – the Big One – television, which came to a head in the sixties. 'They're all media,' declared McLuhan. 'Tell us about it,' responded a million media pundits. And he was only too happy to oblige.

From 1964 until 1968, McLuhan was at the height of his fame, courted by business executives, avant-garde artists and countercultural politicos alike. But he always felt most comfortable in Mediaville. He understood the way it worked, invented the sound bite before there was a name for it. If you wanted a snappy and predictably outrageous quote on anything from waterbeds to Watergate for your chat show then you paid for this long, gangling professor to fly in from Toronto University and pontificate in your studio. Where he would no doubt uncoil his limbs, ceremoniously light a cigar – flicking the ash at intervals into his trouser cuffs – look round at the lights and cameras and gravely inform you that if television had been invented twenty years earlier then the Holocaust would never have happened.

It was an act, as was all the mystical stuff he came out with about Discarnate Man, cathode ray angels, the electronic Pentecost. But that didn't mean there wasn't a kernel of truth inside some of his nutty pronouncements. The Holocaust quip is a case in point. It offended a lot of people, but McLuhan was making a serious point about the comparative sensory effects of a 'cool' medium like television and a 'hot' one like radio. Hitler's hysterical rhetoric benefited from radio's built-in tendency to amplify the imaginative passions of the listener, to hypnotize them, but would have seemed ridiculous on television. The inclusive, implacable gaze of television numbs the viewer; it takes a more ambiguous, less defined personality to have any chance of stimulating curiosity (a Kennedy rather than a Nixon).

And McLuhan was as ambiguous as they came. Maybe because of this, he managed to stir up as much resentment as excitement. Either he was a sinner or a saint, while for some poor impressionable souls he managed to be both. Take our own good doctor of the arts, Jonathan Miller – surely the classic example of the disciple turned apostate. In 1965 he fronted a report for the BBC arts show *Monitor* in which he breathlessly celebrated McLuhan as the Freud of the twentieth century, a psychoanalyst of that age's own 'dark continent': the flickering landscapes of the media. Six years later, with McLuhan's reputation perceptibly on the wane, he published a book in the Fontana Modern Masters series which was a skilful piece of character assassination. Suddenly, McLuhan was no more than a spoiled priest anxious to discover in the technological rituals of broadcasting an ecumenical substitute for the fading power of Catholicism, his theories 'a gigantic system of lies'.

McLuhan initially thought Miller's volume was an elaborate practical joke. Never one to take criticism lightly (or even at all, come to that) he responded by putting down his critic as 'a clown with the habits of a sixth form debater'. It's a suggestive remark. McLuhan himself was not averse to the donnish pleasures of chop logic while insisting to his often baffled audiences of university students – or, at the height of his fame, corporate executives – that he was merely a jester, a prober, a Delphic tease. McLuhan was sensitive to all contradictions but his own.

One figure who managed to touch on the genuine complexities of this charismatic *idiot savant* was Tom Wolfe. In 1965, when the buzz over *Understanding Media* was just picking up and McLuhan himself was on a lectureship tour of the corporate conference rooms of the West Coast, he was commissioned to write an article on the whole phenomenon for the Sunday magazine of the New York *Herald Tribune*, and turned in a sharp, funny and not unsympathetic portrait of an academic innocent abroad turning the tables on the 'business studs' who flocked to hear him speak.

Wolfe's story broke McLuhan in the States, complete with anecdote about a visit to a topless bar in San Francisco ('Everyone was struck dumb; everyone, that is to say, except McLuhan. Inside of thirty seconds he had simply absorbed the whole scene into ... the theory'). McLuhan recognized good publicity when he saw it, only half-jokingly describing the article as 'a major asset to McLuhan Inc.', and ordered a dozen copies of the magazine. The title of the piece became an oft-repeated tag line for the whole McLuhan phenomenon: What If He Is Right?

Well, what if he was? Recent events have tried to supply some kind of answer to this question. After protracted negotiation and much wrangling, McLuhan's legacy of private papers – some 600,000 notes, diaries, letters and unfinished works – were finally acquired by the Canadian Public Archives in 1984. Since then they have formed the basis for a steady stream of books and selected odds and ends – most significantly the letters recording his correspondence with everyone from early literary heroes like Wyndham Lewis and Ezra Pound to later political favourites like Canadian premier Pierre Trudeau – put together by a surviving inner circle of friends and relatives.

As far as they're concerned, McLuhan's celebrity got in the way of his scientific credibility. One of the more recent books edited by his son, Eric, is overprotestingly titled *Laws of Media* and attempts to paint McLuhan as a new Darwin or a new Freud, a Grand Thinker. A big mistake. What's attractive about his books is that they're aphoristic, packed with quotations, speculative propositions and out-and-out wind-ups, which, in perhaps the biggest wind-up of all, he insisted on calling media 'probes'. Unfortunately a lot of people – pro and con – took McLuhan at face value, leaving behind a legacy of misinterpretation and disinformation that clouds the current revival of interest in his work. Luckily, if there's one thing this revival has produced it's a thorough critical biography: *Marshall McLuhan: The Medium and the Messenger* (Random House) by Philip Marchand. Marchand has made extensive use of personal material from the Public Archive and his book has as a result stirred up a small hornet's nest of controversy, with McLuhan's inner sanctum alleging distortion of facts and invasion of privacy (he *was* a good husband; he *didn't* neglect his kids).

But Marchand is no Albert Goldman. He is scrupulously fair to his subject and has produced an acute, precise, if not entirely glowing, portrait of a man of almost effortless contradiction. Here was an old engineering student preaching the end of industrialism, a Canadian student of English literature, a Joyce scholar obsessed by the media. Here was the son of staunch Baptists a converted Catholic, a huckster who seemed to believe in the Second Coming, a faultless host convinced that people were plotting against him behind his back. More striking, even comic, is the news that the Oracle of the Electronic Age was the last person on his block to buy a TV in the fifties (even then it was kept in the basement).

Maybe because he was so oblivious to his own complexities, McLuhan was immensely charismatic in person. He was a great draw in the lecture hall, he was always attracting would-be managers and get-rich-quick merchants more than willing to stake their own cash on some harebrained promotional stunt. Throughout his career he was able to hustle grants and donations off the corporate sector to fund all the various projects he had bubbling away – from his ground-breaking journal of cultural anthropology, *Explorations*, published in the late fifties, to his 1968 subscription newsletter *DEW-LINE*, a slightly threadbare collection of his greatest one-liners which came complete with a pack of predictive playing cards.

By the seventies, however, his media career was effectively over. He remained a professor at Toronto University, which had put him in charge of a special Center for Culture and Technology during his glory days, but when he died in 1980 at the age of sixty-nine, most of his books were out of print. All that remained was a handful of slogans – 'the global village', 'the medium is the message' – hurriedly consigned to the remainder bin of history along with love beads, Crosby, Stills and Nash albums and conspiracy theories.

What went wrong? A clue is provided by going all the way back to his first book, *The Mechanical Bride*, published in 1951. This is a summary of the work he had been doing in the forties on what he called 'the folklore of industrial man' before he became fascinated by the newer electronic technologies of the fifties and sixties (his pet name for *Understanding Media* was 'The Electronic Call Girl'). Meeting his students on their own ground, he applied all the lit crit skills he'd learned from studying modernists like Pound and Eliot to the close reading of everything in the pop playpen from Coke ads to Tarzan comics.

Lucid, witty, breathtaking, these semiotic set-pieces anticipated Roland Barthes's *Mythologies* by over a decade. More significant though is McLuhan's defence of his method, which he characterized as a form of 'civil defence against media fallout'. Just as the sailor in Poe's tale, 'A Descent into the Maelstrom', saves himself from shipwreck by co-operating with rather than struggling against the whirlpool that threatens him, so McLuhan substituted 'amusement' for 'moral indignation' in his handling of pop culture.

In other words, his interest in the media was tactical, a form of cultural jujitsu. Like any other cranky old professor of the period, he wanted to save Literature from the corrupting influence of mass culture. It was only his method that was strange, not his aims.

All well and good. But once he got sucked into the vortex of a celebrity career, it's uncertain how firmly he was willing to hold onto his original values. Co-operating with the tug of a whirlpool is one thing, surrendering to it unconditionally is quite another. McLuhan in the end just tried too hard. He garnished a lot of his later pronouncements with the kind of embarrassing references to flower power, mini-skirts, Happenings and the 'English Beatles' that were guaranteed to alienate his original constituency. The last thing you want an oracle to do is talk your language, particularly if he gets it ever so slightly but significantly wrong.

By the end of his life, if McLuhan was remembered for anything it was for his brief cameo in *Annie Hall*, dapper, slightly strained, conjured out of nowhere by Woody Allen to clinch an argument with a pompous know-it-all in a cinema queue. Marshall McLuhan: an esoteric joke.

What's the verdict today, though? Twenty-five years on is surely time enough to go back to McLuhan and sort the Fraud from the Freud. How do *Understanding Media*, *The Mechanical Bride* and other books like *The Gutenberg Galaxy*, *War and Peace in the Global Village* and *The Medium is the Massage* stand up today?

The first thing to bear in mind is that they are very much hit and miss affairs. About 30 per cent of McLuhan's probes are either facile or ludicrous or both – like the one about how the Soviet objection to the American U-2 spy plane was really down to the fact that it was an aural and not a visual culture (bugging would have been OK, then), or the one explaining how the civil rights movement owed its success to the socially levelling effects of the automobile in the South (so much for all the lunch-counter protests).

But the upside to this is that 70 per cent of McLuhan is stimulating and worthwhile. All of his books, with the exception of his first, *The Mechanical Bride*, are really playing around with four Basic Ideas. These were systematized by *Laws of Media* into an analytic tool called a 'tetrad', which is supposed to be capable of taking apart any cultural artefact but which makes more sense as an intriguing box of interpretive tricks.

The first two ideas are unoriginal and rather questionable. Idea Number One is that technology is an extension of the human body, one that has the effect of altering the equilibrium of the senses. Thus the automobile externalizes human motor power; the media extend the central nervous system. It's uncertain whether this itself is anything more than an extended metaphor – although David Cronenberg certainly had a lot of fun with it in his 1982 movie *Videodrome*, what with its veined TV sets and human video recorders (James Woods in one of the stickier roles of his career).

Idea Number Two meanwhile is even dodgier: that any technology, any medium, when pushed to its limit will overheat and flip into reverse. Thus cash becomes credit; conspicuous consumption becomes conspicuous waste, expenditure, destruction. It works for these examples, sure, but what about something like TV? Push that to an extreme and all you get is *Santa Barbara* four times a day on sixty channels.

But then, for McLuhan, content doesn't count: the Medium is the Message. And, let's face it, he's right. What's significant about any new technology isn't the way it looks; it's the way it changes the landscape. His second two ideas deal with this theme and, compared to the first two, they are fresh and challenging. They hit the mark.

Idea Number Three is that the content of a new medium is always an older medium. Thus cars right up until the beginning of the sixties tended to be designed as sturdy chariots, 'horseless carriages', while the introduction of television, to return to

McLuhan's favoured obsession, was made acceptable by the wholesale buying up of old movies from the ailing Hollywood studios. Look, too, at how the compact disc has revived record company back catalogues or how the personal computer was initially designed as a typewriter with a built-in screen.

This is an important insight. It explains Rupert Murdoch's apparent willingness to lose millions of pounds a week on Sky Television. He surely has an intuition that at some point in the future satellite broadcasting will no longer be a matter of repeating old episodes of *Moonlighting*, but will move into an as yet undefined but lucrative new territory. That's the thing. You can never predict how technology is going to get used. Who could have guessed that the biggest market for radio pagers would be crack dealers?

The flipside to this point that upon its initial introduction technology always cloaks itself in the comforting guise of the past is the idea – Idea Number Four – that once an old technology has been displaced by a newer one it immediately makes a comeback as art, having only really become visible for the first time. Thus when steam power in the early nineteenth century pushed aside older forms of agricultural technology, the environment they had made possible was immediately reclaimed as a new genre of painting – landscape. In the same way, the commercial product of the Hollywood studio system was re-evaluated as high art by the Cahiers du Cinema crowd precisely at the time that television had taken over its mass audience.

Today the same kind of retrieval is at work in the post-industrial scene. There's not just the recent creative salvage art boom, with its transformation of scrap metal into sculpted objects, but also the larger scale reconstructions of old coal mines and workshops as heritage museums. Where will it all end? The Ford plant at Dagenham turned into a theme park?

It's not as crazy as it sounds. McLuhan was a writer balanced on the cusp of history, sensitive to the receding tides of industrialism, the disappearing Fordist regime of assembly-line mass production, yet open to the approaching sweep of new electronic technologies, the materializing world of information and of simulation we live in today. He was a Janus figure facing both ways, his antennae picking up signals from the folklore of industrial man, the mythologies of telematic man. As such, he fits his own definition of the artist, of a figure alert to the ebb and flow of media who attempts to fashion from his predicament a compelling image, a binding spell.

In this challenging age of fax machines, smart missiles, Sony Watchmans and virtual realities it's becoming obvious that we need someone of his intelligence and vision to point out the shifting signs in the landscape, cast the runes of the future. And ultimately it's for this reason, not for any hankering after mystic excitements, that McLuhan deserves to be read again.

Perhaps recognizing this, the University of Toronto reopened his old Centre for Culture and Technology in 1983, having closed it down after his death. Appropriately rechristened the McLuhan Program, its aim is to explore how revolutionary advances in communications technology change the way we think and behave, the way we live. As its new director David Olson admits, this would have been something inconceivable before McLuhan. 'He's got his place in history, he's a significant figure. He won't be looked back on as a new Descartes, Galileo or Freud, as was thought at the time, but he certainly set out a new perspective. He got the ball rolling.'

Free theory DJ

i-D, no. 106, July 1992

The line from Berkeley crackles with static. Avital Ronell is struggling to be heard. But then, it's always been like that. She may be a professor at the University of California now ('teaching spoiled upper-class brats, you know?'), but she's had a long and difficult career as a nomadic theorist and freethinker. She has lived in Tel Aviv, New York, Berlin. She wrote a philosophical essay on AIDS in 1983 before it had been publicly recognized. In 1989, she published *The Telephone Book: Technology, Schizophrenia, Electric Speech*, a densely constructed meditation on technology, time and life at the end of the line, which transformed her into a cult author in the intellectual subworlds of Europe and America.

Now comes *Crack Wars: Literature, Addiction, Mania* (University of Nebraska Press), a less clotted and more accessible work, which, besides being an extended critique of Flaubert's *Madame Bovary*, is also a historical account of the cultural psychopathology of addiction. According to Ronell, if being itself can be considered the archetype of addiction, then both drugs and electronic media become counter-attractions to that primal drag. Everyone is 'on drugs' in one way or another.

Ronell lists her interests as 'technology, anti-racism, state torture and electronic culture'. She is distressed by the cutbacks in American higher education and has opened her classes to the public ('I get a lot of flak for that but I get a lot of interesting people who are kind of spinning on their own'). She has also set up a radio station called Radio Free Theory in an attempt to get her ideas across to a wider public.

What follows is the edited transcript of a telephone conversation that took place with Avital Ronell on May 22 this year.

SB: What is your response to the LA riots?

AR: What interests me is the way these riots are an effect of media technology and the mutations that that implies in our relation to race . . . The Rodney King event occurred at the moment that video, testimonial video, sent out an alarm to television, which was a kind of discourse of effacement and it sent out the alarm precisely at the moment when the Gulf War was being non-covered. I think what happened here was that television refused to show the war; there was a refusal to disseminate, a refusal of violence; and at that very moment a metonymy of the Gulf War erupted on the screen and we suddenly saw a police action take place that involved beating a black body (our whole rhetoric around the Gulf War was that it was a police action). So I think in America what happened was the undisclosed and effaced Gulf War was switched onto this channel of a local metonymy and I think that the very fact that the cops went on trial . . . if one follows this kind of allegory, then there was a hearing for war crimes, for crimes of police force, and they were let off.

SB: How could that happen?

AR: One thing that I think this eruption of the testimonial video has produced for us in America is a real shock because since the sixties I think most people assumed that if it could be said that the whole world's watching, an ethical response and a kind of calling to justice would occur. Now that will have to be rigorously revised because the whole world was watching and suddenly we recognized that that's not enough. And this is a major mutation in our sensibilities – in World War Two we assumed that if there had been witnesses things would have been different. So that has sent shock waves in America – that you could show anything now and it wouldn't elicit a kind of ethical response. So I think people are extremely shocked and that's why in part there has to be a violent rupture – because this is a rupture of and in ethics.

SB: The cops came up with this story about how they thought Rodney King was this dangerous black guy pumped up on PCP, didn't they?

AR: What you have here is a few things. First of all, because they interpreted the video in terms of a frame-by-frame analysis, they transformed it into the chilling effect of a freeze-frame. Now anyone who's read some Barthes and Derrida and Benjamin knows that a picture is always related to phantoms. So what happened was he became part of that whole vocabulary of racist designation; he was a zombie, he was a ghost, he was a phantom... what started the false narrative engine going was this hallucination on the part of the police force that this guy was necessarily on PCP. The point would be that this violence can only be articulated as legitimate and let off the hook if one assumes that drugs is at the core or at the base of it. So this is the war on drugs, the ethnocide that I've been very anxious about that's being carried on in the name of drugs, but in fact we have the police force hallucinating about this guy, so they're the ones that are on the drug of all sorts of lies and rhetorical deceits.

SB: How do you interpret George Bush's war on drugs?

AR: Don't forget that I'm not convinced that the war on *drugs* is a war *on* drugs, but that drugs – because they can't be defined or pinned down or arrested as concepts or objects – permit a wide range of displacement. So as with the Rodney King event one had to assume that to make war on this body one had to assume he was on drugs – it just got rid of a lot of civil liberties. The war on drugs is a way of really busting people without any regard for their civil liberties – without there being any probable cause necessary. It's a kind of way to start a video game; it's the code to start it off – suspension of civil liberties. If one can project on to the Other – and usually it's an impoverished and destitute Other – that he possesses or she is on drugs (which has no real definition as such prior to testing and all that), then one can do anything to that body without going through the much slower and laborious routes of defending the Other's civil right and liberties.

SB: So is the war on drugs a class war?

AR: It's something that can pass through a number of class boundaries or other types of frontiers and barriers and that receives different types of evaluation depending on where it's being dispensed or administered. So some people said to me, 'Why didn't you write about counter-culture or ghetto culture in *Crack Wars*?' I said, 'Precisely because I felt my task was to demystify the zoning ordinances with which we locate drugs; they're totally a part of our metaphysical culture; before we go just marginalizing them to the bad ghetto neighbourhoods we have to see how we've always been on drugs and once they pass a certain passport control and go into the lower classes then we start beating the shit out of them.' So I had to ... for example, one of the major arguments now is how can you support the African-American people who are looting their own neighbourhoods and property, and [US Vice-President] Quayle recently said it's a poverty of values not poverty as such that is the problem. And then you have to say, these people have been expropriated from the start. You can't just say that this is their property that they're destroying, or their neighbourhoods. And don't forget looting is something that goes on at the highest level – think of the S&L scandal.

SB: Also, drugs are used routinely by the American armed forces, aren't they?

AR: Things are becoming more and more ambiguous and difficult and one has to start understanding the valuation wars that are taking place. Because, indeed, when drugs are assimilated to the war machine they become an altogether other entity. In other words, they're assimilated to equipmentality; they're part of the performance, part of the test drive of our military machine. So that all the guys who were on those excessive sorties – they would take attack-dosages of pornography before they dropped on Iraq and they took uppers and downers. At that moment... first of all, there's no definition of drugs... at that moment they become part of our technological performance... So what interests me is to show that there is no drug-free zone, that this is a totally irresponsible hallucination promoted by, if you will, the ruling classes.

SB: How does the war on drugs relate to the globalization of capitalism?

AR: The drug traffic and economies are a phantom and double of capital and the flow of capitalism. And it's Deleuze who reminds us that capital isn't just capital; it's a kind of – he doesn't say a drug – but it's certainly a locus of intense desire, of symbolicity, of passage and of intense activity which organizes all sorts of symptoms, desires and needs – and on a highly symbolic and abstract level. So capital itself is not itself but relies on this kind of gold value; so it's the mother of all values – in a sense it's a maternal empire which has to be mapped and found and around which one wants to circulate and conquer and so on. So the libidinal flow of capital shouldn't be underestimated. So even capital is already its own ghost with a kind of reserve of value and desire. So drugs are, if one wants, a moment in capital's eruption as an attempt to be an object. So I do think it's a very complicated thing and has a lot to do with doublings or the capital that is and is not real and is the production of all desire and so on and so forth.

SB: Any last thoughts on the LA riots?

AR: I think that what's very odd speaking about this from California is that it does follow the fault line of earthquake behaviour. I think we're all expecting the Big One, you know?

Fetish boys

You're moving house. Sorting through the review debris – books, magazines, papers – that you've allowed to accumulate in the back of a cupboard for the last ten years, you're faced with a challenge: how to decide what to trash, what to keep. You remember the imported American superhero comics that you prized as a boy for their shiny covers and hermetic thought balloons (fetish: the overestimation of value that accrues from cultural misrecognition). They now moulder away somewhere in a parental attic. Some of the bedroom zines sent to you in your capacity as popcult gatekeeper on a style mag have relatively low production values. Their hermeticism does not attract. You resist the temptation to throw them away. Stewart later tells you that you should offer to donate them to the V&A small press archive.

Talent spotter

i-D, no. 159, December 1996

Wolfgang Tillmans is tucking into a mess of fried eggs in his studio just off Old Street. It's a good space he's found – bare boards, high ceilings, plenty of light. A bed is crammed into one corner, photographs from magazines are taped to the walls, a tiny kitchen doubles as a dark room and a pile of artfully crumpled clothes lies on the floor as if awaiting the tender gaze of Tillmans's camera. He tells me how he signed the lease during a four-hour stopover in London when he was still meant to be living in Berlin.

Tillmans is not alone in having set up here. A whole posse of graphic designers, photographers and Britpop artists have moved into the light industrial units that peel off north and south from the arterial strip of Old Street. It's cheap, it's central, it's hidden away. Tillmans likes it because the London Apprentice is just up the road. 'It's a good place for a drink and a dance late at night. Pub prices, nothing trendy. Completely unlike the Old Compton Street scene.'

He finishes his dinner and we begin to talk about the reason I'm here. His latest anthology of photos, *for when I'm weak I'm strong* (kunstmuseum wolfsburg), has just been published and he's preparing to participate in a group show of 'new photography' at New York's Museum of Modern Art, which lasts until February 4. 'A hundred thousand people are expected over the Christmas period,' says Tillmans. 'Shoppers from Venezuela, Hong Kong and Germany will be in town. It looks like the whole world will be passing through.' Anybody who's been paying attention to the pages of *i-D* over the last few years will be familiar with Tillmans's work – the oddly refined youth portraits with their air of feinted vulnerability; the impressionistic shots of the dance scene; the interest in subjectivity, trivia, keepsake desire. Now, it seems, the rest of the world is catching up.

So who is Wolfgang Tillmans and how did he get to be so famous? He was born in 1968 in a small town called Remscheid just off Autobahn 1 between Düsseldorf and Cologne. After leaving school, he hooked up with the Social Services for twenty months as an alternative to doing time with the Army and began to mess around in his spare time with one of the first Canon laser copiers. 'I was distressing found images and holiday snapshots which I'd take with my mother's viewfinder camera. The last thing I thought about was becoming a photographer. I figured there were enough images in the world.'

Tillmans has no interest in what he calls 'the debate about authenticity'. The still lifes in *for when I'm weak I'm strong* are appetitive exercises in form and colour which freely mix natural objects with cultural signs – hyperreal vegetables wrapped in cellophane, expressively folded garments that stand in for the absent human body, brilliant fruits lying amidst discarded magazines, totemic debris filling a kitchen sink. 'I don't care if a still life is manufactured or made out of plastic or not because that's not the issue. It's the same with music. This whole debate about hand-made music versus electronic music is similar. I resent it. I remember when I was thirteen, I loved Divine songs – which were the stupidest but hardest electro-beat that was available at the time – and everyone in my class would say, How superficial. But importance is to be given to these superficial things because they have a certain kind of feeling.'

Tillmans moved to the red-light district of Hamburg in 1987 and got caught up in the acid house boom. By this time, he had begun to play around with a camera ('I discovered I was good at it') and his images of the scene he inhabited were snapped up by a whole pile of 'dodgy German style magazines' he would rather forget. Tillmans's emblematic shot of Mike Pickering presiding over the decks like a priest at a mass Dionysian cult dates from this period and contributed to his reputation as an artist who had his finger on the pulse of the dance tribes of Europe. 'My pictures of the club scene have been different because I've been in it not because of the fashion or *actualité* aspect of it. I just wanted to understand the activity of dancing and intoxication and losing control as a general human experience. It was that moment that allowed me for the first time to join my art work and my practical or earning-a-living work.'

Tillmans has exhibited throughout his career and sees himself very much as an artist rather than an eye-for-hire. In the last year alone he has had six solo shows and eighteen group shows, all of which have involved significant expenditures of energy because of the way he likes to treat each event as a site-specific installation. 'A lot of my work is about this. I use magazine images and postcard images of my work taped to the wall alongside a fine hand print. It's probably the first time MOMA will have done this but I like working on all these aspects of representation.'

Tillmans killed off a successful career in Hamburg as a style photographer to move to the UK. He chilled out in the seaside resort of Bournemouth between 1990 and 1992 when he was a student at the town's art college and after that began to get his work in *i-D*. He had always been fascinated by the magazine because he saw it as 'the pipeline to London', full of people living lives of 'immediacy and excitement'. The other publication that influenced him was *Time* magazine. 'The photos in *Time* are so without artifice but perfect and that's what good art should be. They give you this strong sensation of being alive, of the twentieth century, of modernity. In that sense, *Time* is like *i-D*.'

The 'look' that Tillmans has patented is much in demand among the fashion and advertising industries at the moment. Douglas Coupland gave the style merchants a tag-line for early nineties youth; now they seem to think that Tillmans is the photographer-by-appointment to Generation X. It's a thought that appals him. 'I actually get embraced by people I'm not sharing similar concerns with and that's really weird. I was trying to say with my portraits that every person is a strong individual in control of his or her life and is very consciously deciding what clothes they are wearing and is full of struggle and contradictions. I was actively working against the way people are represented in the media. But now these pictures have become iconic of the early nineties there is a huge demand for that kind of imagery. The thing is I'm not willing to provide it.'

Instead he lets his work get ripped off and allows others to get on with the business of reinventing the 'cult of the photographer'. Tillmans is an original. He has no agent, no assistant and does all his own printing. He keeps his overheads low so he can move in, take the shot, and move out with one more memento for his personal *Wunderkammer* or 'dictionary of my world'. His work is essentially nomadic, trivial in the deepest sense (*trivium*: crossroads). 'I was always working on this way of how can I record what is in front of my eyes in the most direct way, so that it actually feels like that afterwards on the picture. It's a very fragile thing because it requires such concentration. That concentration may only last for a second but it's informed by a lifetime's experience and study and struggle – this struggle of how can I do this impossible thing of taking a picture.'

Otaku

i-D, no. 99, December 1991

In July 1989, a twenty-seven-year-old Japanese guy called Tsutomo Miyazaki was charged with the abduction and murder of four young girls and the attempted molestation of another. His Tokyo flat was searched and the police discovered high-rise stacks of *manga* and a collection of 6,000 videos, which included horror movies and kiddie porn. This was his real life. Everything else – his job in a printing shop, the mundane tasks of eating, sleeping, even waking – was a dream.

Or so Miyazaki's defence counsel maintained. They argued that he had been mainlining videos and comics for so long that he had lost all sense of perspective and could no longer tell the difference between the media, the outside world and his own fantasies. Everything blurred into the same brightly coloured ball of confusion. Killing a four-year-old girl was the same as watching it happen on video was the same as dreaming about it. What did it matter? There was always the rewind button.

The Miyazaki trial crystallized public concern over a new breed of teen information junkie that had already been tagged with the name *otaku*. The latest, and craziest, subculture to emerge from Japan, *otaku* describes the type of audiovisual obsessive who shuns body contact and spends all his time gathering data on the most trivial bits of media. According to Volker Grassmuck in *Mediamatic* magazine, some 'hunt for photographs of the music industry's synthetic starlets, some are fanatically into computer games, many are immersed in comic-books much of their waking day, others are plastic-model maniacs, and yet others prefer hacking into car-phone conversations'.

There are as many different types of *otaku* as there are media. Not all are as dangerous as Miyazaki. But all are as crazy. What is significant for each of them is not the act of consumption but any and all information concerning the conditions of production. A rock-*otaku* does not do anything as naïve as actually listen to the tapes he buys. Instead, he finds out the details of their composition and recording – which means everything from who the studio engineer was on a particular track to who would have been the backing singer if they hadn't had a prior commitment. Then he spreads the information he has learned across a computerized bulletin board for other rock-*otaku* to gawk at.

It's the same with computer-*otaku*, fashion-*otaku* and *manga-otaku*. They are all 'radically bored' information fetishists, more concerned with the dimensions than the worth of their chosen field. They all have their own underground electronic networks, whether they are computer-*otaku* or not. Grassmuck defines an *otaku* as 'a person who is into something useless'. It's easy to see what he means.

Item: Haruki is a computer-*otaku*. He has no friends and only one interest. Most of his waking hours are spent crouched over a bedroom console surrounded by a support structure of potato crisps, Instant Ramen and soft drinks. He sports an interchangeable array of jeans and T-shirts and hardly ever speaks to his parents. What he likes to do is hack into corporate mainframes and destroy their data. Why? Because he can. He spreads viruses just for the hell of it.

Item: Tetsuo is a *manga-otaku*. He collects comic-books like *Shonen-Jump*, *Gundam* and *Ultraman* and stores them – shrink-wrapped, tagged and individually indexed – in his living room. The mix of violence, fantasy, technology and pornography is something he can't get enough of and he is likely to spend all day Saturday in the local bookstore in Shinjuku. Recently, he has started to draw his own strips, which he circulates to other *manga-otaku* by mail.

Item: Akira is an idol-*otaku*. He has selected, at random, thirty baby doll singers of the type that dominate the Japanese airwaves and proceeded to collect everything he can about them: posters, T-shirts, magazines, records and concert tickets. He has even compiled tapes of each of their individual TV appearances. His favourite idol is Yui Haga because she literally does not exist. As a media construct built from several different elements – one girl's face, another's voice, someone else's biog – she symbolizes quite neatly the contours of his obsession.

Item: Shigesato used to be into fossils. Then it was tropical fish. Now he is a techno-*otaku*. He scans police radio transmissions, builds electronic time fuses to fit inside the hypothetical bomb he has prepared mentally, has a real police siren on the roof of his car and wonders about the feasibility of interrupting satellite transmissions. He is not a subversive, just a prankster. Yesterday he built a stun-gun from the condenser of his disposable camera.

People like this exist. They are distinguished from the earlier generation of *shinjinrui* – that's to say, 'New Humans', or Japanese yuppies – by their devotion to the immaterial realm of simulation and information at the expense of the immediate environment, the plodding world of gravity and time. They don't hang out, they simply jack in. The rituals of social dressing or even of simple body maintenance have no attraction for them.

The thing about the *shinjinrui* was that they were narcissists. They spent a lot of time looking after themselves, which meant not only pursuing the usual round of conspicuous consumption – with its litany of fad gadgets and brand-name designs – but also taking the whole business of self-display very seriously indeed. One fashion amongst the *shinjinrui*, for example, was the left-arm suntan. Why? Because it showed the person had a prestigious imported vehicle, one with a left-hand wheel drive.

The *shinjinrui* were hyper-consumers, the spoilt brats of the eighties. They wore Gaultier, read *Brutus* and partied at Gold's. They cultivated a self-consciously decadent image and there was still a degree of *affect*, some emotional tone – whether it was ecstasy, nihilism or melancholy – attached to their posturings. The *otaku*, by contrast, subvert the process of consumption. They break products down, turn them inside out, deploy them in unexpected situations for radically transformed ends; they manipulate media and deconstruct signs. They are the new consumers of the nineties – non-emotional, non-professional, non-lifestyle.

This, combined with the Miyazaki case, has given sociologists of all persuasions a field day. Some see the *otaku* as the children of the media. With Pop a salaryman out at work all day and Mom a bored housewife heavily into flower arranging, they were effectively auto-parented: brought up in front of the TV, weaned on comics, toys and gadgets. The world of media and technology was their primal scene.

Others see them as the product of the Japanese education system, with its emphasis on rote-learning rather than comprehension, its interpretation of knowledge as a relentless accumulation of facts. Still others see them as acute symptoms of the 'game show' mentality of Japanese postmodern culture, which tends to break down organized systems of knowledge into easily manipulated info bits. Grassmuck, meanwhile, speculates about a relationship between the techno-sophistication of the *otaku* and traditional Shintoist nature animism, arguing that both 'treat humans as things and things as humans'.

What is certain about them is their compatibility with the evolved forms of hyper-capitalism. For all their interest in jamming police radio broadcasts or manufacturing fuses for hypothetical briefcase bombs, the *otaku* look set to provide the Japanese media economy with the skills and resources necessary for its future development. They are functional outsiders. The territory they occupy may be a cultural underground but it is also an economic testing ground.

In that sense, the *otaku* are an avant-garde labour force. Whereas the celebrated figure of the Japanese postwar economic miracle was the 'corporate warrior' who worked in a hi-tech fortress, drank in a karaoke bar and slept in a capsule hotel, the model citizen of the future seems to be a computer nerd who works from home, doesn't drink, hardly sleeps and never has sex.

For the moment, however, the public image of this strange breed is defined by the horrific career of Tsutomo Miyazaki. Whether the term *otaku* (conventionally used as a polite form of address between speakers uncertain of each other's social standing) will become more of an insult than it already is, whether the state will crack down on the circulation of *manga* and videos, whether the underground electronic networks that sustain the culture of the *otaku* will survive – all these are questions that remain to be answered.

Film fan

The Face, vol. 2, no. 23, August 1990

What makes a Movie Brat? Some, like Paul Schrader, are ex-film critics, scholarly, impassioned, austere. Some, like Martin Scorsese, are ex-film buffs, obsessive, mannered, quixotic. And others, like Joe Dante, are ex-film *fans*. Excitable, manic, perverse. The difference is clear. While Schrader was toiling away composing his doctoral thesis on the Japanese master craftsman, Yasujiro Ozu, and Scorsese was scurrying around the art houses trying to catch the latest Michael Powell screening, Dante was lolling in front of the goggle-box with his tongue hanging out, trying to figure how they did the special effects on *Attack of the 50 Foot Woman*. He's probably the only director on the Hollywood payroll who can claim to have once written for *Famous Monsters of Filmland*.

And it shows. His movies are like animated scrapbooks, short on coherent organization, on *plot*, but crammed with cult performers, collector's item cuts and celebrated one-liners. Serial snatches. Fading auteur signatures are doodled in the margins, clipped images threaten to split the binding, there are pages stuck together, pages missing, pasted cut-ups coming unglued and pictures torn at the edges. And then there are Dante's own deranged contributions. Ballpoint annotations in red ink, arrows and dotted lines, dumb jokes and vile graffiti, everything either scribbled over or violently discoloured. A mound of crazed fan mail to backlot Hollywood.

It's no surprise to learn that Dante originally wanted to get involved in the cartoon business. Not only are his movies shot through with constant references to figures like Tex Avery, Frank Tashlin and Chuck Jones (who crops up in *Gremlins*), they have the same violent energy as the old Warner Brothers cartoons, the same elastic surrealism and slapstick obscenity. Looney Toons in all but name. Even Dante's habit of using the same crowd of B-movie character actors adds to this feeling. Dick Miller (*A Bucket of Blood*), Edward Andrews (*The Fiend That Walked the West*), Kevin McCarthy (*Invasion of the Body Snatchers*), Kenneth Tobey (*The Thing*). All have curdled into caricatures of themselves, becoming celluloid stiffs, cartoon characters.

It all fits in with Dante's film fan mentality. Take *The Schlitz Movie Orgy*. Put together with the help of boyhood pal Jon Davison (who went on to produce *Airplane!* and, later, *RoboCop*) and part-financed by the American beer company, this student effort from Dante is nothing less than a reel-to-reel compendium of old clips from creaking Republic serials and fondly remembered B-movies. Then there are the zed-grade movies Dante whacked out for the Roger Corman film factory during the seventies (it was Davison, incidentally, who got him the job). They all share the same occult trademarks: knowing references, hip cameos, genre in-jokes. Secret signs to an exclusive audience.

Hollywood Boulevard (co-directed with Allan Arkush) was typical. A movie about movie-making, its conceptual cues allowed Dante to recycle the crew as the cast, nudge colleagues Paul Bartel and Jonathan Kaplan in front of the cameras, and dredge the Corman vaults for old footage: jungle movies, car-crash movies, monster movies, any old movies. The genre bending continued with *Piranha* – *Jaws* minus the melodrama but with added camp funnies – and *The Howling* – an SFX fix on the Universal werewolf pictures of the thirties combined with grotesque one-liners and skewed social comment. Both scripted by John Sayles, both seriously smart, but both mere doodlings nonetheless.

Dante could have gone on like this for ever, piling up sardonic footnotes to other people's careers, if he hadn't made the Spielberg connection. The Hollywood wunderkind was so tickled by *Piranha* that he added Dante's name to his list of occasional collaborators. A constructive move. *It's a Good Life* (Dante's contribution to Spielberg's *Twilight Zone* anthology), *Gremlins* and now *Gremlins 2* are all genuinely original visions. Spielberg's twinkling suburban cosmology, with its transcendent kiddie consumerism, its operatic uplift, mutates into a grotesque universe of snickering *Snow White* fans and fast-food psychos when introduced to Dante's own ingrown bubble-gum mythology. Dante's cultural inferno: so sweet it's sick, so excessive it's emetic.

This is Dante's slant on the postmodern recycling racket. Pop fragments and consumer disposables not as the raw material for pastiche but as waste matter, mulch, cultural fertilizer for secret transformations and monstrous growths. Think of the goggle-box fiend from *It's a Good Life*: panting tongue, bulging eyes, the perfect distorting mirror for the junk consumer. Or again the pinhead alien in *Explorers* who can only communicate by quoting lines from old movies and Bugs Bunny cartoons: obscene paunch, tentacular fingers, the postmodern channel-hopper as autistic slob. Remember too that in *Gremlins* the little green monsters first emerge from the larval pulp of some old *Marvel* comic-books.

With these grotesque creatures Dante has tapped straight into the faecal stew of the collective unconscious, the gloop that creeps through the cracks of MTV suburbia. They are made of exactly the same stuff as the perverse urban legends and sick gags that also seem to sprout everywhere in his movies. Rumours of bodies buried in garbage bags in *The 'Burbs*, folk memories of babies burned in the microwave in *Gremlins*. Even the 'gremlins' themselves are an old WWII myth: electrical demons responsible for freak technological accidents and inexplicable deaths.

But all this doesn't mean that Dante has quit indulging his passion for parody. *Innerspace*, which had Dennis Quaid cruising the internal organs of a geeky Martin Short in a microscopic submersible, was *Fantastic Voyage* replayed as splatter comedy. While the stand-out scene in *The 'Burbs* is an acute – and very funny – take-off of *Once Upon a Time in the West*: Tom Hanks squaring up to pay a daring social call on the neighbours, complete with Sergio Leone-style wide-angle close-ups and sub-Morricone twang. Even *Gremlins* was characterized by its director as *It's a Wonderful Life* crossed with *The Birds*.

Dante will forever have his nose buried deep in the Hollywood back-catalogue. It's just that now he's starting to make some personal contributions of his own.

Conspiracy buff

i-D, no. 128, May 1994

The pessimistic French historian of knowledge Michel Foucault once theorized that 'crime' is what the victors of the class war call the defeated actions of their enemies and that it is the responsibility of the cops not to stamp it out but to keep it running smoothly. Just one of the thoughts prompted by a quick reading of Steve Aylett's brilliantly quick-witted *The Crime Studio* (Serif).

A collection of interlinked short stories that all take place in the mythical American city of Beerlight, the book traces the violently changing fortunes of a motley crew of losers, chancers and tossers as they tear up the street, get their names in the papers and bounce from the bar to the slammer and back again. What distinguishes this post-Gotham brand of urban tech noir is the constant, nervy recourse to the semiotics of crime. When Chief of Police Henry Blince announces his intention to halve crime, the narrator observes that this ignores 'the old Zeno principle that if you keep halving something indefinitely you'll never get rid of it'. When the owner of the Delayed Reaction Bar, Don Toto, attempts to influence the crime rate through calculated rumour-mongering, he understands that there is a 'cop/underworld deal' but can't make up his mind who needs who most. And when Jesse Downtime tries to perfect the art of the minimal crime he moves from stealing paint a lick at a time to the synaptic crackles of pure speculation ('Surely no one could tell him what to think? But this was America.').

Aylett's prose hotwires Burroughsian deadpan cool with tough-guy Runyonesque flamboyance and manages to conjure a voice that is mordant, suave, ironic and lyrical all at the same time. An exceptional achievement, given that the guy was born in the London suburb of Bromley in 1967. Make no mistake, Aylett knows his stuff. Influences ranging from Tank Girl to situationism blip away in his comic universe like so much background cultural radiation; there are references to *Mondo 2000* and *Taxi Driver* and vicious jokes are cracked at the expense of John Updike novels. Imagine Mark Leyner on Saturday morning TV and you've got some idea of the liberties Aylett takes with the form of the short story. The orchestrated mayhem of some incidents stretches the stuff of reality as if it were a Tex Avery cartoon, characters dissolve and reform like psychedelic putty, outrageous similes roll in and out of the action like hand-grenades and there are some wonderfully balanced pay-off lines.

Aylett takes the mid-twentieth-century city of film noir (and Foucault) and cracks it apart under the force of a gaze that is thoroughly postmodern. All the Kroker concepts ripped off from Baudrillard – panic, hysteria, dread, boredom – motivate the ecstatic animation of his prose. When paranoia surfaces, it is not (as it is in Burroughs) a comically rational defence mechanism but an almost random act of simulation that gets lost in the reality of its own execution. So that, for example, Carl Overchoke, in the brilliant 'Back and to the Left', starts behaving as if he were under surveillance, soon attracts notice, is picked up by the cops, but can have nothing proved against him. All of which suggests that the coding of the city has changed since Foucault's time and we have to search for new mapping systems. *The Crime Studio* is as good a place as any to start.

Doll collector
i-D, no. 124, January 1994

If *Blade Runner* is often cited as one of the founding texts of postmodernism, this has more to do with its vision of an imploded, retro-fitted Los Angeles than with its interest in cyborgs and sci-fi detectives. Richard Calder's debut novel, *Dead Girls* (HarperCollins), however, is a reminder that there is more to the movie than its art direction. There is a whole archaeological history of the cyborg condensed into the figure of J.F. Sebastian, toy-maker, genetic engineer and prematurely aged delinquent. The point seems to be that the cyborg's cultural antecedent is not the robot (basically a servo-mechanism standing in for the old industrial proletariat) but the automaton (ultimate refinement of the society of the spectacle). The cult of the automaton, of the animated mannequin able to mimic human actions, took off as a result of developments in clock-making miniaturization in the eighteenth century and whole collections of automatic dolls were created by craftsmen and inventors over the next hundred years.

Linked to a parallel fascination with doppelgängers, moving statues and clockwork toys, the automaton soon became a permanent feature of the literature of the uncanny. Which is where *Dead Girls* comes back in. The central figure hovering at the back of the novel's events is Dr Toxicophilous, a reclusive toymaker whose expertise in 'fractal programming' and 'quantum electronics' enables him to construct lifelike dolls for the luxury fashion market. The only problem is that he was reared as a boy on the gothic literature of the 'Second Decadents' of the 1990s and his head is so full of fantasies of vampire women that he unconsciously programmes his creations in the image of his darkest desires. The result is a 'doll plague' that breaks out in London and threatens to consume the world. The novel's narrator is Ignatz Zwakh, a teen lost boy from a ruined future London who flees to Bangkok with his doll baby, Primavera, and gets caught up in a plot involving Thai 'pornocrats', American CIA guys and a secret society of dolls bent on world domination.

In fact, Calder flips the switches of his plot so many times that the novel threatens to shatter into a mosaic of enigmatic images. Written in a dense, abstract, slangy register, it comes alive best in the extended sequence where Ignatz travels into the space at the back of Primavera's head to become a character in her dreamtime. The impossible environment that Calder attempts to describe draws on Lewis Carroll's looking-glass world as well as William Gibson's cyberspace to model its features – the skylines of Bangkok and London superimposed, Primavera's face everywhere – and manages to forge the difficult connection between science fiction and English romantic gothic that only Michael Moorcock has really pulled off in the past.

Calder has fashioned quite a reputation for himself with the stories he has written for *Interzone* and *Science Fiction Eye*, and *Dead Girls* in many ways reads like three or four variations on a theme rather than a complete novel. It is clumsily constructed and lacks any real narrative rhythm, but this is a small criticism to make of a novel so skilful at the art of compressed cultural observation (Brick Lane's Bengali community displaced by immigrant Slavs of the Soviet diaspora, 'photomechanical' living posters, Proust's take on memory as the poor man's virtual reality).

Letters

You lend your copy of William Gibson's *Neuromancer* to Jim and upon his return from Thailand he sends a letter to *i-D* chiding its editor for his failure to cover cyberpunk. The commission comes through within the week and pretty soon the pair of you have written your story on Gibson together. All the letters you subsequently receive – from curious fans, potential colleagues and prospective publishers alike – remain unanswered. You drift through the 'phantasmagoria' (Walter Benjamin) of the media simulacrum and end up sub-editing the peripherals of a glossy magazine. You begin to understand that the letters page of any magazine is its institutional unconscious – a zone of disguised editorial fabrication where the hierarchy of names on the masthead reappears in condensed and scrambled form. You start to keep a journal (letters to yourself).

Cosmo Landesman and Julie Burchill

personal correspondence 18 July 1991

Dear Cosmo and Julie,

Thanks for lunch last week, I had a great time. Here is the Tim Burton proposal, as promised. What do you think? I reckon it'll work.

Have been rummaging through my index-cards in the meantime and have come up with a few ideas for future issues:

NUCLEAR CINEMA – Not just a listings guide to nuclear jeopardy movies (e.g. *Failsafe, Dr Strangelove, Twilight's Last Gleaming*), but an attempt to link the epic technologies of Hollywood and the Pentagon in terms of their devotion to a fantasy of absolute vision (CinemaScope and the Looking Glass bomber – same thing: Foucault's panopticon gone global, an all-seeing eye blinded by its own penetrating power). Also how this visual dynamic has become obsolescent (compare video games and smart missiles, which are both about real-time monitoring, visual feedback, rather than monolithic spectacle – see Virilio).

AN ALTERNATIVE HISTORY OF MODERN LITERATURE – Short, jokey, belligerent piece which insists that *Gray's Anatomy* is a better novel than *Ulysses*, the Warren Commission Report on the JFK assassination a more challenging 'postmodern' text than Pynchon's *V*, etc.

BLADE RUNNER BOYS – What is it with this thing about Tokyo? Why does every hip downtown white boy (David Byrne, Bill Viola, Nigel Coates) insist on seeing it as a metaphor of the postmodern condition, a riot of signs, axis of multinational cultural traffic. Is a New Orientalism beginning to emerge here? One that substitutes an iconography of hi-tech emergency (sexy corporate conglomerates, weird science, picturesque destitution – all on the same block!) for the older hackneyed imagery (opium dens and geisha girls). Could tie this in with the autumn Japan Festival – especially the V&A show, with its computerized fortune-telling stunts and all-purpose techno-fetishism.

Anyway, get in touch if you want me to do anything.

Yours sincerely,

Paul Dave
personal correspondence 1991

Dear Paul,

A response to the first draft of your document:

1 'What happens when technologies of disciplinary power outlive the social they were once indistinguishable from?' They become visible for the first time (Baudrillard's answer to the question in *Forget Foucault*). But what does this 'outlive' imply? Does it mean that discipline now merely chugs along indifferently somewhere near the bottom of the social heap, underfunded and grotesquely inefficient, going through the motions of a project that is now obsolescent for the majority of the population (i.e. workfare, government training schemes, the

armed services). Or does it mean – as you seem to imply – that discipline has been retooled and updated, shifting its base of operations from 'bio-power' to 'eco-power', that it has simultaneously contracted (serving that same majority of the population, the new middle classes) and expanded (its object of attention no longer the human population but the global environment: bacterial life-forms, the weather, non-renewable resources – if I understand you correctly)? And if the latter is the case, is it still possible to talk about 'discipline' any more?

2 'Radical humanism . . . had to bracket "man" to save us from disaster.' But this has already been accomplished by developments in spare-part surgery, genetic engineering, tailored viruses, virtual reality. 'Man' does not have to be theorized away; the intersection of consumerism and techno-culture has already done the job (and this, incidentally, provides another gloss on Paul Virilio's notion of the 'consumption of security': the body no longer as a productive force but as a new field of social relations). Does a new kind of hyper-technicized 'discipline' begin to emerge here? If it does, then it is only for the rich and privileged (the retired, a lot of the time: those pampered baby boomers, still calling the shots even in their senescence). 'Cyber-power' seems to me to be a much more plausible model of disciplinary reinvention than 'eco-power'. As for the 'disaster' you refer to, this has only been sidestepped by some, the lucky ones. For everyone else – the sub-social, the Fourth World, the disenfranchised – the disaster has already happened: AIDS sweeping the inner cities of the US, drug addiction, begging lawlessness (this notion of 'plague' is not just some fancy metaphor). The New Right cultural commentators (e.g. Tony Parsons) do have a point about the disenfranchised (even if they completely ignore their own complicity in producing them as a class) – they are nasty (because civilized behaviour is the result of collective self-restraint – see Norbert Elias – and why the fuck should the Fourth World bother with the effort of subscribing to neo-bourgeois norms of behaviour when they get none of the class benefits?), brutish (ditto) and short (because undernourished; they can't afford the smart drugs and spare-part surgery that is building a new class – not species, as Bruce

Sterling suggests – of 'post-human' creatures). If 'eco-power' has any meaning it is as the underside, the residue, of 'cyber-power': everything that can either be written off (like a tax loss) as surplus to requirements or partially recommodified as grotesque spectacle (what Herman Melville, if you remember – was it in *Pierre*? – calls the 'povertiresque': see *Blade Runner*, *Escape from New York*, etc.). So who is this 'us' that waits to be saved?

3 'A radical molecular energy was sought ... to produce the nonanthropomorphic "swarm" as social model.' Which ends up as Michel de Certeau's office hive of careerist 'subversion'. This is an irony we both see clearly.

4 'Frank Lentricchia notes this double dream of the plague behind the double power of discipline.' His notion of 'saturnalian socialism' is intended as a rebuke to those who misread Foucault's coupling of the king and the crowd at the scaffold: the potential for sovereign triumphalism to flip over into its opposite (compare the situationist dream of spontaneously self-destructing media events). Big deal, says Lentricchia, the real beneficiaries of this struggle were the bourgeoisie. I can see how my own coupling of the new middle classes and the Fourth World falls victim to this same thinking: the assumption that the struggle is significant on its own terms (awarding prizes to the winners and losers), when it may be a new – as yet invisible – class that benefits. Potential candidates? Possibly the 'post-human' super-rich. Then again, maybe moneyed yobs (John Self rather than Keith Talent).[1]

5 'The utopia of the nineteenth-century anarchist becomes the dystopian fulfilment of the twentieth-century left libertarian.' Exactly (de Certeau again). Though not a bad little dystopia, if you can get it (which we certainly can't in the UK).

6 'The carnivalesque social landscape of late capital was immediately claimed in that new right strain of postmodern populism to be achieved social democracy, but the fact was that

---

[1] Contrasting stereotypes of new middle-class success and lumpen failure from the work of eighties career novelist Martin Amis.

it foreclosed any "social" consolidation of the gains made by the new social movements of the sixties.' In other words, the Left lost and the history of '68 has been rewritten by the victors (using the language of the Left – hence the confusion). It is important to remember that some kind of civil war *was* fought in the US during the sixties and that the victory of the New Right, the retrenchment of capitalism, was not inevitable. If you don't understand this then you make your compromises without even realizing what you've gained, much less what you've lost (see P.J. O'Rourke). Also, there is then no possibility of reviving the Left any more (although, as we both agree, the end of the Cold War has been helpful in this respect).

7 'However, Marc Guillaume insists that the old model of epidemia resists.' I absolutely agree with Guillaume. Whether this resistance is successful is another question (a question too hastily answered by those who subscribe to 'saturnalian socialism'). But surely, Guillaume is right? Once discipline begins to wobble, to sink to the depths of the social, to work imperfectly, then the social 'plague' it had apparently tamed at the height of the Fordist era begins to reassert itself with renewed vigour (hence George Romero's zombies: life-in-death bodies that still bear the traces of discipline but are also busy acclimatizing to some new socially disorganized space). This seems to be the major point of disagreement between us.

8 '... the irradiating powers of the disciplinary epidemiology'. I don't get this. My reading of Guillaume is: epidemia/irradiation = Foucault/Baudrillard, discipline/simulation, intervention/projection, welfare/entertainment, hospital/media. Once 'epidemia' can no longer master the plague, then 'irradiation' takes over (i.e. blanket coverage of the population with images). But already, this model of 'irradiation' is obsolescent. 'Narrowcasting' has replaced 'broadcasting'; media images (like smart missiles) target the productive segments of the population, the new middle classes, in the hope of forging a new (non-representational) social bond. The Fourth World is left with whatever is left over: free TV, the crappy end of the media spectrum. The heady days of national TV (the three networks in the US, the duopoly in the UK) represent a transitional

moment: the emergence of new 'irradiating' technologies in the spaces defined by the 'epidemia' of discipline, which, in the post-Fordist era, begin to contract.

9 'Panopticism is reversed; "those who have total power do not need to see".' But this blindness defines the working of panopticism right from the start. It does not suddenly 'reverse': the panopticon is an imaginary construct as much as a real edifice. It does not need to be occupied so long as those subject to surveillance (as a result of an architectural organization of social space) think that it is. In this way, surveillance becomes internalized, becomes productive paranoia (see Lacan). The panopticon is Sartre's keyhole seen (or rather, imagined) from the other side, it is Christian Metz's 'bilateral voyeurism' without the voyeur.

10 'Robert Castel demonstrates that ... the development of new modes of surveillance effectively combine reversible or crude panopticism and superpanopticism.' Obviously I'm going to have to read this guy Castel. By 'superpanopticism', I assume you are referring to polls, systems analyses in the abstract, media projections of social need, massaged statistics, accumulated databases and so on. I fail to see, though, what 'crude panopticism' has to do with any of this: it surely reached its apogee in the nuclear imaginary.

11 ' ... eco-power allows us to see how the subject can get swept up in a general administration of refuse and thus drop below the threshold of political visibility'. An excellent and highly original analysis of the post-industrial metamorphosis of visual technologies, old buddy. Gives a whole new meaning to those ecstatic celebrations of the 'death of the subject', doesn't it? One death for the super-rich (a *theoretical* death that is really a resurrection, an entry into a new 'irradiated' realm of overstimulation, of dizzying images competing for attention: we should really be talking about a 'hyper-subject'), another for the Fourth World (they become invisible – at last I understand what you mean by this; they certainly cut a figure, but it is not politically significant and in that sense does not register).

12 'The expanded vision of life ... becomes part of the class logic of post-industrial political order.' OK, the Fourth World are invisible. But that still leaves unanswered questions. What do they see? How do they see? Perhaps they still see in an old-fashioned panoptic kind of way. Hence the significance of conspiracy theory: it is not a 'degraded metaphor' of the workings of late capital, as Fredric Jameson suggests, but a residual imaging technology, a desperate attempt to see inside the panopticon, to populate its empty interior with various shadowy figures (something only made possible, of course, by the obsolescence of panoptic technologies).

13 ' ... those bodies which cannot acquire a social reality'. I don't see how 'social reality' is in the dispensation of the new middle classes. The Fourth World may be invisible, but they exist. So what does that make them? Ghosts or something, blips on the social radar screen, interference – we're back to Guillaume and his resurgent 'plague'.

14 ' ... surely our dilemma is ... the potential that other living forms have to erase us'. Some of us have already been erased, some of us have been doing the erasing. There is no dilemma, merely a (class) struggle. Or perhaps there is a dilemma for 'us', the members of the intellectual underclass, those who have made their choices and are obliged to collaborate in their own self-erasure (when will this 'life' end and the feared/desired joke life begin?).

15 'Paradoxically the willingness to see more is connected to a linking of this expanded landscape exclusively to the viewing self.' I take your point about how the romantic sublime (expansion of the field of vision appropriated by the bourgeois subject) depends upon an impulse toward 'depopulation' (expansion of the social abolished by an act of aesthetic terrorism). Which is as much to say that the social is repressed by the aesthetic in eighteenth/nineteenth-century bourgeois fantasy. What's missing here, though, is an acknowledgement of how the repressed returns in the gothic imagination of the same period (see Franco Moretti on vampires in *Signs Taken for Wonders*). What is sublime for the bourgeoisie is terrifying for the masses (for them, the prospect of seeing more is dizzying: it destabilizes rather than anchors the viewing subject). Same thing with the nuclear imaginary: apogee of the bourgeois sublime (where it is the globe that is surveyed rather than just the Alps), point of maximum terror (the masses, at the moment of complete socialization, are faced with the spectacle of their extinction). The only difference is that there is no longer any repression. Everything is visible, nothing is disguised. 'Depopulation' is no longer the condition of the sublime, it *is* the sublime.

16 'One of the principal organs of eco-power is the womb.' Surely not? You have already argued most convincingly that eco-power 'targets the anthropomorphic'. The symbology of the womb belongs to the nuclear imaginary – remember that favoured sixties superimposition of the unborn foetus and the mushroom cloud? The logic here is still Foucauldian: 'Go get slaughtered and we promise you a long and pleasant life.'

17 'Stephen Jay Gould's legs are feelers.' Must make it hard for him to get around.

18 'A first definition of the zombie might be ... an untransfigured millennial figure, with the clay and earth still adhering to him.' This seems to be a reference less to Romero's zombies than to the living dead of old-fashioned gothic horror movies (those bodies that rise from their graves). It is still a Fordist scenario (fear of a mob 'uprising').

19 'The zombie as ... "population plague" obstructing the troubled shift from Fordism to post-Fordism.' This is certainly my reading.

20 '... the fallen triumphs of modernity'. Which includes the Hollywood machine. The disaster movies of the seventies are self-referential in this respect; they comment on their own compromised conditions of production within the ruins of the studio system.

21 '... nuclear exterminism ... proved incapable of junking the populations it had conjured out of the ground'. Depends on whether you're speaking literally or metaphorically. And surely the power of 'nuclear exterminism' (which existed under the auspices of an 'imaginary war' – see Mary Kaldor on the Cold War) lay precisely in the fact that it was simulated.

22 '... emblem of bio-power's ability to produce to excess but not to regulate'. An *emblem*, yes. Any consideration of the zombie must distinguish between its use as: (a) a quasi-sociological term used to describe the Fourth World, the sub-social, the disenfranchised of the post-Fordist era, those who may certainly be politically invisible but who nevertheless continue (troublingly) to exist; (b) a cultural stereotype, a figure from the movies that may be the refraction of some political unconscious (Jameson) but may also be inappropriately inflected on the superficial level (for instance, Romero's zombies shadow Guillaume's model of 'epidemic' resistance or obstruction in a way I find politically significant, but they are diegetically represented – quite arbitrarily – in 'saturnalian socialist' mode).

23 'The zombie problem in Baudrillard's texts... covers the neo-liberal carnival of the eighties.' Exactly. The consumer no longer as a passive dupe (Fordism) but as an active collaborator (post-Fordism), a busy shopper, a figure saturated with the demand to make choices – which are all so wonderfully different and all so utterly idiotic ('molecular hell').

24 'Meanwhile the populations of zombies, the former masses, remain comically impossible but certainly not the... inexorable problem tide they were in the 70s.' The Fourth World is 'comically impossible' only from the point of view of the new middle classes, for whom they are no longer politically visible; they are no longer a 'problem tide' in terms of the way they are culturally represented (which they aren't any more). But beyond the threshold of political visibility defined by the new middle classes, beyond the (contracted) orbit of professional middle-class culture, they are all too possible and not at all comic. Their numbers increase daily. Soon, perhaps, they will become a problem tide in their own right – no longer in the movies but on the streets. Which should prompt us to look at things from the other side. How do the zombies of the Fourth World see the new middle classes?

25 '... the emphasis on plague and contagion is politically mistaken in the context of eco-power'. Politically necessary, I would have thought (the mistake of the *Zone 1/2* contributors lies in their 'saturnalian socialism', the *value* they place on the plague metaphor).

26 '... we are not in a post-disciplinary order ... but locked into a malign version of discipline's double power'. Which, as far as I'm concerned, is so far removed from Foucault's disciplinary order that it merits the p-prefix.

27 'Therefore the task ... should be to articulate that "unthinkable" interface.' Yep, and we're just the boys to do the job. Welcome to the wonderful world of the intellectual underclass.

28 'The model of "identification" in operation under the Superpanopticon ... is the forcible matching of human and other material to predetermined profiles.' I'm really unhappy with Mark Poster's use of the term 'Superpanopticon'. This, for me, describes the functioning of the nuclear imaginary, where the perspectival technologies of the Renaissance reach their point of maximum exposure: a total visual field (the globe) combines with a still notional human observer (the President, who has the option of not bothering to keep watch: see Reagan). The surveillance technologies used in the Gulf War are properly 'post-panoptic' because they reverse the old formula: the visual field is partial and obscure, so the human observer must be alert and watchful.

29 'In Oliver Stone's *Salvador* Foucault's disciplinary technologies outlive their benign "social" to reappear as instruments of torture.' Exactly. They do not reappear under the sign of 'eco-power' (as you seem to argue earlier); they simply persist in the most literal and brutal (and ironic) fashion (see also Mike Davis on the drugs economy of LA).

As you can see, we differ. But not by much.

Yours,

Male subject #1

Arena, no. 21, May/June 1990

May I be the first to say how much I enjoyed reading Nick Kent's interview with Paul Newman (*Arena*, no. 20). Who'd have guessed that Hollywood's leading liberal spokesman would turn out to be such an old grouch? I mean, objecting to Madonna becoming an actress is one thing, going on about the pernicious influence of the freedom of the press quite another.

It's a shame Nick didn't take up Mr Newman on one of his less reactionary judgements: namely, that *Butch Cassidy and the Sundance Kid* was so successful because it was essentially about 'a love affair between two men'. Newman's unabashed homoerotic grace – his calm gestures and accommodating silences – have, it seems to me, always been a large part of his charm.

He is that rarest of Hollywood talents: an actor with the kind of presence that appeals equally to both sexes. Neither a boy's own misogynist (Sly, Big Arnie) nor a male-model narcissist (pick any Brat Packer), his charisma is both slow and sure (maybe only Jeff Bridges has come close to emulating him in recent years).

Kent certainly seemed won over.

Male subject #2

Arena, no. 23, September/October 1990

Just thought I'd drop you a line to say how much I enjoyed the profile on Tom Hanks (*Arena*, no. 22). It's good to see that I'm not alone in my admiration for his considerable talents. Here's a guy who can do more with his eyebrows than Jack Nicholson can do with his whole forehead.

I was also intrigued by the Cary Grant comparison. It seems to me there's a whole other story to be written here. Grant is usually written up in the film books as the epitome of male elegance, the regular guy who's just a little off-beam. Yet there's a subdued hysteria to his best performances (*North By Northwest*, *Bringing Up Baby*), a barely controllable sense of panic which always threatens to fracture his surface charm. Same with Hanks (it would certainly be interesting to see him playing an *homme fatale*, as Grant did in *Suspicion*).

Carry on running stories like this and I might have to think very seriously about taking out a subscription.

André Breton
i-D, no. 166, July 1997

In 1924 André Breton opened a Bureau of Surrealist Enquiries in the Rue de Grenelle and invited the public to bring him their accounts of dreams, coincidences or inventions in order to bring about the formation of 'genuine surrealist archives'. He went on to found 'the most scandalous periodical in the world', *La Révolution surréaliste*, and published the manifestos that went on to make his name ('We have no intention of changing men's habits, but we have hopes of proving to them how fragile their thoughts are, and on what unstable foundations, over what cellars they have erected their unsteady houses.'). Breton was not without his critics among the surrealists – Georges Bataille figured that his idealism distanced him from his own theories of 'base materialism', Pierre Naville implicitly rebuked him for not taking the collective project of the Revolution seriously – but it is his recommendations – the liberation of desire, the celebration of childhood and madness, the cult of the mythical woman, the penetration of the everyday by the marvellous – that have come to define the movement. What is surprising is that it has taken so long to disseminate his most important texts. *Nadja* (1928) was translated in 1960, *Mad Love* (1937) in 1987, *Communicating Vessels* (1931) in 1990 and *Arcanum 17* (1944) in 1994.

Communicating Vessels (Bison Books) is now available as a paperback and deserves to be read as one of the key narratives of the twentieth century. Breton is often dismissed as a mystic but this little book makes clear that he was always aware of the dangers of subjective idealism ('the system based on unhappiness'). The imaginative technique he recommended was to simulate states of suspended animation – dream, paranoia, schizophrenia – in order to reconcile a transfigured view of reality with the material conditions of history. As Maurice Nadeau puts it in *The History of Surrealism*: 'he had chosen to dwell on a number of external incidents: encounters, accidents, unexpected events, coincidences impossible to relate by a logical link but which resolved inner debates, materialized unconscious or avowed desires'. Breton shows how the perceiving subject and the object world are two communicating vessels that remain in continuous contact. He quotes Engels ('Causality cannot be understood except as it is linked with the category of objective chance, a form of the manifestation of necessity') to justify this and goes on to probe the foundations of Freudianism in order to understand the activity of his own imagination (counterposing Havelock Ellis's theory of the dream as fear to Freud's more familiar idea of the dream as desire). *Communicating Vessels* was written when Breton was in a state of abjection and represents his attempt to get out of the hole he had dug for himself. It's a hard task but he manages it in the end and it's well worth following the sinuous and baroque pattern of his thoughts. Or as he himself put it: 'there is ... a door half opened, beyond which there is only a step to take in order, upon leaving the vacillating house of poets, to find oneself fully in life.'

Abysmal simulacra

You are sitting in a Buenos Aires TV studio talking about the latest subcult to emerge from London: psychedelic skinheads. The link you have as a style commentator with the authors of the mass-market *physiologies* of the 1840s, those pocket guides to the urban crowd that worked through the medium of stereotype, is not immediately apparent to you. All you know is that the subcult inventories listed in the style press – rastafarian, trustafarian, pastafarian (satire) – increasingly seem to operate according to the generative logic of structural linguistics; they increasingly 'precede' (Jean Baudrillard) the reality they are supposed to represent. What happens next? Style hacks become the curators of recreational subjectivities, advertising meets editorial to become 'advertorial', industry jokes become job descriptions.

Japan

Modern Review, vol. 1, no. 1, Autumn 1991

'It is with the delicious surprise of the first journey through Japanese streets – unable to make one's *kurama*-runner understand anything but gestures, frantic gestures to roll on anywhere, everywhere, since all is unspeakably pleasurable and new – that one first receives the real sensation of being in the Orient, in this Far East so much read of, so long dreamed of, yet, as the eyes bear witness, heretofore all unknown.'

Substitute a red-and-yellow striped taxi for the panting *kurama*-runner, relax the diction, throw in a reference to *Blade Runner* ('this Far East so much semiologized'), and the sentiment could belong to any hip downtown white boy lost in the neon haze of contemporary Tokyo. Which makes it all the more surprising that the above passage is lifted from a collection of essays first published in 1894. *Glimpses of Unfamiliar Japan* is entirely familiar almost a century later as a specimen of that literary corpus known to the Japanese as 'orientalia'. Heated visions of the East brewed in burnt-out Western minds, dazed dreams of the end of empire, these texts characteristically treated Japan as a magic lantern that screened the gaze of the alienated spectator as if it were something Other, something not his own. They are projected fictions masquerading as recorded facts.

The author of *Glimpses of Unfamiliar Japan*, Lafcadio Hearn, is perhaps the best-known exponent of this kind of Orientalism. He is also the strangest. The story of his life is a textbook example of cultural repression and would make a fine addition to Freud's case histories, those fantastic allegories of desire and disgust that were being composed half a world away in a Viennese study at around the same time that Hearn first found his way into print. Born in 1850, just three years before Commodore Perry's American gunships opened the sealed culture of Japan to the inspection of the West, Hearn was christened Patrick by his Anglo-Irish father, a name he symbolically repudiated at the age of nineteen. The odd-sounding 'Lafcadio' was adopted when he emigrated to America, and is commonly assumed to be a disguised reference to the Greek island, Levkas, where his mother had been first seduced and then abandoned by his father. This primal scene of cultural betrayal was to inform all of his subsequent writings.

Hearn first travelled to Japan in 1890, not as a scholar or an amateur adventurer but as a journalist. Like so many media marauders who were to follow in his footsteps a hundred years later, hot on the trail of computers, corporate conglomerates and cyberpunk excitement, he had been commissioned to bring back a story. Except that once he got there, he never left. He married the daughter of a samurai family, changed nationality, immersed himself in the customs of feudal Japan even as they were being swept away by the tide of modernity and changed his name yet again, this time to Koizumi Yakumo. Wishing to be more Japanese than the Japanese, he became paranoid and vengeful, cut himself off from his Western friends and continued to churn out book after book on his adopted home until his death in 1904.

Glimpses of Unfamiliar Japan is typical. An anthology of impressions culled from his first encounter with a land as 'intangible and volatile as a perfume', it is alert to nuances of colour, mood and gesture, to the poetry of surfaces and the charm of accidental collision. Hearn is intrigued not only by the 'smiling little people in their blue costumes', the 'queerly gabled wooden houses' and 'funny little streets', but also by the lacquered signboards with their dancing ideograms, the extravagant packaging of the commonest items, the rhythmic echo of wooden clogs falling into step on station platforms, the juxtaposition of a shop selling American sewing-machines with a stall of Buddhist icons. The sense of disorientation is surprisingly familiar, even if the iconography is by now obsolete.

The sensibility on display in *Glimpses of Unfamiliar Japan* seems almost postmodern in its ecstatic delirium, reminiscent of that schizophrenic mode of perception characterized by Fredric Jameson as discontinuous and emphatically literal, 'bearing a mysterious and oppressive charge of affect, glowing with hallucinatory energy'. Jameson's psychoanalytic model is borrowed from Lacan, but maybe Freud should not be abandoned so easily. Maybe paranoia rather than schizophrenia is a more useful label to attach to Hearn's predicament. Freud was sketching out his thoughts on paranoia in his letters to his colleague, Wilhelm Fliess, just a year after the publication of *Glimpses of Unfamiliar Japan*, and they received their full elaboration in the Schreber case history (which should more properly be considered an act of literary criticism, given that it was an interpretation of Schreber's memoirs).

Paranoia, according to Freud, is what happens when the repression of some fixation is undone by the mechanism of projection, when an unconscious emotion is reconstructed as an external perception, so that 'what was abolished internally returns from without'. Freud being Freud, this deep and dark desire is figured in terms of homosexuality. But in Hearn's case, what is 'abolished internally' was any secure sense of identity. Before he settled in Japan, he was a drifter, a cultural marginal, a dago to the English, a Mick to the Yanks, a man with no proper name.

Japan allowed him to get a fix on himself, but only in the most negative sense, as a *gaijin*. The cultural contradictions that preyed on his mind could then be played back as a picturesque slide-show, where 'each sample of Occidental innovation is set into an Oriental frame that seems adaptable to any picture'. The clash of old and new in Japan, of Buddhist icons and American sewing-machines, was essential for the successful mediation of his repressed anxieties. At the same time, his identity as a Westerner was something he was desperate to shrug off, in an act of symbolic compensation for his father's original act of cultural (and sexual) betrayal.

Hearn had to be that immaculate figure: a *gaijin* who was absolutely Japanese. The impossibility of the formulation was the motor that generated his furious scribbling; the books he published year after year were the index of a pathological delusion. Which in Freudian terms can be defined as megalomania: 'I do not love at all – I do not love anyone' (Freud isolated three other syndromes that commonly attach themselves to paranoia: delusions of persecution, delusions of jealousy and erotomania).

Just as Schreber believed that the world had been swallowed by catastrophe, that he was 'the only real man left alive', while the figures surrounding him were 'miracled up, cursorily improvised men', so a giddy sense of unreality constantly hovers over Hearn's impressions of Japan, as if they had been desperately conjured in the wake of his dismissal of the Western world, as if the Orient were the circumscription of his own expanded ego. Here he is, for example, describing a visit to a Buddhist temple in *Glimpses of Unfamiliar Japan*:

And suddenly, a singular sensation comes upon me as I stand before this weirdly sculpted portal – a sensation of dream and doubt. It seems to me that the steps, and the dragon-swarming gate, and the blue sky arching over the roofs of the town, and the ghostly beauty of Fuji, and the shadow of myself there stretching upon the gray masonry, must all vanish presently.

This 'sensation of dream and doubt' is exactly analogous to the 'mysterious and oppressive charge of affect' described by Jameson. What he reckons in terms of Lacanian schizophrenia is better understood as a form of Freudian megalomania. The consequences of this revision of his psychoanalytic model are fairly severe for Jameson's theorization of subjectivity. Whereas he insists that the postmodern condition is characterized by the 'death' of the subject, its dispersal across a series of random perceptual events, it is probably more accurate to talk of a dilation of the subject, its recuperation of discontinuity and confusion. Jameson seems to equate the postmodern experience with a channel-hopping sense of dazed exposure. He forgets about the finger on the remote control.

All of which is a means of conceptualizing the current fetishization of all things Japanese. What is it with this thing about Tokyo? Why does everyone from David Byrne to Nigel Coates insist on seeing it as a metaphor of the postmodern condition, a riot of signs, a revolving axis of multinational cultural traffic. Is a New Orientalism beginning to emerge here, a hyper-evolved species of 'orientalia'? One that substitutes an iconography of hi-tech emergency (sexy corporate conglomerates, weird science, picturesque destitution – all on the same block) for the more obvious imagery of a Lafcadio Hearn (forget the cherry blossoms, ignore the Buddhist temples).

Well, yes, probably. Except that Hearn's megalomania is still highly visible in all these fevered dreams of technological excess. Again there is the assumption of a historic Year Zero, this time inaugurated by the B-52 bombers of the Pacific War rather than by Commodore Perry's gunships; again there is an alertness to cultural incongruity, the clash of old and new, East and West, except that now it is heralded by the semiotic blur of *Blade Runner*; again there is a fascination with the proliferation of Chinese and Japanese characters, only this time they are picked out in electric-coloured neon. Again there is distraction, evasion, delirium and a quite phoney sense of self-dispossession.

This reinvention of Japan as a land of hi-tech enchantment, a dream of the neon heart of Oriental darkness, was prefigured in the sixties by the aesthetic musings of Roland Barthes and the street photography of William Klein. What attracted both to Tokyo was the opportunity it afforded for cultural amnesia, ecstatic alienation, serial self-erasure. Or, in other words, the ultimate tourist trip. Barthes in *Empire of Signs* and Klein in *Tokyo* are both engaged in the same project, a voyage of discovery turned inside out, where what is cultivated is the *frisson* of subjective estrangement. The thing that gets left out of the picture, of course, is the meaning, the reality, of modern Japan.

Barthes, in his usual mandarin hip fashion, is quite open about this: 'I am not lovingly gazing toward an Oriental essence – to me the Orient is a matter of indifference, merely providing a reserve of features whose manipulation – whose invented interplay – allows me to "entertain" the idea of an unheard-of symbolic system, one altogether detached from our own.' Having checked out of the West, ditched all excess cultural baggage and made his announcement, Barthes is then off on his semiotic tour of Japan, an itinerary that takes in its language, cuisine, *pachinko* parlours, railway stations, stationery stores, *bunraku* dolls and haiku poetry.

Klein is more circumspect in his self-acknowledgement: 'In India, there is nothing to see, everything to interpret, said Henri Michaux. In Tokyo, I thought: there is everything to see, nothing to interpret, I would be the Barbarian of Tokyo.' But there's the same element of megalomania in his frantic tour of Tokyo's gymnasiums, *kabuki* theatres and sports stadiums, its busy streets, crowded trains and scattered hieroglyphs. Tokyo for Klein is a carnival of signs, where faces on cinema posters are as animated as those of passers-by, where a Sony billboard seems as ancient as the canal at its feet. Barthes's confession in *Empire of Signs* could almost serve as a postscript to Tokyo: 'The author has never, in any sense, photographed Japan. Rather, he has done the opposite: Japan has starred him with any number of "flashes".'

And that's been the story ever since for any number of intrepid New Orientalists. Except that nowadays there is so much more to see, so much less to interpret: *manga*, techno-porn, high-density urbanism, mobile fashion, hyper-violent movies, videophones, fax cameras, hand-held televisions, videogames, disposable buildings, even a new breed of 'radically bored' teen information junkies, *otaku*, who shun body contact and spend all their waking hours gathering data on the most trivial bits of media (according to *Mediamatic* magazine, some 'hunt for photographs of the music industry's synthetic starlets, some are fanatically into computer games, many are immersed in comic-books much of their waking day, others are plastic model maniacs, and yet others prefer hacking into car-phone conversations').

Some of this imagery has inevitably seeped into the multimedia spectacle that is the Japan Festival, a series of exhibitions currently being staged in London to coincide with the centenary of the Japan Society. Budgeted at a total of £15 million, the Festival includes the Design Museum's 'Metropolis: Tokyo Design Visions', the V&A's 'Visions of Japan', the Barbican's 'Beyond Japan', the Whitechapel Gallery's 'A Cabinet of Signs: Contemporary Art from Postmodern Japan' and the Science Museum's 'Robotics Japan' among its highlights. In its latest incarnation as the screen of Occidental fantasy, Tokyo has been transformed into everyone's favourite electronic suburb at the end of the world.

The book that accompanies the 'Beyond Japan' exhibition is the best place to look for examples of the New Orientalism. Written by Mark Holborn in a style that is both delirious and dejected, recognizably megalomaniacal in a post-Barthesian fashion (check the first sentence: 'Japan exists in my memory as if on a television screen'), it draws up the usual list of favourite Japanese things: Issey Miyake's deconstructed designs, Tadanori Yokoo's psychedelic graphics, Eiko Ishioka's supersaturated art direction, Daido Moriyama's photos of urban detritus, Seiji Kurata's photos of Tokyo's neon underworld, Rei Kawakubo's monochrome minimalism. All evidence for Holborn, of course, that Tokyo is a laboratory for the invention of a global culture, intersection of past and future, East and West, techno-utopia.

More intriguing than any of these figures, though, are the Western artists Holborn mentions almost in passing – Wim Wenders, Bill Viola, David Byrne, Nigel Coates, Chris Marker. New Orientalists to a man, all of them working in that familiar megalomaniacal idiom pioneered by Lafcadio Hearn, they typically use Tokyo as a screen on which to project their own sense of cultural dislocation, estrangement, drift. What was for Hearn an individual psychosis, an accident of birth, has now become a global pathology. Who is there who can't say that they feel nowhere at home, that they have become a stranger to their native culture, a postmodern urban nomad, a transnational subject?

This theme is explicit in the architecture of Nigel Coates. Tokyo for him is a 'cultural airport lounge', an international point of exchange that imports the semiotic rubble of the West and reflects back the sign of its distressed transformation. Hence the importance of a prepackaged aesthetic of decay in all his work in the city – TV screens buried under floors as if they were sacred relics, fake archaeology, artfully applied garbage, the superimposition of ancient monuments and hyper-media, cultural dissonance. It is hardly surprising that his latest project should go under the name of L'Arca di Noe; it is as if he treats the whole of Tokyo as a vast ark, or storage-house, for the safekeeping of the ruins of Western culture.

As for the rest of them, cultural incongruity is their stock-in-trade. Wenders's *Tokyo-Ga*, intended as an *homage* to the 'images of the loved and ordered world of the mythical city' of Yasujiro Ozu's movies, was disturbed by a crosscurrent of 'impersonal, unkind, threatening... even inhuman images'; Chris Marker's own filmic testament to Tokyo, *Sans Soleil*, approaches the place as if it were an invisible city, 'crisscrossed by trains, tied together with electric wire', an elusive image on a TV monitor, the lost memory of a scribe working in the Japanese court of the tenth century; Bill Viola's lyrical video, *Hatsu Yume* (First Dream), drifts lazily across the fluid landscape of contemporary Japan, taking in its oceans and forests as well as the electronic illumination of nocturnal Tokyo.

Meanwhile, David Byrne's hyperrealist photos frame the semiotic chaos of Tokyo, its street-corner clash of lines, textures and graphics, in crayon colours and flat perspectives, reducing complexity to dumb idiocy, immediacy to infantilism. The deadpan knowingness is typical of Byrne; he's daring you to think he's been outsmarted by his material (which he probably has if he can make such inane comments as 'there are no aesthetic accidents... even the seeming chaos on the streets is intentional').

The symbolic system lurking behind many of these conjurations of Japan is not hard to find. Ridley Scott's *Blade Runner* is the primal scene of the New Orientalism. Which makes it all the more ironic that it actually offers a partial critique of the megalomaniacal misrepresentations of Lafcadio Hearn and his band of fellow travellers. The future Los Angeles of the movie is recreated as an intensified version of any global city, with its linked vectors of acceleration and corrosion, its hybridized architectural style (Greek, Roman, Modernist, Egyptian, Mayan), its juxtaposition of immigrant crowding and depopulation, poverty and efficiency, its proliferation of subcultures (Oriental merchants, punks, Hare Krishnas, cyborgs, salarymen), its polyglot noise and multiracial blur.

Cultural dispersal, rather than being repressed, is embraced, fetishized, art-directed to hell. Everything is out in the open. Including the mechanism of cultural projection so dear to Hearn. One of the most striking things in *Blade Runner* is the use of the hovering vehicles that illuminate the crumbling cityscape with ads for the 'off-world' colonies. Projecting bright illusory dreams of the Other ('the chance to begin again in a golden land of opportunity and adventure'), they jab the city's demoralized population with spotlights, while above them tower huge electronic billboards displaying here a Coca Cola logo, there a smiling geisha girl. The trajectory of Hearn's touristic gaze is in this instance reversed, with cultural incongruity, the semiotic slippage between East and West, screened directly back onto itself.

All those poor *Blade Runner* Boys. They go to Tokyo expecting it to look like a set from their favourite movie and are instead confronted by something that looks suspiciously like downtown Chicago. No wonder their imaginations start working overtime. No wonder the ghost of Lafcadio Hearn still whispers to them from beyond the grave. For them, Japan will remain the same as it ever was – 'heretofore all unknown'.

Euro Disney

Modern Review, vol. 1, no. 3, Spring 1992

California, Florida, Tokyo and, now, Paris. On April 12, as anyone who has recently opened a paper or turned on the TV will know, the Magic Kingdom comes to Europe. It's a Small World, Cottonwood Creek Ranch, the Pirates of the Caribbean, Phantom Manor, Les Voyages de Pinocchio, Alice's Curious Labyrinth, Autopia and Main Street, USA, are now only twenty minutes away from the native city of surrealism. The Mouse has landed.

Despite last minute disagreements with subcontractors over unsettled accounts, nothing seems likely to disturb the £2.2 billion capital investment represented by Euro Disneyland. Leaf through the publicity brochure and the statistics jump off the page. There are thirty attractions, thirty-two shops, twenty-nine restaurants, six themed hotels with 5,200 rooms, numerous convention facilities and a golf-course laid out in a self-enclosed environment one-fifth the area of Paris. There are 1,051 Audio-Animatronic robots and 12,000 employees. There are 25,259 props, 7,653 lights and 4,358 'signs'.

It is with this last figure that Disney looks like selling itself short. For as anyone who has read their Umberto Eco or their Jean Baudrillard knows only too well, Disneyland is a goddamned semiotic paradise. Haven of 'hyperreality', sanctuary of 'simulacra', it has signs literally coming out of its (round, black) ears. And I don't mean the type that directs the visitor to Sleeping Beauty Castle or the Mad Hatter's Tea Cups. No, I mean the type that stimulates the intellectual observer to flights of rhetorical fancy.

You've heard the theories. That Disneyland is not just a theme park but an exercise in advanced urban planning, a humanization of technology through architecture. That it is a kitsch monument, a conceptual art-work disguised as a tourist attraction. That it is a reinvention of history as pastiche and simulation which spectacularly deconstructs its own nostalgic impulses. That it is an experiment in virtual reality programmed by the logic of consumerism. That, in sum, it is an urban façade, a shopping mall and an exploded TV screen all rolled into one.

You can imagine the fun the semioticians will have with Euro Disneyland's distinguishing attraction, Discoveryland. Supposedly inspired by the works of such Euro-visionaries as Leonardo da Vinci, Jules Verne and H.G. Wells, it is basically a collection of hi-tech carnival rides and wraparound spectacles: Le Visionarium, Orbitron, Star Tours, Videopolis. Here, in this cartoon utopia, the master signifiers of the Enlightenment – Science, Progress, Genius – reach their moment of critical apotheosis – as Fun Technology, Retro-Futurism and Mass Celebrity – and implode. Or so some young punk will undoubtedly try to tell you.

Over the last few years, 'theme park' has become the sovereign trope of postmodernism, the defining term of the zeitgeist. Link it with any eligible signifier and you get instant results: a sexy phrase which means fuck all. Theme park economics, theme park politics, theme park fashion, theme park philosophy. All very entertaining, but not exactly very precise. As a conceptual buzz word, 'theme park' is a bit, well, Mickey Mouse.

Time was when an intellectual wouldn't have been caught dead admiring anything as gross as Disneyland. There were just too many ways in which it was politically incorrect. First, it was bourgeois, a synthetic island of tranquillity in a sea of mass urban pleasures, of noisy funfairs and boisterous carnival parades. Then, it was an agent of cultural imperialism, domesticating Third World cultures by turning them into collections of picturesque stereotypes. Plus, it was a form of exploitation, with people literally doing Mickey Mouse jobs for chump change. Finally, it was an ideological mystification, a digest of American consumer capitalist values disguised as harmless entertainment. In short, it was an insult to the people it was designed to attract.

The only problem was that people loved it. All of which left your old-fashioned intellectual in a bit of an ideological jam. On the one hand, he was on the side of the masses; on the other hand, if they did insist on guzzling hot dogs on the Big Thunder Mountain Railroad then they were nothing better than a pack of brainless zombies.

Something of this dilemma survives in Patrick Wright's recent injunction to his fellow critics of the heritage industry to stop 'sneering' at theme parks. His specific point is that 'nostalgia' has a wide remit which can include engagement with a radical historical consciousness; his more general point is that intellectuals ought to get hip. Or as he says: 'If you're actually dismissing the whole thing, you're really not doing anything better than those old sods sneering at *Coronation Street*.'

Now, given the amount of intellectual energy that has been wasted on extolling the subversive significance of Bet Gilroy's earrings, this warning sounds more than a little quaint. Things have moved on. The problem now is not so much that commentators are prone to sneer at theme parks, it's that they are eager to exalt them.

Why, only the other day, Gilbert Adair wrote a column on Disneyland that concluded by celebrating the 'collective, uncomplicated, lump-in-the-throat happiness' of its crowds. (Incidentally, the man surely deserves some sort of a prize for managing to get 'hyperreal', 'simulacrum' and 'virtual reality' all in the same sentence.) Meanwhile, Suzanne Moore, in an article on the related subject of shopping malls, has characterized them as 'public spaces for private experiences', which offer the scope for an ambiguous but quite real 'collectivity'.

Can this really be true? I have my doubts. The central objective for most people planning a visit to a theme park or a mall is to beat the crowds. 'Collectivity' is the last thing they want (although it may be thrust upon them, as it is in traffic jams and mass panics). As for 'happiness', in my dictionary the word comes beneath 'hap', meaning 'chance, fortune, accident'. This gets to the real business of postmodern collectivity. It is random movement in a social vacuum, Brownian motion, chaos theory in action. It is the predictable agitation of particles, monads, consumers. Zombies in a new, hyper-alert, non-alienated, 'happy' way.

A measure of this paradoxical sense of collectivity can be gleaned from the fact that, when Disneyland first opened, its designers waited to see where people actually walked before they constructed the layout of paths and walkways. The aimless trajectory of the average visitor is thus not only simulated in advance, it is fed into a larger calculation of mass mobility which acts as a 'virtual' social horizon. The individual belongs to a collective without knowing it.

How did we get to this woeful state of proposing the theme park or the shopping mall as possible models of collectivity? The culprits are not hard to find. It was Eco who started it all. His 'Travels in Hyperreality' was written in 1975 as a calculated rebuke to the cultural guardians of high modernism. Essentially, he was recommending a new aesthetic capable of appreciating the merits of the Madonna Inn, the Getty Museum and, of course, Disneyland. At the same time, he was setting himself up as a kitsch Columbus, the European discoverer of a secret America of the Absolute Fake and the Almost Real.

'Travels in Hyperreality' was an ironic exercise in comparative aesthetics before it was a paean of praise to Uncle Walt. Now, it reads like an ancient manuscript. As Eco wrote: 'we must in fairness employ this American reality as a critical reagent for an examination of conscience regarding European taste'. Well, I think we've all been more than fair on that score.

Eco sidestepped ideology in favour of aesthetics. It was left to Baudrillard to sidestep aesthetics in favour of simulation. In his 1981 essay, 'Simulacra and Simulations' (also known as 'The Precession of Simulacra'), he made the point that Disneyland is only there to make the rest of Los Angeles (and, implicitly, the postmodern world) look real. It is a 'deterrence machine' designed to save the reality principle. That is why it is so infantile, why it offers such a reduced, frozen image of America. It is an unmistakable imaginary world to counterpoise to the more ambivalent hyperreal environment of the postmodern city.

This is a remark that has been much repeated over the last ten years. There is no denying it is extremely clever and witty, but what it tends to disguise is the extent to which the critical distance operating in American urban space is no longer between the imaginary and the hyperreal but between the insulated and the exposed. A city like Los Angeles, in its new capacity as capital of the Third World, is now divided between the fortified enclaves of the super-rich and the outdoor poor-houses that are the streets.

All of which leaves Disneyland in an uncomfortable position. It is an artificially protected environment but anyone with the price of admission can get in. So what is its current urban status? And what, more specifically, is the significance of Euro Disneyland opening its gates to a 1992 Europe that is lifting its barriers to internal immigration while sealing its borders to the Third World?

Perhaps the modish name to drop is not Umberto Eco or Jean Baudrillard but Paul Virilio. Although Virilio has not written much on theme parks, he has theorized extensively about the kinds of technologies that are a conspicuous feature of Euro Disneyland. According to his way of looking at things, a white-knuckle ride like the Big Thunder Mountain Railroad is a cinematic vehicle before it is a means of transport; by putting the body so violently in motion it transforms conditions of perception and alters subjectivity.

As if to emphasize this point, the more sophisticated rides in Euro Disneyland incorporate hypercinematic simulations into their movements. The Grand Canyon Diorama, for example, simulates a helicopter drop with the aid of a wraparound movie screen (handrails are provided for the queasy), while Star Tours uses flight simulator technology to narrate a trip through space (the whole auditorium bucks and tilts to coincide with the screen action).

The American cultural critic Scott Bukatman has supplemented Virilio's theories by arguing that these new technologies have a social function. He suggests that a ride like Star Tours serves to accommodate its participants to the dislocations in store for them outside the Magic Kingdom in the fast-moving world of telematic society. Disneyland is shock therapy for the masses, a form of induced nausea whereby technology 'creates the conditions for its own acceptance'.

This is all highly persuasive. But it does not admit the fact that the social function of technology may change. And in the meantime a body of knowledge has been accumulated concerning the high-speed processing of concentrated human populations within an enclosed space. This is where the popular imagination of Disneyland as a smiling bureaucracy of terror begins to take shape. Some of the other relevant statistics about Euro Disneyland, for example, include the fact that it expects 11 million visitors in its first year and that the throughput of the rides are measured in seconds.

Maybe the implications at work here are melodramatic, but the figure of apocalypse does lurk somewhere behind the scrubbed corporate image of Disneyland. If one side of the theme park is defined by the Edmonton mall, that fabled monument to conspicuous consumption in Canada, then the other is defined by Biosphere 2, that microcosm of a threatened global ecology installed beneath a plastic bubble in Arizona. Superimpose the two and you have an impression of the theme park as a protected environment of consumption, a life-support system for a way of life that is nearing its sell-by date.

In these recessionary times, in which capitalism finds itself haunted by the spectre of underconsumption, perhaps the theme park – like the monastery in the Dark Ages – is playing a vital role in preserving old skills. Perhaps, in the future, a visit to Euro Disneyland will be the equivalent of getting shipped to a re-education centre or checking into a rehab clinic. Perhaps there might come a time when the Mouse is no longer a pop icon but an emblem of emergency. Are we having fun yet?

Sovietland
i-D, no. 160, January 1997

Jack Womack made a bit of a name for himself in the slipstream of the cyberpunk movement with Future America novels like *Ambient*, *Heathern* and *Random Acts of Senseless Violence*. He maintains he fell into the SF genre because its narrative logistics supplied the only ready-made way he could find of tackling his sense of how contemporary New York was falling apart under the pressure of free-market capitalism. The received myth of New York was so strong that Womack had to travel into the future to look back on the present. When William Gibson wrote *Virtual Light* he was able to draw on Mike Davis's sociological researches in *City of Quartz* to demonstrate how Los Angeles was turning into a city inhabited by two classes – the rich and the rest. Womack had to do his own research in New York. In fact, that seems to have been his primary motive for writing SF in the first place. With *Let's Put the Future Behind Us* (Atlantic Monthly Press), Womack has turned his attention to Moscow and discovered that things have got so weird over there since the arrival of capitalism that the old Soviet myths have been completely demolished. There's no need for him to go back to the future to write about contemporary Moscow. The place already feels like a Jack Womack SF novel. This is the reason why *Let's Put the Future Behind Us* is set in the present but still boasts creative input from William Gibson. It is studded with the Womack trademarks – black wit, restless intelligence, narrative depth and a clairvoyant sense of political emergency – and easily adds up to one of the best novels of the late nineties. It follows the accidental rise to the top of Moscow operator Max Borodin as he gets caught up in a dodgy business deal that involves him with ex-Soviet bureaucrats, fascist demagogues, mad Georgian Stalinists, Brighton Beach Mafia psychos and the flotsam and jetsam of the New Russia. Max's Universal Manufacturing Company supplies forged documents to order and pays off its partners in the currency of their choice – dollars, rouble 'candy wrappers', Barbie dolls or consumer opiates. The commodification of everything including the past and the future is Womack's major theme in the novel. Max is uncertain whether the deal he has got himself into depends upon his being able to supply phoney papers, forged banknotes or hard drugs and in a way it doesn't matter. The signs can be read any way you want in the New Russia – Old Russia comes back as a Sovietland theme park while the contaminated legacy of Chernobyl floats onto the market in the form of a cache of radioactive religious icons. Even the bone-ash from a corrupt crematorium finds its uses as a drug contaminant. Which is as much to say that even death fails to deliver its usual exit line. *Let's Put the Future Behind Us* is that wicked.

Burbclave

i-D, no. 108, September 1992

It's now almost ten years since the invention of the term 'cyberpunk' and you might have thought it was time to find a new word for this particular cognitive mapping of technology, language, politics and capitalism. At the very least, the marketing departments of the big sci-fi imprints must be getting impatient; 'cyberpunk' always was a useful way of hyping a mass of disparate material, from the postmodern bit-lit of William Gibson to third-rate shopping and hacking novels. One thing that has become increasingly problematic in light of cyberpunk's interrogation of the info-domain of computers, fibre optics, TV screens and satellite links is the fact that it is encapsulated in one of the world's oldest communication technologies: the book.

Gibson has been trying to get to grips with this paradox. He is considering rewriting his 'Sprawl' trilogy as a software package and has recently collaborated with the artist Dennis Ashbaugh to produce a viral text, *Agrippa* (the title refers to a brand of photo album common in the twenties), which is only available on disk but which wipes itself as soon as it is scrolled (a neat comment on the trade-offs between human and computer memory, between the storage and the processing of information). One of the thrusts of cyberpunk was that the whole idea of 'literacy' needed to be redefined as the global spread of hyper-media corrupted the older sanctity of print media. The hacker ethic represented a potential democratization of hieratic systems of knowledge, a liberation of the secret files of corporate conglomerates as various as the church, the state and the multinational. As long as you could work a computer, it didn't matter if you couldn't read that well. This is perhaps one reason why Neal Stephenson originally conceived his post-cyberpunk LA meltdown novel, *Snow Crash* (Bantam Spectra; US import), as a computer-generated comic. What better medium could there be for a new genre of science fiction than the hi-tech ideogram? In the end, Stephenson couldn't bring it off and had to go back to the old technology. But you can see where he was coming from. *Snow Crash* speeds along like a Frank Miller graphic novel. It's got a samurai hacker called Hiro Protagonist as the good guy, a resourceful skateboarding courier chick as his sidekick, and a mutant biker with a nuclear bomb in his sidecar as the bad guy. It's got big guns, tiny computers and lots of violence. It's a riot. At the same time, it reads like Jean Baudrillard crossed with Erich von Daniken. Stephenson's central conceit is to compare postmodern America with – wait for it – the culture of Ancient Sumeria. This helps him to get a handle on a media-saturated society divided between an 'infocracy' of the computer-literate with access to a 'Metaverse' of virtual reality and a 'biomass' of ignorant consumers who have to survive in a material world of fortified 'Burbclaves', lawless streets and corporate franchise operations like the Reverend Wayne's Pearly Gates, MetaCops Unlimited and CosaNostra Pizza. Stephenson has certainly done his homework on the Sumerian stuff and you will find more here than you ever need to know on pre-Biblical mythologies of creation and apocalypse. The surprise is that it is all integrated into an elegant disquisition upon that favourite cyberpunk trope – the virus. Stephenson makes the expected connection between the 'infection' of cybernetic and biogenetic systems, but he goes on to examine both religion and capitalism as viral phenomena. Pentecostal religions that encourage 'speaking in tongues' are considered as forms of neurolinguistic programming, while the franchise culture of consumer capitalism is figured as a recursive informational 'growth'. Everything comes together in Stephenson's use of the Fall of the Tower of Babel. What this mythical event heralds is the fragmentation of the means of human communication into a multiplicity of different languages, an 'infocalypse' that is benign to the extent that it strengthens immunity to viral control mechanisms. Hence the linguistic density of *Snow Crash*, its neologisms and abbreviations, its borrowings from specialist technical domains and hijacking of ghetto slang. If all this makes the novel sound like a chunk of mutant theory, then it should be emphasized that this is also a funny and scabrous sci-fi yarn. A groundbreaking achievement.

Media wars

You are drinking in the Eagle on Farringdon Road with the spillover crowd from the Wagadon do upstairs. Before Nick Logan became a glossy magazine publisher he was an editor of one of the music inkies and some of the old lot have dropped by tonight. You meet one old timer whose by-line you dimly remember. He tells you tales of Fleet Street before Murdoch broke the power of the print unions. How you could never rely on getting your freebies safely because the post room guys always got first turn in the media division of spoils. (The moral? Always get 'em biked over.) Some years later you are working as a copy-writer for a new media content provider and participate as a bystander in the weekly office meetings. The employees all sit in a circle and politely clap the announcement of each new contract.

Slacker

i-D, no. 119, August 1993

The cover of *13th GEN* (Vintage, US) looks dire. A shot of a white guy standing against a brick wall wearing jeans and a black T-shirt, the picture cropped just above the neck. You immediately know what you're going to get: a work of pop sociology that attempts to pin down the identity of faceless youth, a quick cash-in on the whole slacker/gen x phenomenon. The design of the book even mimics the Mac aesthetic of Douglas Coupland's *Generation X*, with its visual drop-ins, stat boxes and random pop quotes. Meanwhile, the authors, Neil Howe and Bill Strauss, seem to have invited a member of the lost tribe they are documenting to comment on their findings as they proceed. It all looks very gimmicky. The interventions of the third figure, Ian Williams, are particularly disconcerting, tricked up as they are in terms of unauthorized interceptions of a master text. At least there is the simulation of a dialogue, even if it has to be dramatized in terms of a generation gap: two crinkly baby boomers engaging with a slacker who has hacked his way into their system. Once you get down to the text, though, things become more interesting. Howe and Strauss have done their homework. They understand which cultural events have shaped the experiences of the '13th generation', as they refer to the clutch of young Americans born between 1961 and 1981, and go on to name-check everything from *The Brady Bunch* to *River's Edge*, Jeff Spiccoli to Bart Simpson, *Sesame Street* to Lollapalooza. They also have an admirably clear understanding of the economic circumstances that have propelled this 'sacrificial generation' into a low-wage Ronald McDonaldland of terminal pessimism and social atomization. They are also alert to the way that '13ers' have been scapegoated on all sides as stupid, shallow and superficial, when they are precisely the individuals who will have to clean up all the big messes (drug abuse, pollution, the budget deficit) left behind by the baby boomers. Their general thesis of a culture gap existing between post-sixties Clintonite neo-liberalism and post-punk Reaganite neo-survivalism seems incontestible. Howe and Strauss provide useful documentation of the feelgood psychology books of the sixties and early seventies which rationalized the guilt of a generation as they tuned in to their inner selves and blanked out their kids. There is also some interesting material on the ambivalence that young people reserve for the legacy of seventies identity politics, which wants to police racial and sexual difference in terms of a 'politically correct' but socially divisive language. When Howe and Strauss attend to specific cultural detail, their thesis comes alive. It is when they become too ambitious that things veer wildly off track. The attempt to read twentieth-century American culture as the secret history of the clashes between generations (the G.I. generation, the Silent generation, the Boomer generation, the 13th generation) is absurd, as is their attempt to compare their precious 13ers with F. Scott Fitzgerald's original 'lost generation'. History never goes in circles. Which is why the subjects of *13th GEN* may manage to escape the rather dire future that Howe and Strauss have conjured for them, in which they will be expected to work hard for their money to save America. Much better to kick back and watch MTV.

Mod

Arena, no. 21, May/June 1990

Dick Hebdige has got a lot to answer for. This is the Goldsmith's College lecturer who ten years ago published a book on punk, mod – the whole teen thing – and in the process popularized the equation Subculture equals Style equals Subversion. It was a neat formula, one that went on to become a mainstay of polytechnic sociology seminars and a cliché of pop punditry. Political protest may have been something staged in the street but it was no longer inscribed on banners and placards; instead it was calibrated in the width of an Italian lapel, the weight of a crepe sole, the texture of a shrink-wrapped record sleeve. The politics of style had arrived.

Recently, though, things have started to get out of hand. Suddenly it's not just the music and fashion of wasted youth that are deemed to be subversive; it's everything in the downtown culture mart from TV game shows to rock videos, paperback romances to Hollywood spectaculars. Now that the Age of Teen is over and youth movements are thin on the ground, popular culture has taken over as the new first term in the old subcultural equation. The method remains the same: if it moves on the street, nail it (preferably with a hefty foreign name like Gramsci or de Certeau). The field of play, however, has opened right up.

Welcome to the wonderful world of Cultural Studies – the only academic discipline for which the epithet 'Mickey Mouse scholarship' would probably be viewed as some kind of compliment.

A pointer to this peculiar academic fashion can be gleaned from flipping through the pages of its eponymously titled house journal. Nestling alongside the predictable and now rather dated essays on postmodernism (last decade's fad) in the latest issue of *Cultural Studies* (Routledge) is a revealing little item that goes under the helpful title 'How to Watch *Star Trek*'. The writer, a teacher at some obscure institute of higher education called Drake University, informs us how she spent six months boldly going where no grant-funded researcher has gone before in investigating the whole Trekkie phenomenon.

Several syndicated reruns and many exhaustively quoted interviews later, she comes to the hardly earth-shattering conclusion that *Star Trek* fans are not at all the passive, alienated dupes of popular academic myth but manipulative, sophisticated consumers. They know what's going on, they're hip, they're *subverting* the practices of couch-potato viewing.

It's the same with all the books published under the Cultural Studies rubric. If it's popular, it must be subversive. Last year Manchester University Press published a weighty tome by Martin Baker which did the job on comics. This year Routledge have put together a list that includes at least two classic examples of this rapidly expanding academic fad.

In *Popular Film and Television Comedy* (Routledge), Steve Neale and Frank Krutnick start off with the questionable proposition that 'comedy is inherently subversive' before going on to take a look at such radical examples of the form as *The Two Ronnies* and *Bless this House*. Meanwhile the University of Naples professor Iain Chambers is publishing a book called *Border Dialogues* (Routledge), which attempts to get to grips with a heady mix of 'gender, ethnicity, fashion and computers'. Very provocative. This from the man who in his last book, *Popular Culture*, asked the plaintive and entirely unrhetorical question: 'How do we locate signs of resistance ... in the television audience of *East-Enders*, amongst readers of *Cosmopolitan* and *Mizz*, or in the quiet style of a Cecil Gee suit?' How indeed?

Thankfully, Routledge is also publishing one book at least that tries to make sense of it all – Patrick Brantlinger's *Crusoe's Footsteps: Cultural Studies in Britain and America* (Routledge). Bratlinger speculates that the success of Cultural Studies in universities on both sides of the Atlantic can be put down to two things: the disillusionment of Class of '68 campus radicals with countercultural politics (having failed to change the system, they're settling for changing the syllabus) and the penetration of the ivory towers of old by market forces. (NBC would prefer to employ someone who knows how to watch *Star Trek* than how to read *Moby Dick*.)

That these two factors add up to a commercially viable pseudo-radicalism should come as no great shock. It's a definition of Culture we've become used to over the last few years.

As Jon Savage observes in his penetrating contribution to the selection of essays edited by Simon Frith, *Facing the Music: Essays on Pop, Rock and Culture* (Mandarin), 'the psychic states that were once the province of deviants or marginals are now at the heart of the Western consumer machine'. The academic career move that swaps subcultural semiotics for Cultural Studies is thus hardly surprising.

What is surprising is that it's taken the academics so long to ditch all their cherished illusions about the mind-rotting effects of mass culture (or the 'culture industry', as they rather sniffily used to call it). Maybe it was only guys like these who were ever dumb enough to believe in the first place that viewers of *Star Trek* were themselves so dumb that they couldn't see through its intergalactic frontier mythology as easily as they could William Shatner's stretch nylon uniform.

This is obviously something that's missing from Bratlinger's analysis – the fact that, back in the sixties and seventies, academics were sweating so much blood in the library trying to sort their Adornos from their Althussers that they didn't actually have any time to sit down and watch *Star Trek*. Now they've finally got round to it and discovered that hey, this popular culture stuff is real cool, they're trying to put one over on the rest of us by insisting that it's *subversive* as well.

The biggest offender in this respect is John Fiske, a professor of 'communication arts' at the University of Wisconsin-Madison who is the unofficial Godfather of Cultural Studies. Two recent books – *Understanding Popular Culture* (Unwin) and *Reading the Popular* (Unwin) – reveal him busily setting out his stall in all its tacky splendour. 'I have strong vulgar tastes and my academic training has failed to squash my enjoyment and participation in popular pastimes,' he proudly huffs.

And what you see is what you buy: ripped jeans, window-shopping, *The Wheel of Fortune*, Mills & Boon novels, tabloid newspapers, Madonna, *Dallas*, video arcades, even surfing. Here – according to the theory – is a cultural bazaar of diverse pleasures from which the consumer, that happy postmodern shopper, mix'n'matches meanings to his heart's content. Thereby transforming the ideological snares of mass culture into the subversive gains of pop culture in one fell swoop.

There's just one thing. If the customs of the 'people' – as Fiske rather mistily insists on calling the shopping-mall hordes – are so wonderful, why doesn't he write in a language they can understand? Why all the guff about 'producerly texts' and 'sociocultural allegiances'? If he was really serious about the subversive dynamics of pop culture, he'd have written his books in tabloid headlines.

He hasn't, of course, because that would jeopardize his intellectual credibility. It would make him no better than one of his celebrated surfers or Madonna fans when he has to believe that he knows something they don't. Otherwise why speak on their behalf?

Why indeed? This is something Dick Hebdige, at least, clearly understands. In an essay on the Sublime in a recent edition of *New Formations*, the rather more stiff-necked companion periodical to *Cultural Studies*, he appreciates with studied relish the irony of his latest involvement with subculture and the meaning of style – namely, trooping round to a neighbouring squat at three o'clock in the morning and telling the motley crew of anarchist musicians inside to keep the noise down.

His parting thought is something that Fiske and the whole Cultural Studies crowd would do well to consider: 'Released from the obligation to "understand", I was free to sleep – at last! – the dreamless sleep of the *senex* or the fool.' Which is as much to say: the sleep of the just.

New romantic #1

Arena, no. 36, November 1992

First, I have a small confession to make. I hate Salman Rushdie, David Hare, Harold Pinter, Howard Brenton, Richard Attenborough, Jonathan Miller, Clive James, David Lodge, Malcolm Bradbury, Martin Amis (sort of), Ian McEwan (kind of), Alan Bleasdale (well, not really), Derek Jarman (I'm starting to make this up now), Pete Townshend (this is getting out of hand) and Michael Ignatieff.

Make no mistake, I can hate with the best of them. I hate the

Arts Council and I hate the Booker Prize. I hate the NFT, the RSC, the BBC, and, er, the MCC. I hate them, too. OK?

I hate the left-liberal establishment as much as your average contributor to the *Modern Review*. But I don't think that makes me a radical. I mean, jeez, I voted Labour in the last election.

Now can we have a serious discussion about culture?

The great culture debate hasn't really been up to much so far. From the way people have been carrying on, you'd think that punk never happened. David Hare proposes that, given the choice, he would prefer Keats to Dylan. Wrong! Keats or Dylan? The obvious answer is *neither*. Or else it's Shelley (Percy *and* Pete).

As editor of the *Modern Review*, the pop-cult paper for postmodern grown-ups, Toby Young is having nothing to do with this elite distinction between high and low culture. For most people, he cheekily suggests, a more pertinent question is whether *Star Trek VI* is better than *Star Trek V*. Well, Toby, I'm sure we don't need an Oxford graduate to answer that. Why don't we just poll the kids on the street?

John Carey has also pitched into the fray. As Professor of Literature at Oxford University, this is a guy with credentials. In his recently published book, *The Intellectuals and the Masses*, he comes out against high modernism (all those horrible snobs like Virginia Woolf), pegging it as a form of cultural mystification. So he's on the side of populists like Young.

Then there have been various toings and froings in the *Guardian*. Robert McCrum weighs in on the side of Hare and other liberals when he defends elitism in the arts against what he sees as the vulgar commodification of culture by nasty old capitalism. Back shoots Cosmo Landesman, a contributing editor of the *Modern Review*, with the line that McCrum is a snob and culture would be nothing without capitalism.

Hey, guys. Give these liberals a break! They can't help it. They're old and feeble and out of touch. To keep hacking away at them is cultural triumphalism. Have some respect.

This is no culture war. This is a media turf battle. On the one side, you have all the old farts who don't know their Barthes from their Bart Simpson, and on the other you have all the young dudes who want in. 'Culture' is merely the nominated stake in an entertaining career game.

If we want to talk seriously about culture then we're going to have to go back to the late fifties and re-examine the work of Raymond Williams and Richard Hoggart. Williams in *Culture and Society* and Hoggart in *The Uses of Literacy* were both concerned with broadening the definition of culture to take account of the everyday experiences of a newly emancipated working class. Culture was no longer just about theatre and opera but about jazz, football and gardening. At the same time they insisted on the value of aesthetic discrimination. Some things – like 'juke box boys' or 'the latest Tin Pan drool' – were beyond the pale.

This kind of informed populism fits very well inside the pages of the *Modern Review*. At the same time, the broadened anthropological definition of culture is something that matches the brief of the Department of National Heritage. A Ministry of Culture in all but name, the new Department has jurisdiction over sports, tourism, museums and libraries, broadcasting, film and the arts in general.

This coincidence has seemed suspicious to liberals. They sense a right-wing plot. 'Be careful!' they say. 'In the eighties the New Right targeted the trades unions, the schools and universities, the legal and medical professions, and local government. Now they've got the cultural sphere in their sights. Watch out!'

Uh, huh. Look, I hate to spoil everyone's fun, but the real culture war happened back in the seventies and it was called 'Anarchy in the UK'. As Jon Savage observes, 'there was a real sense in which punk's accurate record of England's tensions hit the desired chord – a clash, not between generations, but between rulers and ruled'.

The left-liberal establishment was rumbled over fifteen years ago. The big problem, and the real historical tragedy, was that punk never developed a political left wing sophisticated enough to match Thatcherism. Instead it was hijacked by the moribund politics of Labourism. Who remembers Red Wedge now?

Stuart Hall was one of the first left-wing theorists to acknowledge the revolutionary, avant-garde nature of Thatcherism when he referred to its 'regressive modernization'. The term hints at an alternative history of the last decade. What price 'progressive modernization'?

Come on. Let's admit it. The New Right won. The culture war is over. The eighties are over. It's time to regroup. And maybe part of that regrouping effort involves a rewriting of history.

So the New Right targeted the universities, eh? Well let's go back and take a look. Specifically, let's go back to Oxford University in Thatcher's first term. Look, there's me in the back row of a lecture hall. No, not the pretty boy with the John Foxx hairstyle. The geek next to him. Yeah, him. (Hmm, thin, isn't he?)

The lecturer is a trendy lefty with a frothy beard. Let's call him D.D. He's gabbing on about *Jude The Obscure*. Thomas Hardy's last novel, published in 1895, is a meditation on the connections between social ambition, the accumulation of cultural capital and the dread of failure. A very apposite text for me and my pals at the time.

For those who have forgotten the novel, I shall summarize. Jude Fawley is a rural stonemason who wants to better himself. As he studies his Homer and Euclid in a West Country village, he dreams mistily of going to 'Christminster' – a thinly veiled Oxford – where he will be able to appropriate middle-class culture and status in one smart move. He 'thought he might become even a bishop'.

The central question of the novel is: are his dreams legitimate or merely delusions of grandeur? Jude may romanticize Christminster as a 'heavenly Jerusalem' but since 1870 Oxford had been trying to keep a lid on working-class demands for adult education because of their explicit link with the desire for social advancement. In those days, a liberal arts education was the prerequisite for a career in the professions and Oxford was a closed shop.

Jude never made it to Christminster. How many thousands were there like him at the time? It wasn't a question my pals and I were interested in. We'd had a free ride to Oxford on the back of the welfare state. We were possibly the last generation to benefit from the 1944 Education Act. It had taken three generations' worth of collective struggle on behalf of the organized working class to finally get us to Christminster. And we thought we'd got there on the strength of our A-Levels.

So there we were. Us and D.D. The Class of '76 being taught about culture and society by a Marxist graduate of the Class of '68. It was no wonder we misunderstood each other so completely.

Jude, D.D. told us, was a snob. What was so great about Christminster that he wanted to go there? My pals and I had already had several suspicions of our own along these lines (Where were the cool people? Had *no one* heard of Scritti Politti? How come we couldn't get any girls?). But to hear a lecturer – a figure of authority – confirming them was radical. It was certainly enough to grab our attention.

D.D. was well into his act by this time. His gown was flapping and his body was rocking. In a seemingly uncontrollable deconstructive frenzy, he pounced on an entirely innocent scene in the novel and declared it to be the master clue that gave the ideological game away. Ah ha!

It was a scene where Jude is courting the pig-farmer's daughter who will eventually drag him down into the muck. They are served beer in an inn and Arabella objects because, after one sip, she can tell the malt and hops used in the liquor have been adulterated. (Ah ha!) This, according to D.D., was practical knowledge of the sort that Jude snobbishly scorned. He went on to joke that Arabella probably had a collection of beer mats back at home to rival any of Jude's own books of the Iliad.

D.D.'s message was clear. All the humanist guff about the moral value of a liberal arts education was a joke. Beer mats, OK? We nodded gravely in approval. Then we trooped back to our rooms, put on Heaven 17's 'We Don't Need That Fascist Groove Thang' and read about Derrida in the *NME*. Let me tell you, we thought we were pretty cool.

So were we conned or what? We certainly had our heads turned. Maybe some of us, like Jude, obscurely hoped that in going to Christminster we would be given the keys to the kingdom. But we'd been through punk so bollocks to that. We were ready for a Cultural Revolution. We'd had Year Zero in pop music: out with hippie bullshit rock and in with whatever Malcolm McLaren was flogging us that week. So it made sense to chuck out Thomas Hardy in favour of beer mats.

But it was all a misunderstanding. D.D. wasn't interested in a revolution. He was interested in his career. We mistook the local rhetoric of a turf battle for a general call to arms. And that had strange and unexpected results.

What D.D. was instructing us in was value-free cultural relativism. It was postmodern anarchy. For him, fighting his local turf battle, this represented a democratic challenge to the traditional authority of the academy. It was a way of opening up an elitist institution to the descendants of Jude the Obscure.

But for some of us, this represented something very different. Once we were out in the big wide world being restructured by Thatcherism, it represented the denial of any authority except that of multinational capital, which tended to flatten the difference between high and low culture, but also between the signs of poverty and the signs of wealth. Lots of my friends who were punks became go-ahead yuppies as a result of overdosing on postmodernism. It solved all their ideological problems. What was the alternative? To do a Hanif Kureishi and compromise with the left-liberal establishment. Much better to forget culture, make money in the City of London and listen to Morrissey on the car stereo.

Oxford Marxists like D.D. will never know how many postpunk Thatcherites they armed and trained.

It is this moment rather than the setting up of the *Modern Review* or the establishment of the Department of National Heritage that marks the terminus of the cultural debate started by Hoggart and Williams. They could afford to expand the definition of culture because they thought the social battle had been won. Poverty had been abolished by the welfare state and everyone had food, clothes and shelter. It made sense to move on to expensive items like 'culture'.

But that was the fifties. Today we've got other problems. But they've got nothing to do with whether Keats is better than Dylan. They've got to do with whether BUPA is better than the NHS, whether student loans are better than student grants, whether low taxation is better than high public spending, whether collective struggle in pursuit of a rational objective is better than individual trusting to luck. Anybody got any answers?

Punk

i-D, no. 163, April 1997

John Williams is a London journalist who has published two previous books in a writing career that has taken him from the *NME* to *GQ* via *The Face*. *Into the Badlands* was his round-up of the American crime writers – figures like George V. Higgins, James Ellroy, Carl Hiaasen and Tony Hillerman – who had inspired him to believe he could write, while *Bloody Valentine* settled his accounts with his punk roots in Cardiff. Now Williams returns as John L. Williams with a debut novel *Faithless* (Serpent's Tail), which attempts to do for London what Higgins has done for Boston or Hiaasen for Miami – claim it as mythic turf. The novel opens with the murder of a young man in a Covent Garden record shop in 1983 and then flash-cuts to 1994 as the man's friend Jeff narrates the events leading up to and surrounding the death. There are two candidates in the frame for the murder – a McLarenesque music biz hipster named Etheridge and a sub-*Minder* gangster type called Charlie Minto. It has to be admitted right from the start that Williams's whodunnit thriller plot doesn't really work. He seems bored by it himself and drops it for whole chapters at a time while he gets stuck into the real business that interests him – documenting the mindset and manners of all those 'who came of age in the years between punk and Thatcher'. The disillusionment that Williams tags as the failure of punk to deliver on its revolutionary promise becomes the material for a disguised rite-of-passage novel about coming to terms with a diminished future and accepting responsibility for the past. Williams has chosen his period carefully – it's the moment when *The Face* takes over from the *NME* as an arbiter of style, when cocktail bars replace dingy pubs, when second-hand Flip finery replaces mock-prole utility clothing, when Roland Barthes replaces Leon Trotsky as a name to drop, when irony replaces authenticity and postmodernism comes too soon. The zeitgeist figure in the novel is a charismatic pop star called Ross (loosely modelled on Green Gartside from Scritti Politti?) who makes the jump from avant-punk radicalism to art-pop posing while leaving his old friend Jeff behind. The switch that Ross has managed to make so effortlessly is one to which it takes Jeff longer to come round, and it is this distance that implicitly measures the rueful pathos of the narrating voice. Williams's eye for historically charged popcult detail means that *Faithless* is bound to be compared to Nick Hornby's *High Fidelity*, but it is a much better novel – smarter, harder, less bound by stereotype. Williams became friendly with Robin Cook (a.k.a. Derek Raymond) late in his life and you can see that the notorious boho London novelist remains a model for him. Williams is aiming high. He may fail to reach Cook's understanding of the metaphysics of evil, but he has succeeded in incarnating himself as an original novelist fully the equal of Hiaasen or Hillerman.

New romantic #2

Arena, no. 40, July/August 1993

I always feel paranoid when I go through Immigration and it's not even as if I've got anything to hide. Not only am I a subject of the United Kingdom of Great Britain and Northern Ireland, I've got a passport to prove it. But do I look the part? This is what makes me nervous when the immigration officer scrutinizes the youthful photo in my passport and compares it to my tired and crumpled features. What signs of betrayal is he looking for? Does he think I'm some kind of impostor? What is the 'normal' profile of a British subject, anyway?

These phantoms flitted through my mind recently as I waited for my passport to be checked at Heathrow after disembarking from a routine flight within Europe. Just a brief anxiety attack. Imagine how I'd have felt if the immigration officer had declared that my passport was not in order. These characters are servants of the Crown. They can drag you off, examine your luggage, examine the insides of your body. They can accuse you of being something you're not. Like an illegal immigrant. And if the

Home Office agrees, you can get turned around and kicked out of the country.

I had no problems with Immigration, of course. I didn't even have any problems with Customs, despite the fact that all the uniformed white guys there looked bored and restless. What criteria do they use for picking somebody up, I wondered.

Out in the concourse, it was like some multicultural bazaar. There were Chinese families with mountains of luggage, Arabs in shades and jellabas, a group of huge American tourists and a couple of African lads with plastic carrier bags. But maybe I was wrong. For all I knew, they could have been British subjects like me.

Heathrow claims to be the busiest airport in the world and I can believe it. But it's got nothing to do with its speed or efficiency. It's down to its occupancy of the Greenwich Meridian Line, international ground zero, one of those invisible little hangovers from Empire that, like British military intervention in Northern Ireland or English parliamentary sovereignty over Wales and Scotland, actually adds up to quite a lot.

Sometimes, it seems that the people in charge of policing our borders have a xenophobic mind-set that wouldn't have been out of place in the Empire.

Take the case of Mira Litobac. After her husband had been conscripted into the Bosnian army, she collected her two sons, quit Sarajevo and drove across Europe to join her sister in London. Grabbed the ferry to Dover and claimed political asylum. The immigration officers actually let her through. It was the Home Office that wanted to deport her.

They pointed to the Dublin Convention. Signed by European Community member states in 1990, it specified that all refugees should claim asylum in the first safe country they come across. As far as the Mira Litobac case was concerned, this meant France, where she had waited three hours for a ferry. Or maybe Germany, which she had driven through. Perhaps Austria? Maybe even Croatia, which is not, after all, as war-torn as Bosnia.

This specious line of Home Office reasoning was in the end defeated by Mira Litobac, who very sensibly obtained herself a lawyer and has now been granted exceptional leave to remain in the country. A happy ending to the story? Well, not quite. In 1991, about 433,300 asylum applications were received by EC member states (out of a global total of 18 million). The UK received 47,000 of these applications. It granted 25 per cent of them, refused 10 per cent of them and gave a full 65 per cent 'exceptional leave to remain'. What this quaint legal formula refers to is the process of shunting an asylum-seeker into a bureaucratic limbo where they pursue their claim until kingdom come.

If you think this is bad, then wait until the Asylum and Immigration Appeals Bill becomes law. This mean-spirited piece of legislation is pernicious in many ways. Not only does it confuse the quite separate categories of immigrant and refugee, but it seeks to reduce the number of refugees granted exceptional leave to remain by speeding up and intensifying asylum procedures. If it had been in place when Mira Litobac landed in Dover in April, then she would have been 'processed' there and then. She would have been fingerprinted, interviewed and no doubt bundled onto the nearest ferry back to France. All with only forty-eight hours to lodge an appeal.

The whole point of the Bill is to establish a fast-track deportation process for those deemed to have a 'manifestly unfounded' claim for asylum. If the Dublin Convention cannot be used to support such an exclusionary judgement, then there is always the possibility of resorting to the stereotype of the 'asylum-cheat'. This phantom figure is the latest and most absurd incarnation of that old Tory bogeyman, the illegal immigrant. He is reckoned to be a cunning native of East Africa or Asia who has faked the signs of political persecution so as to dodge his way into the country and live it up on welfare payments. An absurd idea.

But then the Tories have always had a funny idea of foreigners. If it wasn't illegal immigrants that were exercising their collective imagination then it was immigrants plain and simple. Especially those from the West Indies or India. 'Vote Labour If You Want A Nigger For A Neighbour' was one of their more offensive campaign slogans from the early sixties. But at least it had the virtue of political legibility. Nobody could doubt why they blocked the free flow of immigrants from the Commonwealth and Empire in 1962. It was because they wanted to keep the Mother Country white.

Well, it didn't work, thank god. Otherwise we'd all be living in a bad Ealing comedy. Think about it. The history of Britain this century has been dominated by the long, slowly retreating shadow of Empire (now reaching its terminal phase with Irish bombs regularly exploding in the City of London). A whole mythology of Englishness was invented at the turn of the century to deal with this crisis. Tolerance, humour, understatement, respect for your elders and betters: all these qualities were fetishized by a political elite secretly possessed by guilt, dread and paranoid megalomania.

As a coping mechanism, it has been amazingly successful. But it has produced a dominant culture of stasis, retreat and nostalgia. It has privileged memory over industry, order over excitement and organic community over urban anonymity. Think not just of T.S. Eliot and Evelyn Waugh, think also of William Morris and R.H. Tawney. A romantic vision of England that links the cult of landscape with the mystique of temperament has been remarkably influential across both ends of the political spectrum.

When John Major quoted George Orwell in his April address to the Conservative Group for Europe, this was not so much another example of the Right stealing the Left's best clothes as ancient myths of English nationalism being pressed into the service of a pro-European political cause. Major went on to try to update the imagery when he spoke of Britain being 'the country of long shadows on county grounds, warm beer, invincible green suburbs, dog lovers and pools fillers'. This may have worked for his immediate Tory constituency, but it went down like a weighted corpse in the rest of the country.

Times have changed and the effects of postwar immigration from the West Indies have had a lot to do with it. The urgent, forward-looking rhythms of modernism may have been repressed by High Tory culture for most of the century, but they have been picked up by the dense urban sounds of popular culture. Think not just of the popular press, advertising, music hall, pulp fiction, football, cinema and comic-books, think also of trad jazz, white rhythm & blues, black slang and sixties

London. What this suggests is that the imaginary relation that English pop modernism has historically entertained with a contraband or 'black' America could only be fully inhabited once there was a material black immigrant community to rub shoulders with.

Dick Hebdige has persuasively read the whole carnivalesque parade of English working-class youth cults from the mods to the punks and beyond as a 'a phantom history of race relations since the war'. The cultural transactions that took place between white hipsters and black groovesters were always loaded in favour of the host community. So it was mods as 'white Negroes' and punks as 'white Rastas' rather than the other way round. But you only have to look around on any street corner to see the result. English styles of walking, talking, dressing and generally showing out are funkier and 'blacker' than they were a generation ago.

The history of Afro-Caribbean immigration has changed things around here. And now, the pattern of Asian immigration that occurred ten to twenty years later is also starting to shift cultural bases. The big club story of the last year has been the popularity in Britain's cities of bhangramuffin, a hybrid of Punjabi folk music, Anglo-Jamaican reggae and flash pop stylings. Look no further than the success of Handsworth homeboy, Apache Indian.

Of course, it's always possible to look at things the other way round. It's always possible to take pride in the fact that, for example, a black British soul singer may perform in an American vocal style but speak in a broad Yorkshire accent. But this is to endorse immigrant culture only if it is assimilated into the host community with no complaints, producing another exotic addition to the domestic round of consumer pleasures. If it can be exported to America and make pots of money, then all the better.

The Tories have certainly not been slow to recognize the contribution that post-Beatles pop music has made to the country's balance of payments. It's surprising they haven't been more inventive. Never mind all that guff about 'invincible green suburbs', there is a clear ideological opportunity available now to reconcile the lapsed strains of English pop modernism with the slumbering pulse of High Tory traditionalism.

It would be easy to imagine the cultural canon that would define this English pop nationalism. It has already been sketched out by a thousand and one music critics tracing the genealogy of Suede, that great patriotic project of the moment. It would start with the cockney camp of the Small Faces, or maybe with the flash romanticism of the Kinks (Ray Davies sub-titled one of his albums *The Decline and Fall of the British Empire*). It would continue with the avant-garde anthems of the Who, the suburban angst of the Jam and the music-hall suss of Madness, and perhaps with the languid provocations of the Pet Shop Boys. And it would culminate in Morrissey's aristocratic dabblings with the imagery of English fascism. You can fill in the blanks.

All very cute, but a little too mired in the past for my tastes. A little too reminiscent of what Tom Nairn has referred to as 'the cryptic nature of English nationalism'. If we do need to reinvent an ideology of Englishness, then let's at least try and make it face the future with confidence. And maybe the best way to do that is to grab as many new immigrants as we can, whether they're from Sarajevo or Saigon. You never know, it could be the making of us.

Slow memes

The thesis you are writing for John Kerrigan at the University of Cambridge is capsizing under the weight of your multiple obsessions. You gather up what you can – postmodernism, technological humanism, gothic Marxism, modern primitivism – and begin to stash it inside the popcult cargo destined for the wide-open expanses of the style press. (Jon Savage offers the model praxis.) It's good shit. Some of it is intercepted by vigilant editors (who say things like: Too academic, make it sexy). A lot of it gets through. You like to think of yourself as a smuggler of intellectual contraband. At the same time you yearn for a legitimate media career. (The dilemma: how to buy in without selling out.) 'Pirates: members of a class whose inheritance has been confiscated' (Eric Hobsbawm).

Shadow enlightenment

i-D, no. 159, December 1996

Peter Lamborn Wilson is an itinerant North American scholar, Sufi anarchist, occasional SF writer and perma-dissident who has been responsible over the years for throwing out quite a few buzz words into the pre-millennial utopian mix. His latest piece of para-research, *Pirate Utopias* (Autonomedia), is an account of the republic of Salé on the North African coast of Morocco, which from the late sixteenth century to the eighteenth century functioned as a semi-independent state populated by a cosmopolitan mix of Moorish corsairs and European renegades. Wilson is primarily interested in identifying Salé as an extant historical model for the types of insurrectionary communities that have excited contemporary interest among cyber-libertarians and eco-activists alike. But lurking in the background of his project is something more ambitious. He wants to produce a paradigm shift in our understanding of the Enlightenment and show how its ideals of democracy, public property and free speech are grounded not in the revolutions of America, France and England but in the 'pirate utopia' of Salé that antedated them all. Occultists like Frances Yates have already speculated that the Enlightenment was essentially the creature of a Masonic conspiracy of atheists, neo-Platonists and alchemists which got going in the late sixteenth century. Wilson goes further. He sees Masonic idealism as itself the creature of the 'positive shadow' of Islam that the coast of North Africa cast upon a European landscape wracked by Christianized sexual repression, monarcho-imperialist subjection and the genocidal programmes of capitalism, and speculates that 'heresy' should be understood as a means of 'cultural transfer' and 'social resistance'. *Pirate Utopias* is no fundamentalist Afrocentric rewriting of European history, however. Wilson's tone remains sceptical, tentative and humorous throughout. His model of a utopian community is not one policed by the caste-marks of nationhood but one that is hybridized, porous and essentially impure. Salé was a pirate hangout populated by Moorish aristocrats, Sufis, pederasts, runaway slaves, Irish rebels, heretical Jews, nativized British spies, radical working-class heroes and European converts to Islam. Wilson makes it sound like the ultimate party scene, a hedonistic 'temporary autonomous zone', which through the accidents of history managed to survive for more than a century (and the memory of which attracted Paul Bowles, William Burroughs and other beat renegades to the 'interzone' of Tangier almost two hundred years later). The pirates of Salé made a living by preying on the European merchant vessels that ploughed the trading routes of the Mediterranean, but they cast their net as far wide as the south-west coast of Ireland, the English Channel and even Iceland. Wilson has very little primary research material to go on but what he has managed to unearth he makes the most of. There are enough ripping yarns and rollicking adventure tales in *Pirate Utopias* to keep most action-freaks happy, and it's interesting that although the book is 'anti-copyright' Wilson explicitly reserves 'the right to lucrative Hollywood movie adaptations and other actual booty'. Any bets on Spielberg optioning the book?

Archaic modernity #1

> 'Pop Theory, Bardolatry, Leaving the Twentieth-century Academy' in Steve Beard, *Bloody Banquets: Trash Video, Jacobean Horror, Rewinding Foucault*, unpublished University of Cambridge PhD dissertation fragment, 1990

Forget Derrida

There's been a lot of talk in critical circles just recently about the need to return to history. One way of looking at this is to say that there's been a change in the kind of arcane learning or the *theory* that any self-respecting critic needs to master now to demonstrate his professional competence. A new Parisian idiolect has been imported into the English departments of Anglo-American universities and for literary critics nowadays it's time to talk less about structure, sign and play and more about power and knowledge, less about textuality and more about discourse. Or if you want to get personal, it's time to write off Jacques Derrida and sign up with Michel Foucault. History is back on the agenda.

In the chapter that follows, I shall attempt to place this return to history in context by comparing the recent historicist remodelling of Shakespeare criticism with what at first sight seems an entirely different phenomenon: the acceptance of popular culture as a legitimate object of academic study within many universities. The comparison is not fanciful – Shakespeare's plays can be considered a form of sixteenth-century popular culture, while 'Anarchy in the UK' has more or less been canonized as the *King Lear* of subcultural set texts. Nor is it accidental. I shall go on to demonstrate how each discipline – Shakespeare criticism and media studies, the conceptualization of early modern and postmodern culture – mirrors the other in terms of the formally identical ideological debates they have produced. This in turn will lead me to speculate on an alternative periodization of the modern episteme, one that impinges on the whole vexed issue of postmodernism from a historical rather than – as is usually the case – an aesthetic angle.

A new slogan: proto-modernism

For the last ten years, Derrida's interpretive ethic of deconstruction has been seized on by the English departments of many big Anglo-American universities (especially Yale) as a handy new tool kit for de-engineering the set texts of the Eng Lit canon. It made a striking contribution to the critical overhaul of Romantic poetry and also helped reinvent the Victorian novel. But one area it never really got to grips with was the study of Shakespeare and Renaissance drama. So that when deconstruction fell from favour, criticized as a blinkered exercise in neo-formalism, the return of New Criticism in fashionable guise, and Foucault's theories of discursive formation began to excite interest, Renaissance drama immediately seemed to be the obvious field where they might be profitably applied. Given that Shakespeare's plays were originally constructed not as poetic texts but as dramatic performances, cultural artefacts, 'discourses' staged at court as well as at the public playhouse, Foucault slotted right into historical context here in a way Derrida never did.[1] Plus, it was felt in some quarters – particularly among ambitious young American scholars – to be Shakespeare's turn to acquire a difficult new theoretical language, to refashion itself as a specialist discipline. This was one area of the canon that had remained underdeveloped for too long.

As a result, the critical methodology of Shakespeare criticism has been completely overhauled in the last five or six years. *King Lear* or *Measure for Measure* are no longer considered as hermetically sealed texts that when unwrapped provide an uncomplicated view of E.M.W. Tillyard's *Elizabethan World Picture*.[2] Nor are they treated as silhouetted figures that can be read off against the ground of a Political Unconscious in the manner suggested by the Marxist critic, Fredric Jameson.[3] Foucault's key message for a new wave of Shakespeare critics – chief among them, Stephen Greenblatt – is that literature and history, like politics and culture, are mutually determining. The history of early modern England is constructed by a complex bundle of discourses: state portraits, etiquette manuals, parliamentary speeches, petitions, sermons, proclamations, popular pastimes, everyday customs. And similarly literature, from the sonnet or the court masque to the publicly performed stage play, is defined as a set of cultural artefacts that don't just mediate imaginary ideological relations but perform real cultural labour. The new Shakespeare scholars have responded to Foucault's message by producing a brand of criticism – labelled 'cultural poetics' by Greenblatt – that puts the history back into literature and the poetry back into politics.

As critical fads go, this one has been an immense success, if only in publishing terms. Ever since the appearance in 1985 of *Political Shakespeare* – the trail-blazing volume of essays edited by Jonathan Dollimore and Alan Sinfield with its aggressively unapologetic title matching its iconoclastic contents – the number of books published on this newly conceived Shakespeare has almost threatened to burn a hole in the university presses. The common critical imperative is that the plays demand to be placed in context alongside other publicly performed cultural events if their historical significance is to be fully evaluated. The result is a refreshing change from most conventional interpretations of Shakespeare. Popular pastimes like bear-baiting and the carnival or official pageants like the Lord Mayor's Show and the public execution are as likely to get a look-in as line-by-line readings of the soliloquies in any analysis of the plays.

Although cultural poetics of this sort has been significantly influenced by structural anthropology, especially that of Clifford Geertz, and by the *Annales* school of French historiography, it is nevertheless Foucault who remains the presiding theoretical figure – specifically the Foucault of the seventies, with his interest in discursive regimes of power and knowledge, sexuality and subjectivity. *Discipline and Punish* has been the text of his most frequently quoted, with the 'spectacle of the scaffold' and its ceremonial phrasing of royal power a particularly resonant emblem. The correspondence between this 'theatre of terror', with its ritual brandings and amputations, and the theatre of cruelty that was often the Renaissance stage is striking. Not only were they both concerned with the staging of atrocity, they were both great crowd pleasers, popular entertainments, and the theatres and scaffolds of early modern London were often located in the same recreational areas of the city – like the 'Liberties', that region on the margins of the city that was beyond the jurisdiction of the city fathers.

According to Foucault, public executions were just as much political as they were 'juridical' events; the symbolic torturing of the condemned man was just as much an expression of royal authority as a criminal proof.[4] This immediately leads to the parallel idea that the plays of Shakespeare and his contemporaries were not isolated cultural episodes but political events, discourses that intersected in some way with the public pageantry of royal power. But in what way exactly? The populace of early seventeenth-century London were not only eager to turn up to the free show that was a public execution, they were *required* to. Their physical attendance was necessary for the cultural legitimation of a political ceremony. In the same way that they were obliged to form an admiring audience for the royal entry, that procession of the sovereign through the streets of the city prior to his coronation, so they were also expected to perform 'scaffold service', as Foucault puts it, for their sovereign at Tyburn. What was the exact political status, then, of that other site of popular assembly that dramatized the chronicles of kings and traitors? What was the political significance of the Elizabethan stage?

This is the question asked, in one form or another, by most of the contributors to *Political Shakespeare*. But what's immediately apparent, despite the common interest in cultural poetics, is how the various responses to it polarize quite readily into two groups situated on either shore of the Atlantic. On the American side is what has been labelled – perhaps 'marketed as' is a better term – the New Historicism. It has as its main champion Stephen Greenblatt, who is represented here by his highly influential, even notorious, essay, 'Invisible Bullets'.[5] On the British side is the movement that takes its name from the volume's subtitle: Cultural Materialism. Its most visible proponent is one of the book's editors, Jonathan Dollimore, a critic probably better known for his earlier work, *Radical Tragedy*.[6]

The New Historicists and the Cultural Materialists agree that Shakespeare is political. What they disagree on is the exact nature of his political significance. For the Cultural Materialists

Renaissance drama is a form of popular culture subversive in its intention and oppositional in its effect, while for the New Historicists it is instead a form of licensed misrule ultimately benefiting the exercise of royal power. The Cultural Materialists position Shakespeare vertically along the axis of class struggle, with the plays treated as material forces of cultural change, discourses contributing to the decline of the aristocracy and the rise of the gentry. The New Historicists, by contrast, situate the plays horizontally along the axis of a triumphant absolutism, with stagecraft ultimately nothing more than a disguised form of statecraft.

The differences between Dollimore and Greenblatt are exemplary in this respect. In his introduction to *Political Shakespeare*, Dollimore gives an example of what he means by radical tragedy: the staging of *Richard II* – probably Shakespeare's – in advance of the Essex rebellion of 1601. The climax of the play is the enforced deposition of Richard, a pageantry of royal abdication that had been censored by the Master of the Revels in earlier quartos precisely because Elizabeth viewed it as a challenge to royal authority (the Lord Chamberlain's company had to be bribed by the conspirators to perform it).

After the rebellion was successfully put down, the queen was moved to complain that 'this tragedy was played forty times in open streets and houses'.[7] As far as Dollimore is concerned, Elizabeth's outrage is triggered less by the frequency than by the *location* of these performances. The conventional imagery of royal authority had been paraded in the 'open streets' as an emblem of *vanitas*, of the evanescence of temporal power, rather than as the sign of a triumphant absolutism. The deposition of Richard had been staged as an inverted royal entry, a 'woeful pageant' working to demystify rather than legitimate the sacred signifiers of dynastic succession – what Foucault calls 'the symbolics of blood'.

Dollimore's larger argument in *Radical Tragedy* is that the Elizabethan theatre was in its material structure an 'adversary theatre' opposed to the prevailing institutions of Church and State. The key genre was revenge tragedy, the key dramatic figure the malcontent – stereotypically a resentful and manipulative character whose studied artlessness and fatal charm embodied the larger theatrical challenge to the ideologies of Tudor absolutism, particularly the ideologies of providence and 'Christian essentialism'. And if the message was subversive, the method was proto-Brechtian. Dollimore demonstrates convincingly how much Brecht's theories of estrangement and disalienation were influenced by the Elizabethan stage, and goes on to show how revenge tragedy as a genre was habitually structured by the foregrounding of social contradiction and the exposure of formal device.

Dollimore is pushing a Marxist line here – Elizabethan theatre as a cultural arena that plays the rise of the gentry off against the decline of the aristocracy – but he doesn't neglect his Foucault. Thus the malcontent is not some kind of existential rebel glorying in the individuality of his selfhood, but a theatrically constructed persona, both agent and victim of social corruption. He is 'the bearer of a subjectivity which is not the antithesis of social process but its focus'.[8] In plays like *The Revenger's Tragedy* or *The Atheist's Tragedy*, by Cyril Tourneur, subjectivity is traversed by discourses of sexuality and power, is foregrounded as a site of productive contradiction – hence the theatrical frequency of disguise, game, intrigue. The malcontent self-consciously parades himself, he simulates a self that becomes elusive, fragmented, discontinuous, impossible to essentialize.

The flipside to this process, of course, is that the social order itself is exposed as no more than an artificial construct, an effect of discourse. The malcontent subverts the legitimacy of power by self-consciously usurping it. His cynicism demonstrates that the solemn rituals of the state are no more than engineered pieces of theatre designed to pay off a legitimation deficit. And although the malcontent is duly found out, condemned and punished in the final act, the restored social order which takes it upon itself to judge him has already been bankrupted ideologically. Thus in *The Atheist's Tragedy*, the usurper D'Amville is defeated at the moment of his ceremonial triumph not by providence or the forces of legitimacy but by formal necessity. As he wields the axe that will dispatch the only remaining rival to his power, he suddenly loses his grip ('In lifting up the axe I think h'as knocked his brains out'). Cue the victory of the forces of good.

In sum, according to Dollimore, the revenge play's subversion consists of 'the inscribing of a subversive discourse within an orthodox one'[9] – a process that he elsewhere calls 'transgressive reinscription'.[10] This is a persuasive analysis of the cultural effects of the Elizabethan stage. It's possible to quibble over the details, but the central point about the adversary nature of the theatre as a cultural institution, or discourse, remains a strong one.

Greenblatt's argument in 'Invisible Bullets' is entirely the opposite. For him, the Elizabethan theatre was not adversary but co-optive, a manifestation of 'the process whereby subversive insights are generated in the midst of apparently orthodox texts and simultaneously contained by those texts'.[11] Resistance, in other words, always serves the interests of power. Greenblatt is here using Foucault against Marx. For him, the class struggle is a myth, an illusory effect of discourse, an ideological fiction rehearsed by the state theatre of power.

Greenblatt uses Foucault, just as Dollimore does, yet he comes to a completely opposite conclusion. This initially surprising fact becomes less perplexing when it is remembered that there are two different models of power, and hence of discourse, at work in *Discipline and Punish*.[12] Dollimore seems to base his idea of adversary theatre upon Foucault's interpretation of the public execution and its attendant discourses, while Greenblatt's notion of co-optive theatre seems to take its cue from Foucault's theorization of the prison.

For Foucault, the invisible 'disciplines' of the prison displaced the public execution as means of regulating 'popular illegality', precisely because of the inefficiency, the vulnerability to popular challenge, of the spectacular theatre of terror. Although the people were required to perform scaffold service for their monarch, this always carried the built-in danger of carnivalesque inversion and revolt. The act of extreme violence licensed at the scaffold could often flip over into its saturnalian opposite, where the executioner, the king's champion, would be mocked by the crowd and the condemned man cheered. Indeed, sometimes the condemned might be snatched from the hands of the executioner at the last minute.[13]

In calling up the solidarity of the people to legitimize the ceremonial staging of his power, the monarch thus risked his own humiliation. The economy of power pursued by the public execution was discontinuous, often issuing in 'disturbances around the scaffold'. And in the same way, the discourses of confession and repentance produced by the event, the stereotypical 'gallows speeches' circulated to the larger population in broadsheets and pamphlets, were also equivocal. The strong possibility that they were often apocryphal, or prepared for the condemned in advance of the execution, is not the point. What is significant is that they were 'two-sided discourses'. Intended to authenticate crime and legitimize punishment, they often had the opposite effect – crime was glorified, punishment shrugged off. What was supposed to be an official example became instead a popular festival.[14]

Gallows literature, particularly the 'last words of a condemned man' genre, was one point at which official ideology and popular culture intersected, becoming 'a sort of battleground around the crime, its punishment and its memory'.[15] This zero-sum analytic of power might seem to offer a plausible theoretical model for the functioning of Dollimore's adversary theatre, until it is remembered that its class dividends accrue not to some hypostatized mass – the people – but to that nascent bourgeoisie, the gentry. As Frank Lentricchia points out in his lucid critique of *Discipline and Punish*, 'Michel Foucault's Fantasy for Humanists', the 'saturnalian ritual' of the scaffold may momentarily license popular revolt, but it ultimately invokes a bourgeois backlash which, under the hypocritical banner of humanist 'reform', substitutes the disciplinary for the spectacular, rewrites the literature of crime as fine art along the way, and exorcizes the spectre of collective insurrection much more efficiently than any princely pageant ever could.[16] The adversary theatre of the Jacobean period is very much the anticipation of this pre-emptive bid for power – an examination rather than a mirror of the public execution.

Having said that, Dollimore's celebration of the critical edge of Jacobean drama does tend to float free of any explicit theorization of class. Everything has to be inferred from a few cursory references to Lawrence Stone, the celebrated historian who tied the causes of the English Revolution to the early seventeenth-century crisis of the aristocracy and rise of the gentry.[17] Furthermore, he does tend to downplay the Foucauldian sense of discursive struggle in his actual readings of the plays. Thus, the subversive discourses at work in *The Revenger's Tragedy* or *The Atheist's Tragedy* are untroubled by the orthodox discourses within which they are inscribed – they are intended authorial messages waiting to be decoded by an informed audience. Orthodoxy, in these terms, is not a competing frame of reference, an interruptive force, but the transparent alibi of subversion. For Greenblatt, it's the other way round – subversion as the alibi of orthodoxy. Plays like *King Lear* and *Measure for Measure* are 'centrally and repeatedly concerned with the production and containment of subversion and disorder'.[18] Their theatricality is not set over against the operation of state power but is the central mechanism of absolutism – it is of a piece with the theatricality of the royal entry and the public execution. He isolates three devices that define this theatre of power – testing, recording, explaining – and goes on to specify the way they work in *Henry IV*, Part I. Thus, in his soliloquy at the end of the first tavern scene, Hal *explains* to the audience that when he embraces the role of rake, of drunkard, this is not an act of moral corruption but the scheme of a larger political redemption, a preparation for his later role as king. When he carouses with Falstaff and his cronies, he is operating as a double-agent in enemy territory, *recording* the glossary of the tavern in order to discipline its carnivalesque energy. Hal continually risks exposing himself to the audience as a spy and a fraud, but then his willingness to take this risk is the source of his attraction. The play as a whole *tests* the subversive hypothesis that royal power begins in force and deception precisely as a means of celebrating princely glory.

This whole theory of containment would be halfway plausible if only it weren't so muddled. Greenblatt insists that the Elizabethan stage and the public execution are similar in effect because both are theatrical episodes, but then goes on to describe a finely calibrated dynamic of theatrical power – testing, recording, explaining – that has little to do with the portentous atrocities of the scaffold. The public execution and the Elizabethan stage play plainly belong to different economies of power

– something implicitly recognized by Greenblatt in a later essay, 'Shakespeare and the Exorcists', where he distinguishes the complicit involvement of 'theatre' from the unquestioning assent demanded by 'ritual'.[19]

This is a useful distinction and one that corresponds quite nicely with Foucault's own in *Discipline and Punish* between the spectacular power of the scaffold and the disciplinary power of the prison that superseded it. In fact, Greenblatt seems to model his whole problematic of the theatrical on the imaginary but nevertheless real network of power relations that, according to Foucault, sustained the functioning not only of the prison but also of the school, the army barracks, the workshop and the hospital as they emerged in the early seventeenth century. At work here was an immanent 'micro-physics of power' – invisible where the spectacle of the scaffold was all-too visible, evenly distributed where it was discontinuous, imaginary where it was symbolic.

A new 'political technology of the body' came into effect, no longer concerned with the ritual marking of the body of the condemned so much as with the punitive correction of the body of the 'delinquent'. Techniques like the examination, the case history and the timetable appeared, devices whose surface obsession with the minutely individuated organization of knowledge didn't mean that they weren't at the same time unavoidably implicated with the secret diffusion of a whole nexus of power relays. Quite the opposite: institutional knowledge of the delinquent was the measure of his subjection. Disciplinary society was continuously sustained by the hidden operation of 'power-knowledge relations' – their defining language that of the social sciences, their day-to-day mechanics that of Bentham's Panopticon. Surveillance, partitioning, normalization: these became the order of the day.

Power, according to this analysis, is no longer repressive but productive; it 'produces domains of objects and rituals of truth'.[20] So far, so plausible. It's when Foucault leaves the minute particulars of history behind and begins to generalize about how power is 'not possessed as a thing, or transferred as a property' but 'functions like a piece of machinery' that he veers dangerously close to formalism.[21] Lentricchia goes further, arguing that at such moments 'power tends to occupy the "anonymous" place that classical treatises in metaphysics reserved for substance: without location, identity, or boundaries, it is everywhere and nowhere at the same time'.[22]

This is nowhere more the case than in Foucault's elaboration of the 'analytics of power' in the introductory volume to *The History of Sexuality*. Here, the existence of power 'depends on a multiplicity of points of resistance', which 'play the role of adversary, target, support or handle in power relations'.[23] Power can't make an appearance, in other words, until called up by some kind of resistance. But then again, conversely, resistance can only take shape against the operation of power. This is a model of power that is entirely relational and not a little mythical. Power and resistance form a proportionate couple – as power intensifies, so does resistance; as resistance dissolves, so does power. It's certainly in marked contrast to the catastrophic or absolute model of power that characterizes the scaffold, where the victory of power depends upon the elimination of resistance and vice versa. The two-sided discourse of the gallows speech has been superseded by something more nebulous: the 'tactical polyvalence of discourses', as Foucault puts it.

It's this mythical analytics of power that Greenblatt picks up on in his interpretation of Elizabethan theatre. Even then, he misappropriates it by eliminating Foucault's insistence on the mutually determining relationship between power and resistance. What he comes to theorize in the end is a totalitarian model of power. Dollimore, in order to push his argument in favour of subversion, may tend to flatten the sense of struggle in Foucault's theory of discursive formation; Greenblatt, in order to argue the opposite, makes a virtue out of steamrollering it completely. He concedes that plays like *King Lear* and *Measure for Measure* are indeed subversive, but their subversiveness is 'not the negative limit but the positive condition' of power.[24] Resistance produces power, whereas power contains resistance; power needs resistance in order to make an appearance, but it is never threatened by it, it always contains it. This is as much to say that power manufactures resistance in order to give itself an excuse to function, whereas for Foucault, as Dollimore observes in his essay 'Subjectivity, Sexuality and Transgression',[25] containment is as potentially productive as resistance.

The implication of Greenblatt's argument shorn of its metaphysical gloss is that Shakespearean drama was a proto-modern cultural event, an anticipation of the disciplinary mechanisms that, according to Foucault, would reach their most extreme point of social colonization in the eighteenth and nineteenth centuries. This is a fully plausible theory and one not logically incompatible with Dollimore's larger argument in favour of subversion. In fact, this point of contact between Dollimore and Greenblatt offers a promising point of departure for a new conceptualization of the Elizabethan stage – one that retains its radical politics while articulating its hybrid status as both theatrical and ritual event, site of surveillance and also of spectacle. So far, however, only one of the New Historicists, Steven Mullaney, has been willing to explore this line of argument. In his book *The Place of the Stage* he suggests that the theatre did indeed function as a site for the development of new disciplinary technologies, or 'incorporative' powers as he calls them, but that these operated not as a supplement to the faltering spectacular economy of the scaffold but as a mobilization of nascent bourgeois resentment against sovereign power.[26]

So although Greenblatt lays out the ground plan for a more complex consideration of the theatre than does Dollimore, his central argument in favour of containment is implausible. The test case for his theory is provided by the plays of Christopher Marlowe. Figures like Tamburlaine or Faustus deliberately set out to transgress the political and religious sanctions of Tudor absolutism. What effect do they have? For Dollimore, the Marlovian rebel 'focuses the inherent contingency of, and potential contradictions within, power'.[27] But for Greenblatt, as he makes clear in his book *Renaissance Self-Fashioning*, Tamburlaine and Faustus remain embedded within Renaissance orthodoxy – 'they simply reverse the paradigms and embrace what the society brands as evil', and in so doing 'they imagine themselves in diametrical opposition to their society, when in fact they have unwittingly accepted its crucial structural elements'.[28]

Power, according to Greenblatt, envelopes everyone within its operation, even, or rather most especially, the rebels and the blasphemers. The only intimation of release from its embrace is in the end provided not by transgression but by 'a peculiarly intense submission whose downright violence undermines everything it was meant to shore up'.[29] The truly rebellious figure for Greenblatt is not Tamburlaine or Faustus but Desdemona. She protests her innocence of the crime of adultery even as she surrenders to the smothering embrace of Othello in the marital bed; she even revives sufficiently to be able to clear her husband of his crime by claiming that she has killed herself. All very noble, but hardly something that's going to shake the foundations of society.[30]

Young upwardly mobile literary critics

The Cultural Materialists and the New Historicists offer two models of power, of discourse, which, in order to be more fully understood, must be set into context. It is no accident that the Cultural Materialist interpretation of Shakespeare as a radical dramatist should have taken hold in Britain, while the opposing New Historicist view of him as a compromised figure should be specifically American. Although, as stated earlier, Shakespeare criticism has reinvented itself as an academic discipline over the last few years, it has done so for very different motives depending on which side of the Atlantic it has been pursued. If the central tenet of both the Cultural Materialists and the New Historicists is that Shakespeare's plays must be considered as historical discourses that don't merely reflect but actively intervene in the formation of culture, then the logical conclusion to be drawn is that criticism itself is a discourse in the same way. It has real cultural effects, whether intended or not. Furthermore, if the methodology of 'cultural poetics' insists that literature is a discourse like any other – like folk tales, private diaries or royal proclamations, for example – then this immediately throws into question the singularity of literary criticism. What is so special about literature as opposed to any other discourse? Why should its study require a discipline all to itself? The critic who begins by expanding the dominion of his discipline soon ends up in danger of writing himself out of a job.

None of the new Shakespeare critics are quite willing to go that far, but the Cultural Materialists habitually theorize their critical practice in ways that the New Historicists do not. Take Graham Holderness. In a series of books, most significantly *Shakespeare's History*, he has attempted to contest the 'ideological reproduction' of Shakespeare as a reactionary force in British national culture. He tackles head-on the 'inherited myth' of Shakespeare – 'its long history of assimilation into the apparatus of culture, its incorporation into received traditions of the "canon" of literature, its implementation in systems and structures of education'.[31] For him, the historically determined perception of Shakespeare as a radical dramatist is simultaneous with a more contemporary struggle to subvert his received image as transcendent national bard. Shakespeare criticism becomes in its most acute form a cultural rescue mission, a way of making the plays respond not only to past but also to present political struggles. Cultural Materialism as a discourse intends 'to recover the literary text, not as a self-contained repository of meaning, but as a specified arena in which particular struggles for meaning ... once took place, and can therefore be taken up again'.[32]

The New Historicists have no such larger political ambitions.[33] The main reason for this is that Shakespeare doesn't exist in the States, as it does in Britain, as an oppressive national monument waiting to be toppled or undermined, but is instead diffused across a more heterogeneous cultural scene. An American degree in English Literature can be gained without ever having to look at a Shakespeare play and for most Americans the bust of Shakespeare so familiar to the tourists of Stratford-upon-Avon as a national icon is probably better known as the prop Adam West manipulates to get to the Batcave.

As Don E. Wayne points out in a recent overview of New Historicist and Cultural Materialist criticism, if any Shakespeare 'myth' can be identified in the States, then it is more properly liberal rather than conservative in its inflection. Although the Arnoldian heritage of literature as repository of moral values is common to both countries, in Britain it has trickled down through the cultural elitism of a reactionary figure like F.R. Leavis, while in the immigrant culture of the United States it has instead been interpreted, via Lionel Trilling, as a forum for assimilation and even empowerment.[34]

As a consequence, the political reappropriation of Shakespeare in the States is problematic in a way that it isn't in Britain. For the Cultural Materialists, reacting against critical orthodoxy and recovering a historically subversive Shakespeare are both part of the same political project. It's possible to be fashionable and progressive at the same time. For the New Historicists however, this is a contradictory imperative. The reaction against critical orthodoxy that fashion demands can only distinguish itself by coming up with a radically totalitarian Shakespeare – a political move that chimes uncomfortably with the neo-conservative reaction against the thirties' New Deal in the wider political scene. For the New Historicists to theorize their professional practice would thus involve the tabling of a number of potentially troubling political questions.[35] How far is their undermining of institutional authority within the academy itself recaptured by more dispersed cultural trends? Aren't they the victims of their own theory of containment? Even if they aren't, isn't their obsession with the mechanics of power in England four hundred years ago a way of avoiding the question of how power operates in America today?

At stake here is the whole often ignored issue of professional careerism within American and British universities. The Cultural Materialists and New Historicists represent a new wave of scholars eager to roll back the frontiers of academic tradition in order to make a reputation for themselves. It is entirely logical for the Cultural Materialists to hitch their professional fortunes to a progressive political project, given the attacks on tenure and cuts in funding pressed by the Thatcher government on the British universities (especially in the humanities departments). But in the States, the study of English literature is a much more secure and better rewarded profession. Name critics are traded between the universities as if they were football stars seeking to maximize their earning potential before they burn out. What then is the exact motivation for the radical challenge to academic tradition that has been mounted by the New Historicists?

This is the question posed by Wayne, who observes that for the last ten years 'we have been in a professional environment characterized by ever more sophisticated debunking of an earlier cultural tradition', where 'the content of much of this critical debate (by which I mean something like its *motive*) often remains obscure'.[36] He links this process to the 'assertiveness of the generation of the 1960s' – which is undoubtedly true, but only tells half the story. Elsewhere in America, in law, in banking, in the sunrise industries, the radical assertiveness of the *Easy Rider* generation has transformed itself into the radical careerism of the *Big Chill* generation. It's a process that the universities haven't been immune to. Literary criticism is increasingly becoming, quite literally, a culture industry that every few years or so needs to redesign its basic product – the Eng Lit canon – with the aid of some fancy new French stylings. The latest new theory is imported from Paris, gravely inspected and perhaps tinkered with, before finally being put to work producing fashionable new readings of all the set texts. Scholarship, like anything else in the States, is becoming commodified. It increasingly takes its cue not from the disinterested pursuit of knowledge – that old myth – but from the capture of a market defined by all the bright and shiny new periodicals where it's possible to put down a career marker. To be a respected scholar nowadays is to be a dedicated follower of fashion.

The last subcult: postmodernism

Is this too cynical an interpretation? Perhaps it simply carries the wrong emphasis. Perhaps 'fashion' is too prejudiced a notion, too loaded with suggestions of fickleness and venality, to describe accurately the way in which critical practice is commodified. The Australian critic Meaghan Morris has offered an alternative to it with the Japanese concept of cultural 'boom'. To characterize a form of criticism as fashionable suggests that real, dependable scholarship is still taking place elsewhere and will gain its recognition in due course. To talk about a boom suggests instead the ways in which academic activity is determined and directed by the market. It 'admits greater frankness in discussion about the politics of intellectual work as it relates to, and moves in and out of, commodity circulation'.[37] Meaghan Morris draws this distinction between fashion and boom in an essay, 'Banality in Cultural Studies', which intersects in interesting and significant ways with Don E. Wayne's own essay and opens up the politics of Shakespeare criticism to the larger cultural questions defined by the contemporary postmodern debate. Morris fashions an argument around childhood memories of watching *I Love Lucy* in Sydney by drawing on an opposition between two radically different approaches to the conceptualization of popular culture. On the one side is what John Fiske has championed as 'British Cultural Studies', an emancipatory interpretation of popular practices largely derived from the seventies work of Stuart Hall and the University of Birmingham Centre for Contemporary Cultural Studies (BCCCS) on youth subcultures like mod and punk.[38] On the other side is the ecstatic prophet of doom Jean Baudrillard. The most notorious poststructuralist theorist to emerge from Paris since Derrida, he takes a much more nihilistic line on things, insisting that subcultural styles are always recuperated as commodities, as signs or, more specifically, as both simultaneously – as 'commodity-signs'. For him, patterns of consumption have no political significance beyond providing new input for the media.

Cultural Studies – or Pop Theory as it might more profitably be described – is at the moment, going back to Morris, enjoying its own boom in Britain, especially in the polytechnics and trendier redbrick universities. If the new rallying cry in the humanities departments is to abandon formalism and get back to history, then the talk in the Cultural Studies seminars is of pensioning off literature altogether in order to catch up with what's happening outside on the street. Meanwhile Baudrillard has carved out a fashionable subcultural niche for himself by cleaving ambiguously to the twists and turns of the media and jettisoning not only literature, not only history, but even reality itself in the process. His theorization of the 'hyperreal', developed in a series of books during the late seventies that have only been translated in the eighties, has found a particularly receptive intellectual audience in the instant-history environments of Canada and Australia, and has also set the theoretical agenda for some of the more successful 'simulation' artists of New York.[39]

All of which makes him the perfect academic folk-devil for the Pop Theorists. Baudrillard and a critic like Fiske may agree on the main idea of postmodernism: the erosion of boundaries between modernism and the media, the museum and the culture industry. They may even both latch on to television as the focus of this fragmented cultural scene. But where they differ is in their opposed angles of approach. For Fiske, TV shows like *Magnum, P.I.* or music videos like Madonna's 'Material Girl' are actively appropriated and transformed by their users into something politically charged and potentially subversive, whereas for Baudrillard, conversely, the active participation of the viewer is something solicited by TV – indirectly with the semiotic puzzle of some of its ads, more explicitly with its phone-in polls and charity telethons – in order to maintain the fiction of an independent reality against which it can articulate itself. Fiske translates mass culture – as marketed by the advertising agencies and the media – into pop culture – as appropriated and enjoyed by the consumer – and then situates it along a vertical axis of ideological struggle that takes in not only the Marxist category of class but also other signs of division like race and gender. Baudrillard collapses the distinction between mass culture and pop culture into a media feedback loop whose totalitarian sweep makes questions of class or ideology irrelevant, almost quaint.

Sounds familiar? It's uncanny how this opposition between Cultural Studies and Baudrillard seems to duplicate the contours of debate between the Cultural Materialists and the New Historicists. Fiske quotes the Italian Marxist Antonio Gramsci rather than Foucault, but nevertheless manages to come up with a theorization of popular culture remarkably similar to Dollimore's own conceptualization of Elizabethan theatre. Just as Foucault's theories of discourse permit Dollimore to characterize *The Revenger's Tragedy* as an example of adversary theatre, so Gramsci's notion of 'hegemony' allows Fiske to consider television as a potentially subversive popular practice. The similarity between hegemony and discourse has even been commented on by another Pop Theorist, Iain Chambers, although he frames the comparison in an unhelpful direction.[40]

Hegemony has become an important touchstone for Pop Theorists on the Left ever since the translation of Gramsci's *Prison Notebooks* in the seventies[41] – the same time indeed that a lot of Foucault's own ideas began to gain currency. According to Gramsci, hegemony refers to the way in which 'dominant' ideologies are mediated through popular culture as well as through the institutions and discourses of everyday life – the home, the church, the school, the workplace, the political party and trade union – in order to win the consent of the 'subordinate' classes. Hegemony refers to a diffused cultural process whose ideological aim is to negotiate a stable political settlement that at the end of the day leaves the subordinate classes relatively content with their lot.

But just because this is the aim, it doesn't mean that it is necessarily achieved. Hegemony cuts both ways; it 'posits a constant contradiction between ideology and the social experience of the subordinate that makes this interface into an inevitable site of ideological struggle'.[42] Like Foucault's double-edged literature of the scaffold, popular culture considered as a hegemonic force is something that's up for grabs. Cultural Studies habitually latches on to the discourses of television, genre fiction, Hollywood cinema, comic-books, fashion magazines and pop music in order to demonstrate how their normalizing power can flip over into its opposite: the celebration of aberrancy, the rejection of imposed stereotypes. Hegemony is not a fixed power relation, but operates, again like Foucault's gallows speeches, according to a zero-sum model of power. The more the products of the culture industry are reappropriated by consumers for their own ends, the less effective they are at performing their ideological task; the more resistance increases, the more power loses its grip. What this all adds up to in the end is a politics of consumption, an enabling theory of pleasure.

The new bad guys, according to this scenario, are no longer the corporate cabals of old, but the unreconstructed Marxists of the Frankfurt School, like Theodor Adorno and Herbert Marcuse. Because they suppose that the culture industry is always able to manipulate the masses into a state of false consciousness, they can't see popular culture as anything other than a vast international capitalist conspiracy: the System, the Combine. But for the Pop Theorists, consumers are not 'cultural dupes', in Stuart Hall's phrase, but active users and abusers of pop culture. They remotivate the imagery of the culture industry, prise it free from its original ideological context and reinvest it with their own dreams and fantasies.[43]

Take *Magnum, P.I.* Its hegemonic aim is obvious – to put over the ideologies of authoritarianism, individualism, and masculinity by persuading the viewer to identify with Tom Selleck's macho clone. A classic Frankfurt School-style critique would see this as reason enough to slam it, end of story. But for Fiske, identification is never complete and viewers will 'negotiate' their own reading of the show. Hormonal suburban teenagers might interpret Magnum as a vigilante who doesn't mind stepping on the toes of the law to secure justice; bleary eyed corporate Joes might console themselves with the thought that Magnum would be nowhere without the solid professionalism of his back-up team; bored housewives might use his refusal to get close to any woman as an invitation to recast him as a prop in their daytime sexual fantasies. Take into account the politics of pleasure, in other words, and suddenly *Magnum, P.I.* ends up as a show that is variously anti-authoritarian, anti-individualist and post-feminist – and possibly all three at once.

A neat theoretical trick, but this is literally bargain-basement Marxism. Fiske is obviously correct to insist that the consumer, no cultural dupe, is an active and critical user of mass culture. His mistake is to assume that this transformation of mass into popular culture is by definition radical or subversive – the right-on vision of 'cultural democracy' he conjures is in the end too good to be true. The template for the kinds of resistant practices he has in mind was originally hammered out by Dick Hebdige in his semiotic analysis of British youth subcults – the mods and their fetishistic customization of production-line scooters like the Vespa and the Lambretta; the punks and their provocative appropriation of safety pins and bin liners, conventional signs of refuse, waste and unemployability.[44] But once what's true for a subculture becomes simultaneously true for mass culture as a whole, then the possibility of radical aberrancy is lost. As the pop pundit Jon Savage observes in his essay, 'The Enemy Within: Sex, Rock and Identity', it is now clear that 'the sensibility and success of commercial youth culture were harbingers of the economic and cultural state described as postmodernist; the psychic states that were once the province of deviants or marginals are now at the heart of the Western consumer machine'.[45] The logic of Fiske's argument is ultimately self-defeating. If everything in the culture mart is subversive, then nothing is. Each consumer becomes a subculture of one, in which case they might as well remain a cultural dupe. What's the difference?

A brief consideration of the situationist heritage in the art world will perhaps help clarify the blind spot in Fiske's argument – for as the art critic Hal Foster has pointed out in his essay, 'Readings in Cultural Resistance', situationism and subcultural style share exactly the same political inflection.[46] According to Class of '68 situationists like Raoul Vaneigem and Guy Debord, the way to resist the power of the media was to appropriate its language and turn it back on itself. It was the political responsibility of the artist to get out into the street and stage provocative 'situations' designed to jolt the masses from their befuddlement by the 'society of the spectacle' and so make them aware of their historic destiny. Creative play, pleasurable drift, *'detournement'* – or the customization of stereotype – this was the practice. The aim was nothing less than the 'revolution of everyday life'.[47] The trick was that not only would such situations be subversive, they would also prove so irresistible as spectacles that the media would be bound to cover them. At the end of the day, not only would the revolution be televised, but television would be its unwitting accomplice.

In the last few years, appropriation artists like Barbara Kruger, Jenny Holzer and Cindy Sherman have all picked up on this situationist manifesto, appropriating the imagery of the mass media in order to intercept the exchange of stereotype and disarm the power of the language of advertising. Kruger has pasted her feminist photo-collage texts over billboards ('You molest from afar'), while Holzer's provocative Truisms and Survival slogans have appeared on electronic notice-boards and street corners ('Abuse of power should come as no surprise'). Meanwhile, Sherman has produced a series of Film Stills and Untitled photographic self-portraits that comment on the way female sexuality is stereotyped in Hollywood and the advertising industry.

All well and good, but according to someone like Fiske, all massively beside the point. It's no longer necessary for the situationist to intervene on behalf of the masses, because the masses are already out there doing it for themselves. The consumer is nobody's cultural dupe, he or she is too busy remotivating mass-media cliché, transforming cultural stereotype and generally coming on like a card-carrying member of the Situationist International. Popular culture is by definition concerned with the refashioning of everyday life into a microrevolutionary drama. So what is so radical about appropriation art?

Then again, what is so radical about popular culture? Fiske hijacks situationism as praxis and hands it back to the consumer. But in the process he more or less dispenses with the notion of 'dominant ideology' so necessary not only to the BCCCS and the situationists but also to his own theoretical conceptualization of Gramsci. Again like Dollimore, he starts out with a theory of discursive struggle, of ideological contestation, only to flatten it out into a celebration of the perpetual and untroubled victory of the consumer or what he ends up by calling, in rather dewy-eyed fashion, 'the people'.[48] Any workable distinction between the dominant and subordinate classes has by this time collapsed, as has any strategic opposition between mass culture and pop culture. Meanwhile Fiske's original vision of a politicized cultural democracy has disintegrated into a poststructuralist riot of signs.

But for a pop theorist like Chambers this is exactly the point. He specifically invokes the poststructuralist ideas of Derrida as a way out of the ideological prison to which a Gramscian theorization of popular culture can lead. For him 'living inside the signs' means deconstructing 'the contradictory pleasures of fashion, style, television soap, video games, sport, shopping, reading, drinking, sexuality'.[49] Drifting playfully or 'distractedly' with the signs is precisely the way in which they can be fractured, disrupted and a measure of resistance retrieved. Or, in other words, carry on consuming and as long as you've read your Derrida then your political credibility takes care of itself. What a break! As Meaghan Morris has rather cruelly observed,

Chambers is here reduced to acting out the role of the *'white male theorist* as bimbo'.[50]

Baudrillard's argument is, thankfully, entirely the opposite. For him, to deconstruct the signs in this way is to play the media game according to its own rules – and lose. In his 1972 essay, 'Requiem for the Media', he insists on the impossibility of any attempt to reclaim the media as a potential vehicle of emancipation.[51] He criticizes the neo-Marxist critic Hans Magnus Enzensberger for his vain hope of democratizing the media by wresting its control of ideological messages from the dominant class and restoring it to the consumer; he is also sceptical of the media pranks and 'symbolic actions' of those American situationists of the sixties, the Yippies. Both remain dependent on an obsolescent concept of ideology that has no leverage in a contentless world of proliferating media events.

The impingement of this analytic on that of Greenblatt's is striking. In the same way that he conceptualizes Elizabethan theatre as a triumph of containment, so Baudrillard theorizes the media as an exercise in recuperation. Thus the staged 'situations' of the Yippies are depoliticized the moment they infiltrate the media because 'the subversive act is no longer produced *except as a function of its reproducibility* . . . it is produced directly as a *model*, like a gesture'.[52] This is demonstrably the case: once a political act becomes a piece of television trivia, a 'model' rather than an agent of subversion, it immediately loses its impact, its original momentum. Far from sparking any larger chain reaction, it simply short-circuits, becoming just another cliché in the media lexicon of scandal. It may retain its subversive meaning but that's only because all media events are equally meaningless when you come down to it.

Enzensberger makes the same mistake. He assumes that the media can be manipulated or turned against themselves when 'it is not as vehicles of content, but in their form and very operation, that media induce a social relation'.[53] Television is literally an empty vessel, a dead screen, not an instrument of communication. It doesn't matter what ideological messages it transmits – what's significant is its structure, not its contents. For this reason, Enzensberger's attempt to map the opposition between the dominant and subordinate classes onto that between the producer (or transmitter) and the consumer (or receiver) of the media is particularly ill-conceived. For Baudrillard – as for Greenblatt – the class struggle is an irrelevant issue. Television is the site not of an ideological struggle between classes but of a cybernetic feedback loop between reversible input and output stations. Thus, Enzensberger's 'consumers' are solicited by phone-in programmes, by polls and market-research operations to 'produce' an opinion, a sign of response, which is then fed back into the media to be consumed by its 'producers'.

The media define an integrated circuit where 'reversibility' is the positive condition, not the negative limit, of their continuing successful performance. Rather than challenging the operation of the media, something like the provocative spectacles of the situationist or the subversive customizations of the subcultural consumer simply feed their appetite for the scandalous and the freakish. What starts off as a revolutionary act of appropriation or infiltration ends up by being recycled back into the media. In fact, Baudrillard goes further: it's not so much that resistance is recuperated as it is preprogrammed. The radical moment never exists, even for a fleeting instant, beyond the scope of the media regime of power; it is built into its very operation. Resistance is in the end *produced* by the media, it is prepackaged as a 'simulation'. Just like the referendum (or the stock market, for that matter), the media are a system driven by predetermined feedback, they are 'a speech that answers itself via the simulated detour of a response' and their final lesson is that 'the absolutization of speech under the formal guise of exchange is the definition of power'.[54]

The media thus operate – again like Greenblatt's theatre – according to a totalitarian model of power where subversion is only ever a 'model' and resistance a 'simulation'. What is at stake is no longer the ownership of the means of production – the Marxist fantasy – but the monopoly of the 'structural code' regulating input and output. In a system where commodities are produced as signs and signs are produced as commodities, ownership of the material hardware that manufactures these commodity-signs is no longer an issue. What is significant is the way in which they are traded as preprogrammed bits of information, the way their exchangeability is governed by an immaterial code.⁵⁵

This whole business of the 'code', or alternatively the 'structural law of value', is a big obsession for Baudrillard, his very own cybernetic metaphysic.⁵⁶ The code is what makes the electronic world go round. Its aim is indeterminate, its operating logic that of '[c]ybernetic control, generation by models, differential modulation, feedback, questionnaires'.⁵⁷ Just as the genetic code programmes the infinite replication of DNA, so the media code programmes the endless exchange of signs and commodities, of information. We're back to a familiar scenography here: the poststructuralist play of signifiers.⁵⁸ Only now it's seen from the other side. What a pop theorist like Chambers celebrates as an enabling tactic, a form of cultural empowerment, Baudrillard coolly exhibits as the latest state of play in the media game. Living inside the signs represents nothing more than a 'passion for the code'.

Baudrillard offers a more plausible analysis of the way the media works than either Chambers or Fiske. He's less than completely satisfactory when it comes to answering the Big Question: namely, is there any way at all of resisting the absolute power of the code? In more recent essays like 'In the Shadow of the Silent Majorities' and 'The Masses', he suggests that the required tactic is not appropriation or subversion, nor even deconstruction, but rather the renunciation of subjectivity, the 'practice of the object'.⁵⁹ If the power of the media depends not just upon the production of meaning but, even more crucially, upon the production of a *demand* for meaning, then the way to resist it is to refuse this demand by accepting everything and interpreting nothing, by forgetting meaning and running with 'fascination' instead. If transgression is always recuperated, then the only retaliatory gambit available may be 'hyperconformity', the attempt to outcode the code by engaging in infantilism, passivity, idiocy, total dependence⁶⁰ – all examples of 'hypersimulation reduplicating simulation and exterminating it according to its own logic'.⁶¹

Baudrillard typically associates this tactic, or rather anti-tactic, not with the semiotic self-consciousness of disenfranchised subcultures or avant-garde artists but with the untutored idiocy of the masses, of the 'silent majority'. Unlike Fiske's radical consumers, the masses refuse to decode or redirect the images of the media, they refuse to produce signs of deviancy or of protest that the media can consume in its turn. Instead they take everything the media can throw at them straight. Like a black hole – to use Baudrillard's favoured astronomical metaphor – they are quite literally all-consuming: 'You want us to consume – O.K., let's consume, always more, and anything whatsoever; for any useless and absurd purpose.'[62]

Again there's an uncanny echo of Greenblatt here. What Desdemona is for him, the silent majority is for Baudrillard. Hyperconformity is not so much an act of surrender as a 'victorious challenge'. It challenges the media to keep things coming, to up the ante, to simulate ever more absurd and shocking spectacles. The masses play on the media's hope of retrieving some kind of genuine, non-simulated response from them, of getting something to work on. Their fatal charm seduces the media into an escalating production of degraded banalities while hoping they finally collapse from exhaustion.[63] Meanwhile the media itself has to keep on raising the stakes if it wants to call the bluff of the masses[64] and in this way it becomes increasingly hysterical in its solicitations, increasingly shocking and provocative. Think of *Today*'s hung parliament billboard ads from a few years ago – prime sites devoted to giant hoardings of Margaret Thatcher and other leading British politicians each gagging on the noose. How can Barbara Kruger compete with that?

Appropriation as a subversive artistic gesture has been completely outstripped by the world of simulation. As Hal Foster observes, to expose the operation of the code 'hardly constitutes resistance, as is commonly believed: it simply means that you are a good player, a good consumer'.[65] Appropriation artists use situationist-approved tactics like shock and *detournement* to wake the masses from their alienated slump in front of the TV set, but according to Baudrillard this is now more properly the job of the admen: stimulation of the jaded consumer, provocation of the silent majority. As for Fiske's 'good' consumers – who may well indeed be skilled in all the tricks of the situationist trade as they scandalously mix'n'match meanings at the bazaar of mass culture – they are merely cultural dupes in a new postmodern, disalienated way. Perhaps they even know it too, victims of yuppie cynicism, of what Peter Sloterdijk, in another context, has labelled 'enlightened false consciousness'.[66]

But that doesn't mean that the recommendation of hyperconformity as a means of resistance isn't without problems of its own. The tactic itself is plausible; uneasiness sets in, however, when Baudrillard attempts to tie its operation to the practices of the silent majority. Having disqualified disenfranchised subcultures and avant-garde artists from contention as the standard-bearers of transgression, he seems too easily content with falling back for a substitute on that old Marxist standby: the masses. As if they still existed as some kind of historic bloc, as if they hadn't long since been broken down into a series of fragmentary marketing categories: yuppies, sloanes, dinkies, empty-nesters, casuals, woofies, etc. Baudrillard is performing a clever conjuring trick here, reviving and giving a positive spin to the 'practices of the mass ... which we bury with the disdainful terms *alienation* and *passivity*'.[67] He's turning back on itself the Frankfurt School theorization of mass culture – for the System, read the Code; for the duping of the alienated masses read the triumph of the silent majority. It's a neat piece of one-upmanship given that for someone like Fiske the Frankfurt School represents the necessary academic adversary. But that doesn't make it persuasive.

It could be argued in favour of Baudrillard's analytic that the silent majority may not exist as a material body, but that they are nevertheless real in an imaginary sense. The ghost of something long since vanished, they still – as the title of his book suggests – cast their shadow over the present cultural landscape. But that would be to ignore the implications of his set-piece text on the whole phenomenon, 'The Beaubourg-Effect: Implosion and Deterrence', where the masses supposedly triumph over the media-situationism of the Beaubourg museum precisely by the weight of their numbers, by their bodily density: 'summoned to participate, to interact, to simulate, to play with the models ... (t)hey interact and manipulate so well that they eradicate all the meaning imputed to this operation and threaten even the infrastructure of the building'.[68] Beaubourg should have disappeared the day after its opening, according to Baudrillard, 'dismantled and kidnapped by the crowd as the only possible response to the absurd challenge of the transparency and the democracy of culture'.[69] Maybe so. The only problem is it's still standing.

Hyperconformism remains a viable gambit only if associated with the calculating operator rather than the naïve mass, the kind of figure who has gone one step beyond Fiske's plugged-in consumer and knows that it's smart to be stupid, it's hip to be square. This is something obviously appreciated by the New York school of 'simulation artists' like Peter Halley and especially Haim Steinbach and Jeff Koons – all skilled players at what Hal Foster, in his essay, 'For a Concept of the Political in Contemporary Art', has called 'Baudrillard's Endgame'.[70] Halley's Day-Glo canvases, with their colour-coded lines and rectangles, their manipulation of formal geometries, attempt to suggest how the space of the cybernetic social – from the computer to the city – consists of the reproduction of one model, that of 'the cell and the conduit'. Meanwhile, the wall-mounted ready-mades of Steinbach, the glass-cased Hoovers of Koons use Baudrillard in a different way. In their post-Warholian and ironically unironic condensation, rather than displacement, of the commodity aura, they have perfected the art of hyperconformism, of dumb insolence. Koons in particular – with his recent sell-out 'Banality' show featuring porcelain statues of Michael Jackson and Bubbles – seems to have played out Baudrillard's Endgame to its reductive conclusion. Here is art as the black hole of the media cosmology of commodity-signs, fascinating in its meaninglessness, seductive in its banality; here is the artist as destructive simulator of simulation, a hypercynic more cynical than the most cynical of yuppie consumers. Koons's celebrity status as clown prince of the art world is not just the index; it's the necessary condition of his artistic achievement. It's no accident he used to be a Wall Street broker.

Theory as lifestyle accessory

Power is either a tugging and tearing of discourse, a struggle between classes, or it is an effortless containment of subversion;

popular culture is either the ideological site of resistant pleasures or a system of licensed delinquencies, a conjuring trick. The debates are identical whether generated by the study of Tudor absolutism and the plays of Shakespeare or the analysis of late capitalism and the mass media. Greenblatt plays the same kind of endgame as Baudrillard; the Pop Theorists share the same radical credentials as the Cultural Materialists. An intriguing coincidence.

What makes this duplication of arguments even more fascinating is the fact that they are politically orientated in opposite directions. The means of Baudrillard and the New Historicism, of Pop Theory and Cultural Materialism may be similar, but their ends are entirely different. Once these arguments are considered as cultural events in themselves, as discursive performances of the type characterized by Foucault, then their mutual shadowing is suddenly reversed. Baudrillard is revealed to be as institutionally challenging, as radical in his own way, as a Cultural Materialist like Graham Holderness, while the Pop Theorists, for all their talk of subversion, are open to the same charges of opportunism and myopia as the New Historicists.

The growth of Cultural Studies from its initially deprived academic status in Britain during the seventies to its more recent penetration of the American academy has been traced by Patrick Brantlinger in his book, *Crusoe's Footsteps: Cultural Studies in Britain and America*. He puts the success of this new academic package down to two things: first, the thwarted idealism of Class of '68 campus radicals, who, having failed to change the system, are now settling for changing the syllabus; and second, the increasing colonization of the universities by market forces, the demand for graduates to be educated consumers rather than masters of the liberal arts. The obvious conclusion – that this adds up to a brand of commercially successful pseudo-radicalism – is never drawn by Brantlinger, who prefers instead to view the various strands of Cultural Studies as 'authentic and progressive movements of knowledge'.[71] Nevertheless, he has sketched in a picture of compromise and careerism within the ivory towers that bears striking resemblances to Don E. Wayne's own description of how the polemical flames of the New Historicists are fanned by a repressed political guilt.

The urge to debunk received critical wisdom, which Wayne sees as the typical symptom of New Historicist bad conscience, is also a feature of Cultural Studies. In universities on both sides of the Atlantic, theoretical discourses have been mobilized in order to legitimize the study of popular culture and outface the academic establishment. As far as America is concerned, the target remains the same as it is for the New Historicists: the liberal elite for whom the word Pop is an affront to the modernist heritage. In Britain things are slightly different. The adversary is no longer Leavisite moral elitism, in the way that it is for the Cultural Materialists, but the kind of unreconstructed Marxism that still sees popular culture as the opium of the masses. In both cases Pop Theory is reacting against broadly progressive cultural formations. It therefore attempts to trump them by insisting that its object of study is more radical, more empowering than they imagine. It's a rhetorical ploy, but one that its executors are desperate to take literally. Otherwise they have no way of distinguishing their own celebration of the consumer economy, their liberal-bashing and their wilful philistinism from that of the New Right.

Like the New Historicists, the Pop Theorists refuse to theorize their own discursive practice for fear of exposing their secret dissimulations.[72] They are also unwilling to acknowledge the way in which the boom in Cultural Studies marks, as Meaghan Morris observes, 'the beginning of a move to "commodify" an appropriate theoretical style for analysing everyday life'[73] – a style that becomes a form of cultural capital not just in the universities, particularly the American ones, but also in the expanded field of the media (look at how many left-leaning academics have set up shop as independent television producers in London during the last decade). Perhaps the final irony is that this theoretical style, while celebrating the language of the popular, is itself largely impenetrable to anyone without a degree in communication science. If the Pop Theorists were really serious about the subversive dynamics of pop culture, they'd have written their various treatises in tabloid headlines. They haven't, of course, because that would jeopardize their intellectual credibility within the academy. It would make them no better than one of their beloved couch potatoes or Madonna fans when they have to believe they know something these folks don't. Otherwise why speak on their behalf?

Why indeed? This is exactly the question posed by Baudrillard's own celebration of the silent majority. If the indifference of the masses is so radical, then isn't his partisan espousal of their silence redundant at best and disabling at worst? As Lawrence Grossberg – a major player in the Pop Theory game – observes in his essay, 'Putting the Pop Back into Postmodernism', although the recommendation of inertia 'appears to place the masses at the leading edge of history, since only they already live within the simulacrum, embracing the disappearance of agency and activity, it is in reality the critic – Baudrillard – who speaks and even denies the masses the right or the desire to speak'.[74] This is a valid criticism – as argued earlier, there are big problems with Baudrillard's entire conceptualization of the masses – but it doesn't tell the whole story. It fails to acknowledge Baudrillard's consciousness of the paradoxes of his enunciative position, his insistence that theory is pursued only upon the condition that it is itself theorized – not as something supplementary to but as something built into its own operation.

It's at this point – the point of 'theoretical violence' – that Baudrillard begins to diverge from the radical conservatism of a New Historicist like Stephen Greenblatt and link up with the reactive interventionism of a Cultural Materialist like Graham Holderness. As he puts it in his 1987 essay, 'Why Theory?', it is 'not enough for theory to describe and analyse, it must itself be an event in the universe it describes'.[75] Given that this universe is one of simulation and media preprogramming, theory is obliged to risk hyperconformist idiocy if it is to escape recuperation; it must become a 'challenge to the real'. Hence Baudrillard's notorious science fictional metaphysic, his manipulation of tropes borrowed from astronomy and the genetic sciences, his provocations and evasions. All are attempts on his part to outcode the code, to defy the media to accelerate their hyperreal trajectory and overreach themselves. From this perspective, the fact that his championing of the masses is untenable precisely defines its theoretical value – it's one more challenge, another desperate gamble. The masses become his ventriloquist; he becomes their dummy.

Baudrillard is here playing a very dangerous game, his own endgame, in fact, and it's not surprising that his hyperconformism has often been mistaken for mere conformism, for a post-'68 sell-out of the New Historicist type. This is the conclusion Douglas Kellner reaches in his otherwise valuable book *Jean Baudrillard: From Marxism to Postmodernism and Beyond*. For him Baudrillard is merely another ex-Marxist who's jumped ship, a 'court jester of the society he mocks'.[76] A crude judgement. He is closer to the mark when he observes how Baudrillard's ascendant media profile during the eighties, his cult status outside the academy, his celebrity, has coincided with a transformation in the nature of his output, which has become increasingly autobiographical, fragmentary and self-pastiching, with each text 'citing previous references and the same stories ... in an attempt to drive them to the superlative, to the nth degree, to the point of simulation and parody'.[77]

This isn't the cop-out Kellner thinks it is, it's a form of 'refusal by overacceptance', a strategy Baudrillard is quite willing to concede is only made possible by a society whose means of socialization is no longer the repression but the solicitation, the simulation, of speech.[78] In that sense, he is waging the same radical campaign as a figure like Holderness, but on a completely different terrain using completely different weapons. Trapped in the real world of university funding cuts and Shakespeare-led cultural imperialism, Holderness is free to fight oppression by demanding difference, whereas Baudrillard, released into the hyperreal world of media-manufactured situationism and everyday outrage, is constrained to combat simulation by producing only more of the same. He's in a different universe from the Cultural Materialists – the same as the New Historicists, only on the other side, the same too as the Pop Theorists, only one step ahead – a universe in which he has become his own black hole, consuming all speculation about his motives, shedding no new light on his theories. A cynical trader in his own reputation, he transforms his texts into precious bound commodities, his theories into signs of apocalyptic wonder, setting himself up as the willing victim of his own sacrificial logic. Politically, he's got nowhere left to go.

End of an episteme

An intriguing crosshatch of correspondences between two separate academic debates has thus been established – one centring on the political function of the theatrical in the early modern period, the other on the political valency of the popular in the postmodern period. The disciplines are different, but the questions remain the same. Is it power as simulation or power as repression, discourse as one-way street or discourse as two-way mirror? Is it the class struggle as the motor or as the mirage of history? In the end, is it criticism as engagement or criticism as evasion? As I have shown earlier, these are questions that can be answered. Baudrillard is right – the leading edge of the contemporary cultural scene is characterized by the simulation of power and the recuperation of dissent – and the New Historicists are wrong – they unconsciously project this anxious vision of society back into the past. The Cultural Materialists are right – the Elizabethan theatre challenges absolutism in the name of class identity – and the Pop Theorists are wrong – they import this now obsolescent narrative of emancipation into a Baudrillardian world of preprogrammed participations.

These connections between media studies and Shakespeare criticism represent more than just a pleasing formal pattern, a fractal puzzle; they are symptoms of a larger historical crisis. They demonstrate that precipitate exchanges of cultural capital are taking place between the early seventeenth and the late twentieth century, between two very different periods of history that are nevertheless marked by the same signs of transition. The complex of power-knowledge relations that first emerged in the theatres of Tudor England under the sign of testing, recording and explaining is now receding. What was staged for the citizens of London as a full dress rehearsal of Foucault's disciplinary social – the institutional regime that was to permeate all sectors of civil society by the nineteenth century – is put on show for us today as a museum exhibit. The Renaissance and our own time face each other across the centuries like two magnets of opposite polarity. What lies between is a force-field of cultural attraction whose contours are only now recognizable for the first time. It's one definition of modernity.

Archaic modernity #2

notes to 'Pop Theory, Bardolatry, Leaving the Twentieth-century Academy', in Steve Beard, Bloody Banquets: Trash Video, Jacobean Horror, Rewinding Foucault, unpublished University of Cambridge PhD dissertation fragment, 1990

1. For Foucault's theory of discursive formation, see Michel Foucault, *The Archaeology of Knowledge* (London: Tavistock, 1972); idem., 'Nietzsche, Genealogy, History', in Donald F. Bouchard (ed.), *Language, Counter-Memory, Practice* (Oxford: Blackwell, 1977). For a useful summary of the Foucauldian methodology, see Hubert L. Dreyfus and Paul Rabinow, *Michel Foucault: Beyond Structuralism and Hermeneutics* (Chicago: University of Chicago Press, 1982), pp. 44–78, 104–25.

2. See E.M.W. Tillyard, *The Elizabethan World Picture* (London: Chatto & Windus, 1943).

3. See Fredric Jameson, *The Political Unconscious: Narrative as a Socially Symbolic Act* (London: Methuen, 1981), pp. 17–102. For a critique of Jameson's methodology with respect to the study of Renaissance drama, see Jonathan Goldberg, 'The Politics of Renaissance Literature: A Review Essay', ELH, vol. 49, no. 2 (Summer 1982), pp. 514–42.

4. Michel Foucault, *Discipline and Punish* (Harmondsworth: Penguin, 1979; orig. 1975), pp. 32–69.

5. Stephen Greenblatt, 'Invisible Bullets: Renaissance Authority and its Subversion', Glyph 8 (1981), pp. 40–61; reprinted in Jonathan Dollimore and Alan Sinfield (eds), *Political Shakespeare: New Essays in Cultural Materialism* (Manchester: Manchester University Press, 1985), pp. 18–47; also Stephen Greenblatt, *Shakespearean Negotiations: The Circulation of Social Energy in Renaissance England* (Oxford: Clarendon, 1988), pp. 21–65. For other variations on the New Historicist theme see Jonathan Goldberg, *James I and the Politics of Literature: Jonson, Shakespeare, Donne and Their Contemporaries* (London: Johns Hopkins University Press, 1983); Leonard Tennenhouse, *Power on Display: The Politics of Shakespeare's Genres* (London: Methuen, 1986); Steven Mullaney, *The Place of the Stage: License, Play and Power in Renaissance England* (London: University of Chicago Press, 1988); Stephen Greenblatt, *Learning to Curse: Essays in Early Modern Culture* (London: Routledge, 1990). See also Marjorie Garber (ed.), *Cannibals, Witches and Divorce: Estranging the Renaissance* (London: Johns Hopkins University Press, 1987).

6. Jonathan Dollimore, *Radical Tragedy: Religion, Ideology and Power*

in the Drama of Shakespeare and His Contemporaries (Brighton: Harvester, 1984). For other Cultural Materialist texts see Jonathan Dollimore, 'Introduction: Shakespeare, Cultural Materialism and the New Historicism', in Jonathan Dollimore and Alan Sinfield (eds), *Political Shakespeare*, pp. 2–17; Lisa Jardine, *Still Harping on Daughters: Women and Drama in the Age of Shakespeare* (Brighton: Harvester, 1983); Catherine Belsey, *The Subject of Tragedy: Identity and Difference* (London: Methuen, 1985); Graham Holderness, *Shakespeare's History* (New York: St Martin's Press, 1985); also Michael Drakakis (ed.), *Alternative Shakespeares* (London: Methuen, 1985); Graham Holderness (ed.), *The Shakespeare Myth* (Manchester: Manchester University Press, 1988).

7   Dollimore, 'Introduction' to *Political Shakespeare*, p. 8.
8   Dollimore, *Radical Tragedy*, p. 50.
9   Ibid., p. 119.
10 Jonathan Dollimore, 'Subjectivity, Sexuality and Transgression: The Jacobean Connection', *Renaissance Drama*, n.s. XVII (1986), p. 57.
11 Greenblatt, 'Invisible Bullets', p. 41.
12 In *The Dialectic of Nihilism: Post-Structuralism and Law* (Oxford: Basil Blackwell, 1984), p. 179, Gillian Rose writes of *Discipline and Punish* that ' "power" is used in both the Parsonian sense of a circulating resource like credit or purchasing power which can be increased overall ... and in the zero-sum sense according to which one person's power is another's lack of power'. Although acute enough to pinpoint this bifurcation between two models of power, Rose slips when she puts it down to confusion or incoherence. She is rather hard on Foucault generally, accusing him of ripping off everyone from Saint-Simon to Durkheim.
13 See Foucault, *Discipline and Punish*, pp. 59–60.
14 For an examination of the set-piece execution and last dying speech as problematic mechanisms of ideological control, see Peter Spierenburg, *The Spectacle of Suffering: Executions and the Evolution of Repression: From a Preindustrial Metropolis to the European Experience* (Cambridge: Cambridge University Press, 1984), pp. 100–9; Lacey Baldwin Smith, 'English Treason Trials and Confessions in the Sixteenth Century', *Journal of the History of Ideas*, vol. xv, no. 4 (October 1954), pp. 471–98; J.A. Sharpe, ' "Last Dying Speeches": Religion, Ideology and Public Execution in Seventeenth-Century England', *Past and Present*, no. 107 (May 1985), pp. 144–67. For a broader historical context see Douglas

Hay, Peter Linebaugh, John G. Rule, E. P. Thompson and Cal Winslow, *Albion's Fatal Tree: Crime and Society in Eighteenth-Century England* (London: Allen Lane, 1976).

15 Foucault, *Discipline and Punish*, p. 67.
16 Frank Lentricchia, 'Michel Foucault's Fantasy for Humanists', in his *Ariel and the Police* (Wisconsin: University of Wisconsin Press, 1988), pp. 43–9.
17 See Dollimore, *Radical Tragedy*, p. 4. The reference to Lawrence Stone is to his *The Causes of the English Revolution 1529–1642* (London: Routledge & Kegan Paul, 1972), p. 116.
18 Greenblatt, 'Invisible Bullets', p. 53.
19 Stephen Greenblatt, 'Shakespeare and the Exorcists', in Patricia Parker and Geoffrey Hartman (eds), *Shakespeare and the Question of Theory* (London: Methuen, 1985), pp. 163–87; reprinted in Stephen Greenblatt, *Shakespearean Negotiations*, pp. 94–128.
20 Foucault, *Discipline and Punish*, p. 194.
21 Ibid., p. 177.
22 Lentricchia, 'Michel Foucault's Fantasy for Humanists', p. 68.
23 Michel Foucault, *The History of Sexuality*, Volume One: *An Introduction* (Harmondsworth: Penguin, 1981; orig. 1976), p. 95.
24 Greenblatt, 'Invisible Bullets', p. 48.
25 'Rather than seeing containment as that which preempts and defeats transgression we need to see both as potentially productive forces', Dollimore, 'Subjectivity, Sexuality and Transgression', p. 71. See Lentricchia, 'Michel Foucault's Fantasy for Humanists', pp. 92–3, for an explicit account of how Greenblatt has misappropriated Foucault's analytics of power for his own (untheorized) ends.
26 See Mullaney, *The Place of the Stage*, pp. 89–115.
27 Dollimore, 'Subjectivity, Sexuality and Transgression', p. 60.
28 Stephen Greenblatt, 'Marlowe and the Will to Absolute Play', in his *Renaissance Self-Fashioning: From More to Shakespeare* (London: University of Chicago Press, 1980), p. 209.
29 Ibid., p. 254.
30 For a feminist critique of Greenblatt see Marguerite Waller, 'Academic Tootsie: The Denial of Difference and the Difference it Makes', *Diacritics*, vol. 17, no. 1 (Spring 1987), pp. 2–20.
31 Holderness, *Shakespeare's History*, p. 4. See also Gary Taylor, *Reinventing Shakespeare: A Cultural History from the Restoration to*

the Present (London: Hogarth, 1990), esp. pp. 373–411 for a more polemical demolition job on Bardolatry – or, as Taylor calls it, 'Shakespearotics'.

32 Ibid., p. 10.

33 This is something pointed out by Jean E. Howard in her review essay 'The New Historicism in Renaissance Studies', *English Literary Review*, vol. 16, no. 1 (Winter 1982), pp. 13–43.

34 Don E. Wayne, 'Power, Politics and the Shakespeare Text: Recent Criticism in England and the United States', in Jean E. Howard and Marion F. O'Connor (eds), *Shakespeare Reproduced: The Text in History and Ideology* (London: Methuen, 1987), pp. 47–67. See also Michael D. Bristol, *Shakespeare's America, America's Shakespeare* (London: Routledge, 1990).

35 For a related argument, see William Galperin, 'Back to the Future: Historicizing the New Historicism', in E. Ann Kaplan and Michael Sprinker (eds), *Cross Currents: Recent Trends in Humanities Research* (London: Verso, 1990), pp. 43–55.

36 Ibid., p. 57. Lentricchia is under no illusions about the motives for this assault: 'New historicism is another expression of the bitter and well-grounded first-world suspicion that modern history is the betrayal of liberalism', Lentricchia, 'Michel Foucault's Fantasy for Humanists', p. 97. The 'humanist' targeted by the title of his essay is, of course, Greenblatt – though whether he is as bitter as Lentricchia suggests is open to question.

37 Meaghan Morris, 'Banality in Cultural Studies', *Block*, no. 14 (Autumn 1988), p. 15. Much of my critique of Cultural Studies is heavily indebted to Morris. Her reading of Baudrillard, however, is grotesque.

38 John Fiske, 'British Cultural Studies and Television', in Robert C. Allen (ed.), *Channels of Discourse* (London: Methuen, 1987), pp. 254–89. See also idem., *Understanding Popular Culture* (London: Unwin, 1989) and *Reading the Popular* (London: Unwin, 1989), where Fiske expands on his earlier essay by arguing that everything in the downtown cultural bazaar is radical and subversive – from ripped jeans to window-shopping, *The Wheel of Fortune*, Mills & Boon novels, tabloid newspapers, Madonna, *Dallas*, video arcades and even surfing. For other examples of Cultural Studies see Iain Chambers, *Popular Culture: The Metropolitan Experience* (London: Methuen, 1986); Dick Hebdige, 'Post-script 1: Vital Strategies', in his *Hiding in the Light* (London: Methuen, 1988), pp. 208–23; idem., 'After the Masses', in Stuart Hall and Martin Jacques (eds), *New Times: The Changing Face of*

Politics in the 1990s (London: Lawrence & Wishart, 1989), pp. 76–93; Lawrence Grossberg, 'Putting the Pop Back into Postmodernism', in Andrew Ross (ed.), *Universal Abandon? The Politics of Postmodernism* (Edinburgh: Edinburgh University Press, 1988), pp. 167–190.

39 See Jean Baudrillard, *Selected Writings*, (ed.) Mark Poster (Oxford: Polity, 1988) and Douglas Kellner, *Jean Baudrillard: From Marxism to Postmodernism and Beyond* (Oxford: Polity, 1989) for Baudrillard bibliographies. For the Australian reception of Baudrillard, see Alan Frankovits (ed.), *Seduced and Abandoned: The Baudrillard Scene* (Glebe: Stonemoss, 1984). For the Canadian reception see Arthur and Marilouise Kroker (eds), *Body Invaders* (Basingstoke: Macmillan, 1988); Arthur Kroker and David Cook (eds), *The Postmodern Scene: Excremental Culture and Hyper-Aesthetics* (New York: St Martin's Press, 1986); Arthur and Marilouise Kroker and David Cook (eds), *Panic Encyclopedia: The Definitive Guide to the Postmodern Scene* (Basingstoke: Macmillan, 1989).

40 Iain Chambers, *Popular Culture*, pp. 200–21. Chambers comments that with the Gramscian concept of hegemony 'ideology becomes a flexible coordinator, and comes close to Michel Foucault's work on the local organization of knowledge and power: the "discourse" where relations, objects and subjects are positioned according to the unfolding strategy of "micro-powers" exercised by a particular practice: the discourse of the clinic, of the prison, of sexuality', p. 211. This is not quite the way I see it. For the purposes of my argument the operation of hegemony at the level of subcultural style corresponds not to the tactically polyvalent discourse of the prison but to the two-sided discourse of the scaffold. With gallows speeches, as with youth subcultures like punk, there is an equivocal emphasis on spectacle and collectivity that is absent from the panoptic regime of surveillance and isolation that prevails with the prison.

41 Antonio Gramsci, *Selections from the Prison Notebooks* (London: Lawrence & Wishart, 1971).

42 See Fiske, 'British Cultural Studies', p. 259. Compare Chambers, *Popular Culture*, p. 210: 'Under hegemony, ideology is not directly imposed but continually composed through a mobile strategy of shifting alliances and compromises formed in pursuit of a government by "consensus"'.

43 Lawrence Grossberg observes that 'affect is stitched into reality without the mediation of ideology, although the ideological surfaces always provide the sites of reality, the raw material for

its affective economies' ('Putting the Pop Back into Postmodernism', p. 181). Baudrillard would no doubt agree that postmodernism collapses the traditional distinction between affect and meaning, but would question whether this is an enabling scenario.

44 Dick Hebdige, *Subculture: The Meaning of Style* (London: Routledge, 1979).

45 Jon Savage, 'The Enemy Within: Sex, Rock and Identity', in Simon Frith (ed.), *Facing the Music: Essays on Pop, Rock and Culture* (London: Mandarin, 1990), p. 164.

46 Hal Foster, 'Readings in Cultural Resistance', in his *Recodings: Art, Spectacle, Cultural Politics* (Port Townsend: Bay Press, 1985), pp. 169–76.

47 For a comprehensive survey of the heritage of situationism see George Robertson, 'The Situationist International: Its Penetration into British Culture', *Block*, no. 14 (Autumn 1988), pp. 38–53.

48 'Despite ... the hegemonic force of the dominant classes, the people still manage to make their own meanings and to construct their own culture within, and often against, that which the industry provides for them', Fiske, 'British Cultural Studies', p. 286.

49 Chambers, *Popular Culture*, p. 212.

50 Morris, 'Banality in Cultural Studies', p. 22. Compare Chambers, *Popular Culture*, p. 207: 'How do we locate the signs of resistance ... in the television audience of *EastEnders*, amongst readers of *Cosmopolitan* and *Mizz*, or in the quiet style of a Cecil Gee suit?' That this is not a rhetorical question is the perfect vindication of Meaghan Morris's jibe.

51 Jean Baudrillard, 'Requiem for the Media', in his *For a Critique of the Political Economy of the Sign* (St Louis: Telos Press, 1981; orig. 1972), pp. 164–84.

52 Ibid., p. 174.

53 Ibid., p. 169.

54 Ibid., p. 171.

55 See 'Toward a Critique of the Political Economy of the Sign' in his *For a Critique*, pp. 143–63. For Baudrillard, the machinations of the code are defined by the circulation of 'sign exchange value'. It is noticeable, however, that he has very little to say about 'sign use value'. No doubt he would argue that the latter is the

alibi of the former, that the way in which mass culture is actively transformed into pop culture is the precondition of the code's successful operation. And yet it is typical of him not to offer any specific examples.

56 See Joseph Valente, 'Hall of Mirrors: Baudrillard on Marx', *diacritics*, vol. 15, no. 2 (Summer 1985), pp. 54–65. 'Within its sphere, the general code is tantamount to the ultimate theoretical imposition, the predication of a God; it serves as the omnipotent subject and ideal reference point which centers Baudrillard's entire epistemology,' ibid., p. 65.

57 Ibid., p. 156.

58 Jean Baudrillard, 'Symbolic Exchange and Death' in his *Selected Writings*, p. 139. This is an excerpt from Baudrillard's 1976 book, *L'Échange symbolique et la mort*. In many ways his major text, it has been translated piecemeal in various different guises – most visibly as 'The Orders of Simulacra' in Jean Baudrillard, *Simulations* (New York: Semiotext(e), 1983), pp. 83–159. See Kellner, *Jean Baudrillard*, pp. 227–8 for details.

59 Jean Baudrillard, 'In the Shadow of the Silent Majorities' in his *In the Shadow of the Silent Majorities . . . Or The End of the Social* (New York: Semiotext(e), 1983; orig. 1978), pp. 27, 41–8; idem., 'The Masses: the Implosion of the Social in the Media' in his *Selected Writings* (orig. 1985), pp. 207–19.

60 'The Masses', p. 218.

61 'In the Shadow', pp. 47–8.

62 Ibid., p. 46.

63 'Fatality' and 'banality', 'seduction' and 'production' are important terms for Baudrillard in more texts like *Seduction* (Basingstoke: Macmillan, 1990; orig. 1979) and *Fatal Strategies* (London: Pluto, 1990; orig. 1983). It's at this point that my own reading of Baudrillard parts company from that of Meaghan Morris. She sees no irony in his use of the Frankfurt School analytic when she quite happily regroups banality/production under the sign of the culture industry while pegging fatality/ seduction as signifiers of an elitist aesthetic order defined by values like 'rule' and 'discrimination'. See Meaghan Morris, 'Banality in Cultural Studies', p. 19; idem., 'Room 101 or A Few Worst Things in the World', in André Frankovits (ed.), *Seduced and Abandoned*, pp. 108–10. It's more accurate instead to see these terms as mutually defining: the fatal as the hyperbanal, the

     seductive as the hyperproductive (although that doesn't mean the reverse is the case).

64 Baudrillard uses the poker metaphor explicitly during the course of a recent interview. See Judith Williamson, 'An Interview with Jean Baudrillard', *Block*, no. 10 (Spring 1989), p. 18.

65 Foster, 'Readings in Cultural Resistance', p. 171.

66 See Peter Sloterdijk, 'Cynicism – The Twilight of False Consciousness', *New German Critique*, no. 33 (Fall 1984), pp. 190–6; idem., *Critique of Cynical Reason* (London: Verso, 1988).

67 Baudrillard, 'The Masses', p. 218.

68 Jean Baudrillard, 'The Beaubourg-Effect: Implosion and Deterrence', *October*, no. 20 (Spring 1982; orig. 1977), p.7.

69 Ibid., p. 10.

70 Hal Foster, 'For a Concept of the Political in Contemporary Art', in his *Recodings*, p. 146. Foster compares Baudrillard's Endgame unfavourably to the alternative artistic practice of 'neo-Gramscian resistance or interference', as represented by figures like Hans Haacke and Martha Rosler. But because he fails to perceive the links between this Gramscian project and the outplayed situationist aesthetic, he is unable to concede the belatedness and irrelevancy of much of their work (although he does have the good grace to admit to the inadequacy of Barbara Kruger's art). See also Hal Foster, 'Signs Taken For Wonders', *Art in America* (June 1986), pp. 80–91, for a survey of Baudrillard's influences on the art world.

71 See Patrick Brantlinger, *Crusoe's Footsteps: Cultural Studies in Britain and America* (London: Routledge, 1990), pp. 1–33, esp. 11–12.

72 This is something pinpointed – in a slightly different context – by the critic Judith Williamson, who argues that 'the new yuppie-left pop culture craze is peculiarly phoney and non-subjective, for while it centres on *other* people's subjectivity (all those TV watchers who love *The Price Is Right?* or *Dynasty*) it allows the apparently left-wing practitioners of it to conceal theirs'. See Judith Williamson, 'The Problems of Being Popular', *New Socialist*, no. 41 (September 1986), p. 15.

73 Meaghan Morris, 'Banality', p. 16.

74 Grossberg, 'Putting the Pop Back into Postmodernism', p. 175.

75 Jean Baudrillard, 'Why Theory' in his *The Ecstasy of Communication* (New York: Semiotext(e), 1988), p. 99.

76 Kellner, *Jean Baudrillard*, p. 216.

77 Ibid., p. 200. Kellner considers *Fatal Strategies* to be Baudrillard's last 'serious' text. Everything since then is panned: *La Gauche divine: chronique des années 1977–1984* (Paris: Grasset, 1985) as a too easy slag-off of the French Left, *America* (London: Verso, 1988; orig. 1986) as a platitudinous travelogue, *Cool Memories* (London: Verso, 1990; orig. 1987) as a predictable anti-feminist diatribe. Kellner's got a point, but then again, isn't it the same one Baudrillard is trying to make? Isn't this Baudrillard being hyperbanal and therefore – hopefully – fatally seductive?

78 'To a system whose argument is oppression and repression, the strategic resistance is to demand the liberating rights of the subject. But this seems rather to reflect an earlier phase of the system; and even if we are still confronted with it, it is no longer a strategic territory: the present argument of the system is to maximize speech, to maximize the production of meaning, of participation. And so the strategic resistance is that of the refusal of meaning and the refusal of speech; or of the hyperconformist simulation of the very mechanisms of the system, which is another form of refusal by overacceptance' (Baudrillard, 'The Masses', p. 219). Baudrillard doesn't deny that repression still exists, he merely considers it archaic. For him, power is better served by a Freedom of Information Act that releases millions of classified documents into the public realm every year – therefore stymieing all attempts at evaluation – than by some thirty-year rule that keeps Cabinet papers safely under lock and key. Of course, if you are unfortunate enough to live in the kind of society that prefers the old-fashioned methods, then Baudrillard probably has little to say to you.

Index of Concepts

access protocol, 54
adversary theatre, 167–169, 170, 174, 180
advertorial, 125
aesthetic recommodification, xv, 16, 71, 91, 104–105, 106–107, 115, 131–132, 190
aesthetic terrorism, 52, 118–119, 138, 150, 190
ambient photography, 7, 98–101, 129–130, 131
anti-aversion therapy, 138
apocalypticism, 17, 55, 57, 59, 138, 142, 194
appropriation art, 16, 183–184, 188
art gig, 68
artificial intelligence, 70
assassination, 56, 58–59, 63, 86, 113
asylum-cheat, 157
audio voyeurism, 77, 90
auto-destructive art, 141
auto-immune disease, 34
automatic writing, 24
automaton, 110–111, 193
auto-parenting, 104
avatar, 33
aversion therapy, 21

Bardolatry, 163, 176–177, 199
base materialism, 3, 17, 45, 108, 123
beatnik, 74, 162
bestiality, 20, 22, 24, 29, 33
bhangramuffin, 159
bilateral voyeurism, 117, 121
biomass, 141
bio-piracy, 31
biopower, 114, 120
Biosphere 2, 36, 138
biotech, 19, 30, 58, 59, 63, 66, 110, 114, 142
black hole, 71, 188, 190
body maintenance, 22, 41, 104
bondage 26

bourgeois public sphere, xiii, 4, 151
bricolage, 18–19, 69–70, 83
burn-out, 15, 54, 177

cargo cult, 17, 63, 83, 161
castration complex, 32
censorship, 29–30, 55, 113–121, 155, 159
chaos theory, 71
chemical warfare, 66
Christian essentialism, 162, 168
cinephilia, 39, 48, 105–108
class struggle, 49, 54, 55, 57–58, 108, 114–116, 117–118, 120, 151–152, 167, 169, 170–171, 180, 184, 186, 195, 198
club culture, 19, 64–65, 66, 81–82, 99–101
cognitive mapping, 21, 55, 58–59, 70–71, 77–83, 110, 118, 140
Cold War, 116, 120
collective unconscious, 17–18, 57, 108
comix, 44–45, 98, 102, 104, 108, 141, 158, 181
commodification of everything, 44, 71, 140, 178, 179, 186–187, 190, 192
consensual hallucination, 63, 76, 77, 78, 94, 96, 125–133
consensus reality, 76
conspiracy theory, 19, 70–71, 74, 88, 118, 181
consumption of security, 114
co-optive theatre, 169, 171
Cool Britannia, 3, 98, 159–160
corporate warrior, 105
countersurveillance, 79, 83, 92–93
creative salvage, 91
cult studs, 32, 88–89, 145–148, 150, 152–153, 163, 178–183, 184, 187, 188, 191–192, 195, 199–201, 202, 203
cultural engineer, 78
Cultural Materialism, 165,

Index of Concepts

166–169, 170, 173–174, 175–177, 180, 184, 191–192, 193, 194, 195, 196–198
cultural imperialism, 13, 52, 135, 152–153, 159–160
cultural capital, 151, 192, 195
cultural poetics, 165–166, 175
cultural boom, 5, 61, 72, 101, 140, 178–179, 192
cultural dupe, 181, 184, 188
culture industry, xiii, 1, 39, 54, 75, 98, 113, 125, 143, 147, 161, 178, 180, 181–182
culture war, 150–151, 153
cyberculture, 16, 18, 26–39, 41, 52–53, 57–58, 61–74, 77–82, 84–92, 94–95, 102–105, 110–111, 113, 114, 121, 130, 134, 137–138, 140–142, 143
cyberfeminism, 28, 31–38, 41
cybernetic Marxism, 35
cyber-porn, 26–30, 31–32
cyberpunk, 18, 39, 61–62, 63, 70–71, 112, 126, 139, 140–142
cyberspace, 27, 28, 30, 33, 37, 63–64, 76, 78, 81, 83, 111
cyber-totty, 31
cyborg, 18, 90, 110–111, 133

damnation game, 11–12, 13–15
derive, xiv, 183, 184
deterrence machine, 56–57, 137, 139, 180
detournement, 80, 183, 188
Difference Engine, 62–63, 69–70
disalienation, 168
disaster movies, 119
disposable building, 130, 131–132
DIY porn, 35
doppelgänger, 110
double agent, 13, 161, 171
downward social mobility, 49, 113–115, 116, 117, 118, 120, 151
drag king, 31
dream interpretation, 24, 124
drug culture, xiv, 8, 9–10, 12–14, 18, 19, 34–35, 49, 59, 65–66, 74, 76, 93, 94–96, 100, 114, 121, 140
drum'n'bass, 79
dystopianism, 18, 63, 115, 133, 138–139

early capitalism, 162
ecopower, xiv, 57, 81, 114–115, 117–119, 121
elective surgery, 67
Elvis, 16–18, 31
English nationalism, 158–160
enlightened false consciousness, 189, 203
erotic delirium, 20, 128
ethnographic surrealism, xiii, 18–19, 23–26, 54–60, 70–71, 77–79, 82–83
etiquette manual, 164
exhibitionism, 1–2, 4, 20, 41, 104
exploitation films, 12–13, 40, 102, 106–107, 130
extremist sports, 53

false consciousness, 181
fatal woman, 34–35, 47, 111, 123
fetishism, 20, 24, 27, 41–42, 78–79, 98, 99, 105–107, 129, 133, 182
film noir, 7, 14, 15, 72, 109
flaneur electronique, 78
found noise, 78
found imagery, 99
Fourth World, 55, 58, 114–118, 120
fractal programming, 110, 185–187
frottism, 20, 45
functional outsiderdom, 105, 161–162, 169, 171, 173–175, 194

gallows literature, 170, 197–198, 200
gender hacking, 21, 28–29, 30–31, 33
gender reassignment, 30
gender policing, 31
general incrimination, 52
Generation X, 19, 101, 143–144
geomantic information, 83
gothic Marxism, 161
graphomania, 106, 128

hegemony, 180–182, 200, 201, 203
heritage industry, 135–136, 140, 160, 176
Hollywood Playhouse, 40, 49, 51, 68
homicidal mania, 12, 15, 20, 66, 102

Index of Concepts

homme fatale, 11–12, 15, 123
homosexuality, 11–12, 20, 21, 37, 74, 98–99, 122, 127
hotel fetishism, 64
hunt-sab, 79
hyperconformism, 104, 132, 187–190, 194, 204
hyper-consumer, 104, 136, 146–147, 180, 187–188
hyper-media, 141
Hyperreal America, 51, 55, 109, 133–135, 136–137, 137–138, 139
hypersimulation, 187
hyper-subject, 117, 128–129

ideal masochism, 9, 11, 14, 20, 21, 46, 47, 175
identity politics, 144, 180
idol, 103
illegal immigrant, 155, 157
image market, 52, 116
impulse looting, 95, 162
infocalypse, 142
infocracy, 141
information addiction, 63, 102–103, 104–105, 130
Information Revolution, 34–35, 69, 79–80, 142
intellectual underclass, xiv, 118, 121
intelligent agent, 38
invention of tradition, 134, 158
invisible literature, 21, 67
Islamic iconophobia, 68
iteration, 70

kiddie porn, 29, 102
kinotrope, 69
kitsch, 16–17, 19, 20, 106–108, 133–135, 136–137, 144, 190

l'amour fou, 23, 25–26, 123–124
late capitalism, 34–35, 70, 95–96, 105, 115–116, 118, 133–135, 138–139, 142, 143, 146, 149, 153, 191
lesbianism, 20, 22, 28, 37
ley-lines, 83
licensed misrule, 167
longevity doctor, 67
loungecore, 20

lustmurder, 21, 102

macho clone, 182
malcontent, 167, 168
male hysteria, 122
manga, 102, 103, 105, 130
mass avant-gardism, 18–19, 77–79, 147, 182–183
mass panic, 52, 119–120, 136
masturbation, 21, 25, 27, 42, 45
media terrorism, 19, 52, 59, 68
media simulacrum, xiii, 17–18, 51, 54, 55, 57, 78, 102–104, 105, 112, 117, 125, 194
medico-military complex, 34
megalomania, 8, 11, 14, 19, 40, 50–51, 128, 129, 130, 131, 132, 151, 158, 162
messianic comeback, 8–9, 13, 15, 17, 72, 75, 88, 117, 118
metaphysics of substance, 96, 172
micro-physics of power, 172–173
military entertainment complex, 52
mimetic violence, 52
modern primitivism, 161
Mondo 2000, 64–65
moral panic, 29
multiple orgasm, 25

nano-tech, 53
narrowcasting, 116
near-death experience, 9, 48, 53, 76, 93–95
necrophilia, 20
neo-liberalism, 115–116, 120, 144
neologism, 63
neurasthenia, 21
neurolinguistic programming, 142
New Hollywood, 14, 50, 60, 72, 75
new media, 76, 143
New Historicism, 164, 166–167, 169, 171–172, 173–175, 176–177, 180, 185, 186, 188, 191–192, 193, 195, 196–197, 187–199
New Orientalism, 111, 113, 129–133
new social movements, 52, 116
nodal points, 83

Index of Concepts

nomadic war machine, 34–35, 52, 96, 101
non-repressive desublimation, 56
normalization of the psychopathic, 20–21, 57, 105, 172
nuclear sublime, 56, 119, 121
nuclear jeopardy, 56
nymphomania, 20

objective chance, 2, 124
occultism, 74, 76, 77, 78, 82–83, 93, 123–124, 162
Old Hollywood, 8, 10–11, 12, 13, 49, 122–123
organic intellectual, xiii, xiv, 23, 56–57, 64, 92, 113–121, 161
orgiastic cannibalism, 17, 21
orientalia, 126
otaku, xiii, 102–105, 130

pagan media, 17, 34, 81–82, 85–86, 105, 132
panic reaction formation, 31
panopticism, 112, 117–119, 172, 200
pantheism, 8, 105
paranoia, 14, 15, 76, 88, 109, 117, 123, 126–127, 155, 158
parental control filter, 29
patriarchy, 23, 34–35
periodic attractor, 195
perpetual present, 63
pharmakon, 6
photomechanics, 111
police action, 93–94, 156–158
political unconscious, 120, 164, 196
polymorphous perversity, 28
pop modernism, 3, 100–101, 145, 152–153, 158–159, 182–183
popular illegality, xiv, 21, 95, 109, 169
porn, 22–23, 25, 35, 41, 44–45, 96, 103, 111, 130
post-avant-gardism, 4, 41–42, 73, 77–78, 81–82, 155, 187–190
post-cyberpunk, 141
post-Fordism, 91–92, 117, 119, 120
post-humanism, 38, 63, 65, 66–67, 114

post-industrial society, 32, 35, 87, 91–92, 113–114, 116–118, 121
postmodernism, xiv, 18, 44, 70, 71, 83, 105, 107–108, 109–110, 113, 115–116, 121, 128–129, 131, 134–135, 136–137, 141, 145, 149, 153, 154, 161–162, 163, 164–165, 175–178, 179–180, 191–195, 196, 199–204
post-postmodernism, 18
povertiresque, 99, 113, 115, 129, 133
prefabricated archaeology, 69, 132
progressive modernization, 151
proof-piece, 69
proto-modernism, 161–162, 174
psyberspace, 33
psychogeography, xiii, 55, 74, 81–83
psychosexual metamorphosis, 17, 21, 28, 33
psychotechnology, 18, 52–53, 85, 89–91, 137–138
punk, 19, 74, 133, 145, 149, 150–151, 152–153, 154–155, 159, 179, 182, 200
Puritanism, 9, 45, 56–57

quantum electronics, 110
queer subjectivity, xiv, 20, 21, 99–100, 122–123

radical humanism, 114
rave science, 81, 99–100
ready-made, 190
reality principle, 137
recreational subjectivity, 125
refusal by overacceptance, 17, 194, 204
regressive modernization, xv, 150–151
repressive desublimation, 20, 56
revenge tragedy, 167–169
reversible immanence, 90, 118, 120, 121, 133, 186, 190, 193–194
revolt into style, xiv
revolution of everyday life, 183
romantic sublime, 118–119, 148
royal entry, 166, 171

sacred art, 81, 82, 99, 162
sacred trivia, 17, 83, 101

Index of Concepts

sacrificial death cult, 13, 17, 51, 188
sacrificial generation, 144
safe sex, 23, 27
salaryman, 46, 104, 133
sampladelics, xiv, 106–107
saturnalian socialism, 115–116, 120, 121, 169–170
scaffold service, 166, 169
schizophrenia, 1, 54–55, 72–73, 76, 92, 123, 127–129
script doctor, 40
sexual addiction, 27
Shakespearotics, 199
shamanism, 24, 74, 81–82, 83, 84
shinjinrui, 104
shoot-em-up, 32
shudder-novel, 47, 83
sick joke, 37, 108
sign crime, xv, 71, 115, 108–110, 169–170
sign exchange value, 71, 140, 186–187, 190, 201–202
sign use value, xiv, 16, 71, 80, 91, 104–105, 106–107, 132, 201
simulation art, 179, 190
simultaneous orgasm, 24
single-issue fanaticism, 57
site-specific installation, 100
situationism, 109, 115, 183–184, 185, 186, 188, 189–190, 194, 201, 203
sixties counterculture, xiv, 8, 12–14, 58–59, 65–66, 74, 84–85, 86, 89, 116, 146, 178, 185, 191
smiling disease, 46
society of the spectacle, 183
sodomy, 23, 24
sound polaroids, 78
speed, 35, 52, 137–138
spree killing, 59
state torture, 93–95, 121
steampunk, 69–71
stress disorder, 66
structural linguistics, 125
structural anthropology, 165
structure of feeling, 35, 100
style culture, xv, 83–84, 100–101, 125, 145, 153
subjective idealism, 123
Sufi anarchism, 161
suicide, 9, 17, 51

superpanopticism, 117, 121
symbolics of blood, 167
synchronicity, 76, 123, 124

table dance, 41
tech noir, 61, 63, 109
techgnosis, 32, 75–77, 78, 81–82, 84, 85, 94, 102
technological sublime, 18, 129
technological humanism, 57–58, 91, 161
technopagan, 33, 64–65, 81, 105, 132
technophobia, 33, 75
telematic angel, 75, 85
temporary autonomous zone, 63, 81–82, 162
testimonial video, 41–42, 93–94
Theatre of Cruelty, 24, 165–166
theoretical violence, 193–194
transcendental landscape, 16, 51, 158
transgender, 31, 38
transgression, 21, 174–175, 187, 189
transgressive reinscription, 13–14, 71, 161
transsexualism, 21, 32, 33
Trekkiedom, 37, 145–146, 147
troilism, 23

unconscious sadism, 20, 46, 47
underconsumption, 139
uneasy listening, 77–79
union gig, 68
urban legend, 108
urban facadism, 134
utopianism, 35, 36, 65, 115, 131, 133–136, 161–162

vampire, 47–49, 111, 118
virtual reality, 30, 32, 33, 53, 57, 64, 80–81, 111, 114, 134, 136, 141
virus, 34, 74, 103, 114, 141, 142
voyeurism, 24, 41, 48, 56, 117

war on drugs, 34–35, 94–96
war porn, 60, 67–68
white male abjection, 3, 9, 12, 17–18, 20, 39, 45–46, 124
white Negro, 159

white Rasta, 159
working class hero, 72–73, 75–76, 151–152, 162

young British art, 1–6, 98

zombie, 116, 119–120, 135–136

Index of Names

Peter Ackroyd 82
Gilbert Adair 136
Rita Addison 81
Theodor Adorno 147, 181
Akira 103
Albion 198
Alice 133
Keith Allen 6
Woody Allen 89
Robert C Allen 199
Louis Althusser 147
Robert Altman 40
Martin Amis 115, 148
Edward Andrews, 106
Arabella 152
Louis Aragon 23, 24, 25
Jeffrey Archer 18, 83
Ariel 198
Allan Arkush 107
Matthew Arnold 176
Antonin Artaud 23, 24
Dennis Ashbaugh 141
Richard Attenborough 148
Tex Avery 106, 109
Steve Aylett 108–110

Charles Babbage 69–70
Martin Baker 146
Alec Baldwin 72
Lucille Ball 179
J G Ballard 18, 20, 27, 54–60, 67
Lester Bangs 17
Barbie 32, 140
Jonathan Barnbrook 3
P T Barnum 60
Barrie 22
John Barrymore 9
Paul Bartel 107
Roland Barthes 89, 94, 129–130, 149, 154
Kim Basinger 72
Georges Bataille 123
Charles Baudelaire 47
Jean Baudrillard 71, 75, 109, 113, 116, 120, 125, 134, 137, 141, 179–180, 185–190, 191, 193–194, 195, 199, 200, 201, 202, 203, 204
Sleeping Beauty 134
Beavis 26
Lenny Beige 20
Catherine Belsey 197
Walter Benjamin 94, 112
Jeremy Bentham 172
Tom Berenger 7
Hakim Bey 76
Kathryn Bigelow 49
Bill 28
Tony Blair 3
William Blake 83
Alan Bleasdale 148
Henry Blince 109
Humphrey Bogart 49
Frank Booth 8–9
Max Borodin 140
Donald F Bouchard 196
Madame Bovary 93
David Bowie 6
Paul Bowles 74, 162
Circuit Boy 31
Malcolm Bradbury 148
Lloyd Bradley 1
Marlon Brando 7
Patrick Brantlinger 146–147, 191, 203
Perry Bravo 40
Bertolt Brecht 168
Howard Brenton 148
Andre Breton xiv, 23–26, 123–124
Pieter Breughel 44
Jeff Bridges 51, 122
Michael D Bristol 199
Big Brother 26, 29
Tiffany Lee Brown 33
Buddha 127, 128
Scott Bukatman 138
Bugs Bunny 107
Julie Burchill xiv, 112–113
William Burroughs xiii, 65, 72, 73–74, 109, 162
Tim Burton 51, 112
George Bush 59, 94

Index of Names

Butt-head 26
David Byrne 113, 129, 131–132
Lord Byron 47

Nicolas Cage 7, 49
Richard Calder 110–111
Melodie Calvert 30
James Cameron 67, 68
John Carey 149
Lewis Carroll 111
Barbara Cartland 22
Lisa Cartwright 31
Butch Cassidy 122
Carlos Castaneda 84
Robert Castel 117
Louis-Ferdinand Céline 73
Iain Chambers 146, 180, 184–185, 187, 199, 200, 201
Dinos Chapman 5
Jake Chapman 5
Noam Chomsky 1
Jesus Christ 8, 15, 17
Christina 42
Michael Cimino 49–52
Bill Clinton 144
Nigel Coates 113, 129, 131–132
Jarvis Cocker 6
Harry Cohn 10–11, 13
Matthew Collings 3
Christopher Columbus 137
David Cook 200
Robin Cook 155
Francis Ford Coppola 14, 47, 49, 50–51
Roger Corman 12–13, 107
Alain Corneau 72
Douglas Coupland 19, 101, 143
David Cronenberg 60, 90
David Crosby 88
Charles Crumb 45–46
Max Crumb 46
Robert Crumb 44–46
Crumb Senior 46
Robinson Crusoe 146, 191, 203
Valentine Cunningham 151–153

D'Amville 168
Leonardo da Vinci 134
Jeffrey Dahmer 21
Salvador Dali 56
Joe Dante 106–108
Charles Darwin 87

Paul Dave xiv, 113–121
Jon Davidson 106–107
Ray Davies 160
Charlotte Davies 81
Mike Davis 121, 139
Michel de Certeau 115, 145
Christian de Chalonge 48
James Dean 7, 8, 11–12, 14
Julius Deane 66
Guy Debord 183
Gilles Deleuze 29, 34, 83, 96
Cecil B DeMille 60
Jacques Derrida 94, 152, 163, 164, 179, 184
Rene Descartes 92
Desdemona 175, 188
Moby Dick 146
Philip K Dick, 75–76
Charles Dickens 54
Marlene Dietrich 48
Matt Dillon 8, 14
Dionysius 100
Walt Disney 81, 133–139
Divine 99
Dobbin 23
Artful Dodger 54, 71
Jonathan Dollimore 165–171, 173–174, 184, 196, 197, 198
John Donne 196
Jesse Downtime 109
Count Dracula 47–49
Michael Drakakis 197
Hubert L Dreyfus 196
David Duchovny 1
Aidan Dun 82
Emile Durkheim 197
Robert Duvall 15
Andrea Dworkin 29
Bob Dylan 149, 153

Umberto Eco 134, 136–137
Atom Egoyan 41–43
Katie Elder 12, 13
Palmer Eldritch 75
Norbert Elias 114
T S Eliot 88, 158
Havelock Ellis 124
James Ellroy 154
Paul Eluard 23
Tracey Emin 5
Frederick Engels 124
Brian Eno 79

Index of Names

Hans Magnus Enzensberger 185–186
Eric 42
Max Ernst 23, 56
Etheridge 154
Euclid 151

Falstaff 171
William Faulkner 11
Faust 11, 14, 15
Faustus 174, 175
Jude Fawsley 151–152
Raymond Federman 18
Abel Ferrara 68
Leslie Fiedler 11
W C Fields 9
Iris Finz 22
Steven Finz 22, 24
John Fiske 147–148, 179–180, 182–184, 187, 188, 189, 199, 200
F Scott Fitzgerald 144
Gustave Flaubert 93
Wilhelm Fliess 127
James Foley 72
Peter Fonda 13, 16
Henry Ford 91, 116–117, 119–120
Hal Foster 4, 183, 188, 189, 201, 203
Jodie Foster 7, 16
Michel Foucault 21, 25, 34, 69, 72, 108, 109–110, 112, 113, 115, 116, 119, 121, 163, 163–175, 180–181, 191, 195, 196, 197, 198, 199, 200
Gene Fowler 9
John Foxx 151
Francis 42, 43
Frank 22
Frankenstein 38, 47
Alan Frankovits 200, 202
Christopher Frayling 47
Stephen Frears 72
Sigmund Freud 21, 23, 25, 45, 86, 87, 89, 92, 124, 126, 127–128
William Friedkin 50–51
Simon Frith 147, 201
Fritz 44
Sam Fuller 13

Galileo Galilei 92
William Galperin 199
Marjorie Garber 196
Greta Garbo 48

Green Gartside 155
Jean-Paul Gaultier 104
Cecil Gee 146, 201
Clifford Geertz 165
Sybil Gerard 69
J Paul Getty 136
William Gibson 33, 39, 61–71, 76, 80, 83–84, 111, 112, 139, 140–141
Barry Gifford 72
Bet Gilroy 135
Gina 22
Allen Ginsberg 74
Tank Girl 109
John Glenn 37
Crispin Glover 8
God 45, 202
Jean-Luc Godard 14
Paul Godwin 81–82
Jonathan Goldberg 196
Albert Goldman 17, 87
Gordon 22
Stephen Jay Gould 119
Antonio Gramsci xiii, 145, 180–181, 184, 200, 203
Cary Grant 122–123
Volker Grassmuck 102, 105
Henry Gray 113
Stephen Greenblatt 164–167, 169, 171–175, 186, 188, 191, 193, 196, 197, 198, 199
Maggie Greenwald 72
Bruce Greenwood 42
Lawrence Grossberg 193, 200, 203
Felix Guattari 29
Marc Guillaume 116, 118, 120
Stephen Gyllenhal 15

Hans Haacke 203
Yui Haga 103
Hal 171
Judith Halberstam 31
Stuart Hall xv, 150–151, 179, 182, 199
Peter Halley 190
Evelyn Hammonds 31
Tom Hanks 108, 122–123
Victoria Hanover 4, 21, 43, 69–71, 98, 113, 164
Donna Haraway 30, 32, 38
Thomas Hardy 151–152
David Hare 148, 149

Index of Names

Harriet 22
Nina Hartley 36
Geoffrey Hartman 198
Haruki 103
Henry Hathaway 8, 12
Mad Hatter 134
Nicholas Hawksmoor 82
Nathaniel Hawthorne 11
Douglas Hay 198
Brooke Hayward 12, 13
Lafcadio Hearn 125–128, 133
Dick Hebdige 145, 148, 159, 182, 199, 201
Martin Heidegger 32
Jimi Hendrix 79
Elvis Herselvis 31
Carl Hiaasen 154, 155
George V Higgins 154
Kathy High 31
Tony Hillerman 154, 155
Damien Hirst 1–6
Adolf Hitler 85
Elvis Hitler 17
Eric Hobsbawm 161
E T A Hoffman 47
Richard Hoggart 150, 153
Mark Holborn 131
Graham Holderness 176, 191, 193, 194, 197
Jenny Holzer 183
Stewart Home 82, 99
Homer 151
Anthony Hopkins 47, 49
Dennis Hopper 6–16
Nick Hornby 155
Jean E Howard 199
Neil Howe 143–144
Robert Hughes 44, 45
E Howard Hunt 39
Tim Hunter 15

Michael Ignatieff 148
Malcolm Imrie 23
Apache Indian 159
Iseult 40
Eiko Ishioka 131
Eddie Izzard 6

Jack 82
Michael Jackson 190
Martin Jacques 199
Henry Jaglom 14

Clive James 148
Fredric Jameson 70, 118, 120, 127, 128–129, 164, 196
Janus 91
Lisa Jardine 197
Derek Jarman 148
Jeff 154, 155
Joseph Paul Jerrigan 31
Virginia Johnson 25
Chuck Jones 106
Dylan Jones 112, 161
Ben Jonson 196
Janis Joplin 44
Jay Joplin 1
James Joyce 87

Pauline Kael 14
Mary Kaldor 120
E Ann Kaplan 199
Jonathan Kaplan 107
Steve Katz 18
Rei Kawakubo 131
John Keats 47, 149, 153
Harvey Keitel 39
Douglas Kellner 194, 200, 202, 204
James Kelman 54
John F Kennedy 56, 58, 59, 85, 113
Nick Kent 122
Jack Kerouac 74
John Kerrigan 161
Artificial Kid 63
Sundance Kid 122
Rodney King 93–95
Stephen King 18
Mia Kirshner 42
William Klein 129–130
Jeff Koons 190
King Koopa 7
Elias Koteas 42
Hare Krishna 133
Arthur Kroker 79, 109, 200
Marilouise Kroker 79, 200
Barbara Kruger 183, 188, 203
Frank Krutnick 146
Seiji Kurata, 131
Hanif Kureishi 153
Steve Kurtz 30

Louis L'Amour 18
Jacques Lacan 117, 127, 128
Marc Laidlaw 61
Christopher Lambert 51

Index of Names

Henry Lancaster 171
Cosmo Landesman 112, 149
Tony Las Vegas 31
Brenda Laurel 32, 38, 81
D H Lawrence 50
King Lear 14, 163, 164, 171, 173
Timothy Leary 65
F R Leavis 176, 192
Bruce Lee 19
Christopher Lee 48
Michael Lehmann 51
Annie Leibowitz 18
Stalislaw Lem 20
Frank Lentricchia 115, 170, 172–173, 198, 199
Sergio Leone 108
Wyndham Lewis 87
Mark Leyner 18–19, 109
Abraham Lincoln 19
Peter Linebaugh 198
Mira Litobac 156–157
David Lodge 148
Nick Logan 143
Robert Longo 68
Ada Lovelace 34
George Lucas 14
Bela Lugosi 48
David Lynch 7, 8, 46

Mr M 21
Madonna 82, 122, 136, 147, 148, 180, 192, 199
Rene Magritte 56
Norman Mailer 40
Big Daddy Mainframe 31
John Major 158
Nothing Man 73
Philip Marchand 87
Greil Marcus 16, 17
Herbert Marcuse 56, 181
Mario 7
Chris Marker 131
Christopher Marlowe 174–175, 198
Penny Marshall 41
Martin 49
Dean Martin 12
Karl Marx 23, 35, 69, 152, 161, 164, 168, 169, 180, 181, 182, 185, 186, 189, 192, 194, 200, 202
William Masters 25
Marcel Mauss xiii

Christa McAuliffe 36
Kevin McCarthy 106
Jim McClellan 112, 151
Robert McCrum 149
Ronald McDonald 144
Ian McEwan 148
Dorothy McGuire 10
Don McKellar 42
Terence McKenna 19
Malcolm McLaren 39, 153, 154
Eric McLuhan 87
Marshall McLuhan 34, 75, 84–92
Herman Melville 11, 115
Mephistopheles 11
Christian Metz 39, 117
Henri Michaux 130
Mick 127
Dick Miller 106
Frank Miller 141
Jonathan Miller 86, 148
Charlie Minto 154
Elvis Mishima 17
James Mitchell 72
Issey Miyake 131
Tsutomo Miyazaki 102, 104, 105
Mona 62
Michael Moorcock 111
Alan Moore 82
Suzanne Moore 136
Hans Moravec 39
Thomas More 198
Franco Moretti 118
Ted Morgan 72, 73–74
Daido Moriyama 131
Ennio Morricone 108
Meaghan Morris 178–179, 184–185, 192, 199, 201, 202, 203
William Morris 158
Morrissey 153, 160
Paul Morrissey 49
Mickey Mouse 134–135, 139, 145
Steven Mullaney 174, 196, 198
Rupert Murdoch 91, 143
F W Murnau 48

Maurice Nadeau 124
Nadja 123
Tom Nairn 160
Narratron 70
Graham Nash 88
Mr Natural 45
Pierre Naville 123

Index of Names

Steve Neale 146
Neuromancer 62
Paul Newman 12, 122
Jack Nicholson 12, 122
Friedrich Nietzsche 196
Richard M Nixon 85
Elvis Nixon 17
Kim Novak 30

Marion F O'Connor 199
Edmund O'Keane 9
Georgia O'Keefe 16
P J O'Rourke 116
Gary Oldman 47
David Olson 92
Roy Orbison 15
Peggy Orenstein 44
George Orwell 158
Lee Harvey Oswald 59
Othello 175
Carl Overchoke 110
Rifat Ozbek 5
Yasujiro Ozu 106, 132

Camille Paglia 29
Lisa Palac 32
Charlie Parker 9
Patricia Parker 198
Talcott Parsons 197
Tony Parsons 114
Patrick 126
Sam Peckinpah 72
Constance Penley 32, 35–37
Sean Penn 7, 8, 15, 144
Benjamin Peret 23, 25
Commodore Perry 126, 129
Mark Pesce 81–82
Docteur Petiot 48
Pablo Picasso 45
Mike Pickering 100
Julianne Pierce 31
Jose Pierre 23
Pinocchio 133
Harold Pinter 148
Sadie Plant 32, 33–35
Richard Plantagenet 167
Liss Platt 30
Edgar Allan Poe 47, 89
Robert Polito 72–73
Jackson Pollock 18
Mark Poster 121, 200
Ezra Pound 87, 88

Michael Powell 106
Elvis Presley 16–18, 31
Jesse Presley 17
Jacques Prévert 23, 25
Primavera 111
Prometheus 38
Hiro Protagonist 141
Marcel Proust 111
Thomas Pynchon 113

Dennis Quaid 108
Dan Quayle 95
Raymond Queneau 23, 24

Paul Rabinow 196
Randy 22
Man Ray 23
Nicholas Ray 11
Derek Raymond 155
Paul Raymond 27
Ronald Reagan 55, 59, 121, 144
Lou Reed 6
Keanu Reeves 47
Wilhelm Reich 45
Robin Rimbaud 77–79
George Robertson 201
Pat Robertson 36
Mimi Rogers 49
George Romero 49, 116, 119–120
Avital Ronell 32, 92–97
Gillian Rose 197
Norman Rosenthal 4
Martha Rosler 203
Ross 155
Andrew Ross 200
Mark Rothko 16
Mickey Rourke 8, 14, 49, 50, 51
Candida Royale 36
Rudy Rucker 61
John G Rule 198
Damon Runyon 109
Salman Rushdie 148
Winona Ryder 47

Charles Saatchi 5
Saddam Hussein 60, 68
Saint-Simon 197
Jean-Paul Sartre 117
Joyan Saunders 30
Joachim Sauter 80
Jon Savage 147, 150, 161, 182–183, 201

Index of Names

John Sayles 107
Scanner 77–79
Paul Schrader 105–106
Daniel Paul Schreber 127, 128
Arnold Schwarzenegger 122
Norman Schwarzkopf 60
Martin Scorsese 105–106
Ridley Scott 75, 132–133
J F Sebastian 110
John Self 115
Tom Selleck 182
Nicholas Serota 4
Michel Serrault 48
Michel Serres 75
Brian Sewell 3
William Shakespeare 10, 11, 163, 164–167, 171, 173–177, 191, 194, 195, 196, 197, 198, 199
J A Sharpe 197
William Shatner 147
Percy Bysshe Shelley 149
Pete Shelley 149
Alan Shepard 37
Cindy Sherman 183
Shigesato 103
Lewis Shiner 61
John Shirley 61
Martin Short 108
Bart Simpson 144, 149
Iain Sinclair xiii, 82–84
Alan Sinfield 165, 196, 197
Sisyphus 61
Peter Sloterdijk 189, 203
DNA Slut 31
Lacey Baldwin Smith 197
Jeff Spiccoli 144
Steven Spielberg 14, 58, 107, 162
Peter Spierenburg 197
Michael Sprinker 199
Annie Sprinkle 28
Sylvester Stallone 122
Haim Steinbach 190
Neal Stephenson 17, 82, 141–142
Albert Steptoe 45
Bruce Sterling 39, 52, 61–71, 114
Dave Stewart 6
Stephen Stills 88
Karlheinz Stockhausen 79
Dean Stockwell 13
Bram Stoker 47, 49
Lawrence Stone 170–171, 198
Oliver Stone 39, 41, 121

Sandy Stone 32, 38
Dr Strangelove 112
Lee Strasberg 12
John Strausbaugh 17–18
Bill Strauss 143–144
James Stuart 163, 170, 196, 197
Ronald Sukenick 18
Lawrence Sutin 76
Stuart Swezey 39

Keith Talent 115
Christine Tamblyn 31
Tamburlaine 174, 175
Yves Tanguy 23, 56
Tarzan 88
Frank Tashlin 106
Bertrand Tavernier 72
R H Tawney 158
Elizabeth Taylor 7
Gary Taylor 198, 199
Neil Tennant 6
Leonard Tennenhouse 196
Jennifer Terry 30
Tetsuo 103
Margaret Thatcher xv, 150, 153, 154, 177, 188
Thomas 42
E P Thompson 198
Jim Thompson xiii, 72–73
Wolfgang Tillmans 98–101
E M W Tillyard 164, 196
Kenneth Tobey 106
Don Toto 109
Cyril Tourneur 168
Pete Townshend 148
Dr Toxicophilous 110
Travis 55
Lionel Trilling 177
Roger Trilling 39
Tristan 40
Leon Trotsky 154
Pierre Trudeau 87
Elizabeth Tudor 164, 166–169, 171, 173–174, 185, 195, 196
Mark Twain 11

Ultraman 103
John Updike 109
Countess V 21
Joseph Valente 202
VALIS 76
Vincent Van Gogh 10

Index of Names

Raoul Vaneigem 183
Jules Verne 134
Bill Viola 113, 131–132
Paul Virilio 52–53, 113, 114, 137–138
Erich von Daniken 141
Richard von Krafft-Ebing 20–21

Bruce Wagner 39–41
Marguerite Waller 198
Andy Warhol 4, 12, 190
Jack Warner 11
Earl Warren 59, 113
Alfred Watkins 83
Evelyn Waugh 158
DonE Wayne 176–177, 178, 179, 191–192, 199
John Wayne 7, 12
Reverend Wayne 141
H G Wells 134
Wim Wenders 7, 14, 131–132
Adam West 176
Snow White 107
Bud Wiggins 40
Dolly Wiggins 40

Oscar Wilde 21
John Williams 154
John L Williams 154–155
Ian Williams 143–144
Raymond Williams 150, 153
Judith Williamson 203
Robert Anton Wilson 84
Peter Lamborn Wilson 161–162
Cal Winslow 198
Tom Wolfe 86–87
Jack Womack 17, 139–140
Natalie Wood 12
James Woods 90
Virginia Woolf 149
Patrick Wright 135

Koizumi Yakumo 126
Frances Yates 162
Tadanori Yokoo 131
Toby Young 149

Zeno 109
Count Zero 62
Ignatz Zwakh 111
Terry Zwigoff 44–46

Also published by Serpent's Tail

Ian Penman

VITAL SIGNS: Music, Movies & Other Manias

In 1977, the Clash and the Sex Pistols released their debut albums, Vladimir Nabokov died and Ian Penman had his first review published in the *NME*. Britain's leading weekly music paper was just about to embark upon its most glamorous era, with Penman its star writer. Penman would write about great music, and terrible frauds, of brilliant, obscure pop bands, and famous soap opera actresses long before it was the done thing. Perming Barthes with dub, booze and Walter Benjamin, Penman achieved something few music writers can even dream of, he changed the way the subject was written about.

Twenty years on, the Penman signature has bloomed everywhere from the *Face* to *The Times*, obscure academic film journals to German *Vogue*, *Tatler* to *Arena*, consolidating his position as someone who could write about all things cultural with a rare originality, wit and insight, whilst collecting disciples and detractors along the way like some religious cult. From Amis to Zappa, Tricky to De Niro, Fassbinder to Michael Jackson, cartoons & curry, S&M, heavy metal, or test driving crack for *Harpers & Queen* ... this brilliant collection brings together for the very first time Ian Penman's journalism. In doing so it offers a one man overview of the last two decades in culture and politics.

'There's very few things I've wanted but couldn't have, but one I can think of is envy.... When I met Penman ... I finally found someone of my own generation I could feel this most shimmeringly savage and sexy of emotions for. And it felt DAMN GOOD. Reader, in your hands you hold your very own ticket to Heaven, via Hell, and back'

Julie Burchill

Lynne Tillman

The Broad Picture

Lynne Tillman's essays are irreverent, smart, funny – evidence of her playful, rebellious mind. They are collected here together for the first time. Her subjects range broadly and widely, from Matisse and 'reading women' to the issue of race in *The Bodyguard*, from Ray Charles' voice and lyrics to narrative theories, from cat therapy to sex, memory and death. An exceptional writer, Tillman takes the reader on an expansive tour of 20th century life and culture to unearth and enlighten its preoccupations, fears and obsessions.

'Adding to her daring feats in fiction, Lynne Tillman is now an essayist for our times. A private eye in the public sphere, she refuses no assignment and distils the finest wit, intelligence and hard evidence from some of the world's most transient artifacts and allegories. This is a truly memorable book.'

Andrew Ross,
author of 'The Chicago Gangster Theory of Life'

'Tillman's work is always intelligent, always subtle, and very often funny, and the scalpel she uses for slicing it into the American order of things has a decidedly wicked edge to it.'

Patrick McGrath

Jonathan Romney

Short Orders

The nineties has been a turbulent and changing period for cinema. The film critic Jonathan Romney has spent the decade at the pictures making sense of things. *Short Orders* is a collection of his sharp, inquiring and entertaining writings on film, from art house to multiplex, and featuring his unique take on the likes of Tarantino, Jarman, Scorsese and Almodóvar. The collection also includes extended reflections on the end of cinema's first century and Hollywood's entry into the digital age and, with it, the end of the reign of the 'real' on-screen.

'I've long felt that Jonathan Romney was one of the sharpest film critics writing in English. Reading his collected pieces in *Short Orders* has confirmed and deepened this feeling. Moving with breathtaking confidence, from the American mainstream to the more obscure byways of World Cinema, *Short Orders* is bursting with dazzling and provocative observations. Written with verve, bold intelligence and dead pan wit, *Short Orders* is the most exhilarating collection of film criticism in a very long time.'

Howard Schuman

Kathy Acker

Bodies of Work

Kathy Acker's essays map a wide ranging cultural territory. From art and cinema, through politics, bodybuilding, science fiction and the city, they both reflect and challenge these times of radical change and puzzlement. Matching guts to theory, anger with compassion, Acker offers original views on the likes of Peter Greenaway, Samuel Delaney, Burroughs, de Sade, and Cronenberg's *Crash*. Collectively, these essays offer the reader a journey into strangeness, provocation and delight.

'Acker is a postmodern Colette with echoes of Cleland's Fanny Hill'

William S. Burroughs

'Sacrified sensibility, subversive intellect, and predatory wit make her a writer like no other'

New York Times

Matthew Collin

Altered State: The Story of Ecstasy Culture and Acid House

From its publication in 1997, Altered State established itself as the definitive text on dance culture. This second edition includes accounts of the election campaign of Tony Blair, which used an Ecstasy anthem as its musical theme, and the trial of a 19-year-old for supplying the drug that killed Leah Betts, Britain's most notorious Ecstasy death.

Drawing on a wealth of background research and original interviews with key figures on both sides of the law, Altered State examines the causes and contexts, ideologies and myths of Ecstasy culture, dramatising its euphoric narrative from peak experience to comedown and aftermath, and shedding new light on the social history of the most spectacular youth movement of the century.

'At last somebody has written the *real* history of the last ten years, and written it with such wit, verve, empathy and profound intelligence. I can't recommend this marvellous piece of work enough'

Irvine Welsh

'The first full history of the dance boom which, fuelled by Ecstasy, has transformed British culture over the past decade: here you will also find the drive to transcendence, or oblivion, that is at the heart of British pop'

Jon Savage

'Perhaps the most important document written about contemporary British society'

The Scotsman

'Altered State is not just timely; it was crying out to be written'

Independent